50% OFF Online CPCE Prep Course!

Dear Customer,

We consider it an honor and a privilege that you chose our CPCE Study Guide. As a way of showing our appreciation and to help us better serve you, we have partnered with Mometrix Test Preparation to offer you **50% off their online CPCE Prep Course**. Many CPCE courses are needlessly expensive and don't deliver enough value. With their course, you get access to the best CPCE prep material, and **you only pay half price.**

Mometrix has structured our online course to perfectly complement your printed study guide. The CPCE Prep Course contains **in-depth lessons** that cover all the most important topics, **20+ video reviews** that explain difficult concepts, over **1,000 practice questions** to ensure you feel prepared, and over **500 digital flashcards**, so you can study while you're on the go.

Online CPCE Prep Course

Topics Included:

- Human Growth and Development
- Fundamentals of Counseling
- Assessment and Testing
- Social and Cultural Diversity
- Counseling and Helping Relationships
- Group Counseling and Group Work
- Career Development
- Professional Counseling Orientation and Ethical Practice
- Research and Program Evaluation

Course Features:

- CPCE Study Guide
  - Get content that complements our best-selling study guide.
- 5 Full-Length Practice Tests
  - With over 1,000 practice questions, you can test yourself again and again.
- Mobile Friendly
  - If you need to study on the go, the course is easily accessible from your mobile device.
- CPCE Flashcards
  - Our course includes a flashcard mode consisting of over 500 content cards to help you study.

To receive this discount, visit them at mometrix.com/university/cpce or simply scan this QR code with your smartphone. At the checkout page, enter the discount code: **CPCE50TPB**

If you have any questions or concerns, please contact them at support@mometrix.com.

 in partnership with

FREE Test Taking Tips Video/DVD Offer

To better serve you, we created videos covering test taking tips that we want to give you for FREE. **These videos cover world-class tips that will help you succeed on your test.**

We just ask that you send us feedback about this product. Please let us know what you thought about it—whether good, bad, or indifferent.

To get your **FREE videos**, you can use the QR code below or email freevideos@studyguideteam.com with "Free Videos" in the subject line and the following information in the body of the email:

  a. The title of your product
  b. Your product rating on a scale of 1-5, with 5 being the highest
  c. Your feedback about the product

If you have any questions or concerns, please don't hesitate to contact us at info@studyguideteam.com.

Thank you!

CPCE Exam Preparation

2 Practice Tests and Counselor Study Guide
[Includes Detailed Answer Explanations]

Joshua Rueda

Written and edited by TPB Publishing.

TPB Publishing is not associated with or endorsed by any official testing organization. TPB Publishing is a publisher of unofficial educational products. All test and organization names are trademarks of their respective owners. Content in this book is included for utilitarian purposes only and does not constitute an endorsement by TPB Publishing of any particular point of view.

Interested in buying more than 10 copies of our product? Contact us about bulk discounts:
bulkorders@studyguideteam.com

ISBN 13: 9781637754351
ISBN 10: 1637754353

Table of Contents

Welcome

Dear Reader,

Welcome to your new Test Prep Books study guide! We are pleased that you chose us to help you prepare for your exam. There are many study options to choose from, and we appreciate you choosing us. Studying can be a daunting task, but we have designed a smart, effective study guide to help prepare you for what lies ahead.

Whether you're a parent helping your child learn and grow, a high school student working hard to get into your dream college, or a nursing student studying for a complex exam, we want to help give you the tools you need to succeed. We hope this study guide gives you the skills and the confidence to thrive, and we can't thank you enough for allowing us to be part of your journey.

In an effort to continue to improve our products, we welcome feedback from our customers. We look forward to hearing from you. Suggestions, success stories, and criticisms can all be communicated by emailing us at info@studyguideteam.com.

Sincerely,
Test Prep Books Team

FREE Videos/DVD OFFER

Doing well on your exam requires both knowing the test content and understanding how to use that knowledge to do well on the test. We offer completely FREE test taking tip videos. **These videos cover world-class tips that you can use to succeed on your test.**

To get your **FREE videos**, you can use the QR code below or email freevideos@studyguideteam.com with "Free Videos" in the subject line and the following information in the body of the email:

   a. The title of your product
   b. Your product rating on a scale of 1-5, with 5 being the highest
   c. Your feedback about the product

If you have any questions or concerns, please don't hesitate to contact us at info@studyguideteam.com.

SCAN HERE

1

Quick Overview

As you draw closer to taking your exam, effective preparation becomes more and more important. Thankfully, you have this study guide to help you get ready. Use this guide to help keep your studying on track and refer to it often.

This study guide contains several key sections that will help you be successful on your exam. The guide contains tips for what you should do the night before and the day of the test. Also included are test-taking tips. Knowing the right information is not always enough. Many well-prepared test takers struggle with exams. These tips will help equip you to accurately read, assess, and answer test questions.

A large part of the guide is devoted to showing you what content to expect on the exam and to helping you better understand that content. In this guide are practice test questions so that you can see how well you have grasped the content. Then, answer explanations are provided so that you can understand why you missed certain questions.

Don't try to cram the night before you take your exam. This is not a wise strategy for a few reasons. First, your retention of the information will be low. Your time would be better used by reviewing information you already know rather than trying to learn a lot of new information. Second, you will likely become stressed as you try to gain a large amount of knowledge in a short amount of time. Third, you will be depriving yourself of sleep. So be sure to go to bed at a reasonable time the night before. Being well-rested helps you focus and remain calm.

Be sure to eat a substantial breakfast the morning of the exam. If you are taking the exam in the afternoon, be sure to have a good lunch as well. Being hungry is distracting and can make it difficult to focus. You have hopefully spent lots of time preparing for the exam. Don't let an empty stomach get in the way of success!

When travelling to the testing center, leave earlier than needed. That way, you have a buffer in case you experience any delays. This will help you remain calm and will keep you from missing your appointment time at the testing center.

Be sure to pace yourself during the exam. Don't try to rush through the exam. There is no need to risk performing poorly on the exam just so you can leave the testing center early. Allow yourself to use all of the allotted time if needed.

Remain positive while taking the exam even if you feel like you are performing poorly. Thinking about the content you should have mastered will not help you perform better on the exam.

Once the exam is complete, take some time to relax. Even if you feel that you need to take the exam again, you will be well served by some down time before you begin studying again. It's often easier to convince yourself to study if you know that it will come with a reward!

Test-Taking Strategies

1. Predicting the Answer

When you feel confident in your preparation for a multiple-choice test, try predicting the answer before reading the answer choices. This is especially useful on questions that test objective factual knowledge. By predicting the answer before reading the available choices, you eliminate the possibility that you will be distracted or led astray by an incorrect answer choice. You will feel more confident in your selection if you read the question, predict the answer, and then find your prediction among the answer choices. After using this strategy, be sure to still read all of the answer choices carefully and completely. If you feel unprepared, you should not attempt to predict the answers. This would be a waste of time and an opportunity for your mind to wander in the wrong direction.

2. Reading the Whole Question

Too often, test takers scan a multiple-choice question, recognize a few familiar words, and immediately jump to the answer choices. Test authors are aware of this common impatience, and they will sometimes prey upon it. For instance, a test author might subtly turn the question into a negative, or he or she might redirect the focus of the question right at the end. The only way to avoid falling into these traps is to read the entirety of the question carefully before reading the answer choices.

3. Looking for Wrong Answers

Long and complicated multiple-choice questions can be intimidating. One way to simplify a difficult multiple-choice question is to eliminate all of the answer choices that are clearly wrong. In most sets of answers, there will be at least one selection that can be dismissed right away. If the test is administered on paper, the test taker could draw a line through it to indicate that it may be ignored; otherwise, the test taker will have to perform this operation mentally or on scratch paper. In either case, once the obviously incorrect answers have been eliminated, the remaining choices may be considered. Sometimes identifying the clearly wrong answers will give the test taker some information about the correct answer. For instance, if one of the remaining answer choices is a direct opposite of one of the eliminated answer choices, it may well be the correct answer. The opposite of obviously wrong is obviously right! Of course, this is not always the case. Some answers are obviously incorrect simply because they are irrelevant to the question being asked. Still, identifying and eliminating some incorrect answer choices is a good way to simplify a multiple-choice question.

4. Don't Overanalyze

Anxious test takers often overanalyze questions. When you are nervous, your brain will often run wild, causing you to make associations and discover clues that don't actually exist. If you feel that this may be a problem for you, do whatever you can to slow down during the test. Try taking a deep breath or counting to ten. As you read and consider the question, restrict yourself to the particular words used by the author. Avoid thought tangents about what the author *really* meant, or what he or she was *trying* to say. The only things that matter on a multiple-choice test are the words that are actually in the question. You must avoid reading too much into a multiple-choice question, or supposing that the writer meant something other than what he or she wrote.

3

5. No Need for Panic

It is wise to learn as many strategies as possible before taking a multiple-choice test, but it is likely that you will come across a few questions for which you simply don't know the answer. In this situation, avoid panicking. Because most multiple-choice tests include dozens of questions, the relative value of a single wrong answer is small. As much as possible, you should compartmentalize each question on a multiple-choice test. In other words, you should not allow your feelings about one question to affect your success on the others. When you find a question that you either don't understand or don't know how to answer, just take a deep breath and do your best. Read the entire question slowly and carefully. Try rephrasing the question a couple of different ways. Then, read all of the answer choices carefully. After eliminating obviously wrong answers, make a selection and move on to the next question.

6. Confusing Answer Choices

When working on a difficult multiple-choice question, there may be a tendency to focus on the answer choices that are the easiest to understand. Many people, whether consciously or not, gravitate to the answer choices that require the least concentration, knowledge, and memory. This is a mistake. When you come across an answer choice that is confusing, you should give it extra attention. A question might be confusing because you do not know the subject matter to which it refers. If this is the case, don't eliminate the answer before you have affirmatively settled on another. When you come across an answer choice of this type, set it aside as you look at the remaining choices. If you can confidently assert that one of the other choices is correct, you can leave the confusing answer aside. Otherwise, you will need to take a moment to try to better understand the confusing answer choice. Rephrasing is one way to tease out the sense of a confusing answer choice.

7. Your First Instinct

Many people struggle with multiple-choice tests because they overthink the questions. If you have studied sufficiently for the test, you should be prepared to trust your first instinct once you have carefully and completely read the question and all of the answer choices. There is a great deal of research suggesting that the mind can come to the correct conclusion very quickly once it has obtained all of the relevant information. At times, it may seem to you as if your intuition is working faster even than your reasoning mind. This may in fact be true. The knowledge you obtain while studying may be retrieved from your subconscious before you have a chance to work out the associations that support it. Verify your instinct by working out the reasons that it should be trusted.

8. Key Words

Many test takers struggle with multiple-choice questions because they have poor reading comprehension skills. Quickly reading and understanding a multiple-choice question requires a mixture of skill and experience. To help with this, try jotting down a few key words and phrases on a piece of scrap paper. Doing this concentrates the process of reading and forces the mind to weigh the relative importance of the question's parts. In selecting words and phrases to write down, the test taker thinks about the question more deeply and carefully. This is especially true for multiple-choice questions that are preceded by a long prompt.

9. Subtle Negatives

One of the oldest tricks in the multiple-choice test writer's book is to subtly reverse the meaning of a question with a word like *not* or *except*. If you are not paying attention to each word in the question, you can easily be led astray by this trick. For instance, a common question format is, "Which of the following is...?" Obviously, if the question instead is, "Which of the following is not...?," then the answer will be quite different. Even worse, the test makers are aware of the potential for this mistake and will include one answer choice that would be correct if the question were not negated or reversed. A test taker who misses the reversal will find what he or she believes to be a correct answer and will be so confident that he or she will fail to reread the question and discover the original error. The only way to avoid this is to practice a wide variety of multiple-choice questions and to pay close attention to each and every word.

10. Reading Every Answer Choice

It may seem obvious, but you should always read every one of the answer choices! Too many test takers fall into the habit of scanning the question and assuming that they understand the question because they recognize a few key words. From there, they pick the first answer choice that answers the question they believe they have read. Test takers who read all of the answer choices might discover that one of the latter answer choices is actually *more* correct. Moreover, reading all of the answer choices can remind you of facts related to the question that can help you arrive at the correct answer. Sometimes, a misstatement or incorrect detail in one of the latter answer choices will trigger your memory of the subject and will enable you to find the right answer. Failing to read all of the answer choices is like not reading all of the items on a restaurant menu: you might miss out on the perfect choice.

11. Spot the Hedges

One of the keys to success on multiple-choice tests is paying close attention to every word. This is never truer than with words like *almost*, *most*, *some*, and *sometimes*. These words are called "hedges" because they indicate that a statement is not totally true or not true in every place and time. An absolute statement will contain no hedges, but in many subjects, the answers are not always straightforward or absolute. There are always exceptions to the rules in these subjects. For this reason, you should favor those multiple-choice questions that contain hedging language. The presence of qualifying words indicates that the author is taking special care with his or her words, which is certainly important when composing the right answer. After all, there are many ways to be wrong, but there is only one way to be right! For this reason, it is wise to avoid answers that are absolute when taking a multiple-choice test. An absolute answer is one that says things are either all one way or all another. They often include words like *every*, *always*, *best*, and *never*. If you are taking a multiple-choice test in a subject that doesn't lend itself to absolute answers, be on your guard if you see any of these words.

12. Long Answers

In many subject areas, the answers are not simple. As already mentioned, the right answer often requires hedges. Another common feature of the answers to a complex or subjective question are qualifying clauses, which are groups of words that subtly modify the meaning of the sentence. If the question or answer choice describes a rule to which there are exceptions or the subject matter is complicated, ambiguous, or confusing, the correct answer will require many words in order to be expressed clearly and accurately. In essence, you should not be deterred by answer choices that seem

excessively long. Oftentimes, the author of the text will not be able to write the correct answer without offering some qualifications and modifications. Your job is to read the answer choices thoroughly and completely and to select the one that most accurately and precisely answers the question.

13. Restating to Understand

Sometimes, a question on a multiple-choice test is difficult not because of what it asks but because of how it is written. If this is the case, restate the question or answer choice in different words. This process serves a couple of important purposes. First, it forces you to concentrate on the core of the question. In order to rephrase the question accurately, you have to understand it well. Rephrasing the question will concentrate your mind on the key words and ideas. Second, it will present the information to your mind in a fresh way. This process may trigger your memory and render some useful scrap of information picked up while studying.

14. True Statements

Sometimes an answer choice will be true in itself, but it does not answer the question. This is one of the main reasons why it is essential to read the question carefully and completely before proceeding to the answer choices. Too often, test takers skip ahead to the answer choices and look for true statements. Having found one of these, they are content to select it without reference to the question above. Obviously, this provides an easy way for test makers to play tricks. The savvy test taker will always read the entire question before turning to the answer choices. Then, having settled on a correct answer choice, he or she will refer to the original question and ensure that the selected answer is relevant. The mistake of choosing a correct-but-irrelevant answer choice is especially common on questions related to specific pieces of objective knowledge. A prepared test taker will have a wealth of factual knowledge at his or her disposal, and should not be careless in its application.

15. No Patterns

One of the more dangerous ideas that circulates about multiple-choice tests is that the correct answers tend to fall into patterns. These erroneous ideas range from a belief that B and C are the most common right answers, to the idea that an unprepared test-taker should answer "A-B-A-C-A-D-A-B-A." It cannot be emphasized enough that pattern-seeking of this type is exactly the WRONG way to approach a multiple-choice test. To begin with, it is highly unlikely that the test maker will plot the correct answers according to some predetermined pattern. The questions are scrambled and delivered in a random order. Furthermore, even if the test maker was following a pattern in the assignation of correct answers, there is no reason why the test taker would know which pattern he or she was using. Any attempt to discern a pattern in the answer choices is a waste of time and a distraction from the real work of taking the test. A test taker would be much better served by extra preparation before the test than by reliance on a pattern in the answers.

Introduction to the CPCE

Function of the Test

The Counselor Preparation Comprehensive Examination (CPCE) was developed by the Center for Credentialing & Education (CCE) to assess counseling students' knowledge of core subject areas. The CPCE can also give counseling education programs an objective view of the effectiveness of their curricula, offer a benchmark to compare knowledge at different points during students' matriculation, and provide the opportunity to compare their students' data to national and institutional averages.

Target Population

The target population for the CPCE is master's-level students enrolled in graduate-level counselor education programs. These counselor education programs should have courses that cover the eight core areas defined by the Council for Accreditation of Counseling and Related Educational Programs (CACREP) in their Standards for Preparation:

- Professional Counseling Orientation and Ethical Practice
- Social and Cultural Diversity
- Human Growth and Development
- Career Development
- Counseling and Helping Relationships
- Group Counseling and Group Work
- Assessment and Testing
- Research and Program Evaluation

Test Format and Scoring

The CPCE consists of 160 multiple-choice questions with 20 questions per content area. Of the 20 questions per section, 17 will be scored and the remaining 3 will be considered pretest items that will not affect the student's score. The 24 total unscored questions are used to determine question performance for future examinations. The unscored questions will be in the same format as the scored questions and will be scattered among them within the exam. Each student's composite score and their scores for each section will be reported to their institution. CCE will also provide statistics on program performance and national data.

Institutions may choose to add components to the exam, such as supplemental essay questions or questions from specialty counseling areas. Scoring of these additional sections is the responsibility of the institution. Institutions are also responsible for establishing a minimum score for their students.

Candidates will have 3 hours and 45 minutes to complete the exam. The breakdown of questions per subject area is illustrated in the chart below.

Content Area	Percent of Questions	Number of Scored Questions
Professional Counseling Orientation and Ethical Practice	12.5	17
Social and Cultural Diversity	12.5	17
Human Growth and Development	12.5	17
Career Development	12.5	17
Counseling and Helping Relationships	12.5	17
Group Counseling and Group Work	12.5	17
Assessment and Testing	12.5	17
Research and Program Evaluation	12.5	17

Study Prep Plan for the CPCE

1   **Schedule** - Use one of our study schedules below or come up with one of your own.

2   **Relax** - Test anxiety can hurt even the best students. There are many ways to reduce stress. Find the one that works best for you.

3   **Execute** - Once you have a good plan in place, be sure to stick to it.

One Week Study Schedule		
Day 1	Professional Counseling Orientation...	
Day 2	Human Growth and Development	
Day 3	Career Development	
Day 4	Group Counseling and Group Work	
Day 5	Practice Test #1	
Day 6	Practice Test #2	
Day 7	Take Your Exam!	

Two Week Study Schedule			
Day 1	Professional Counseling Orientation...	Day 8	Group Counseling and Group Work
Day 2	Social and Cultural Diversity	Day 9	Research and Program Evaluation
Day 3	Human Growth and Development	Day 10	Practice Test #1
Day 4	Theories and Etiology of Addictions...	Day 11	Answer Explanations #1
Day 5	Career Development	Day 12	Practice Test #2
Day 6	Counseling and Helping Relationships	Day 13	Answer Explanations #2
Day 7	Developmentally Relevant Treatment...	Day 14	Take Your Exam!

One Month Study Schedule							
Day 1	Professional Counseling...	Day 11	Practice Questions	Day 21	Forms of Testing
Day 2	Relationships and Collaboration with...	Day 12	Career Development	Day 22	Practice Questions
Day 3	Credentialing, Licensure...	Day 13	Practice Questions	Day 23	Research and Program Evaluation
Day 4	Practice Questions	Day 14	Counseling and Helping Relationships	Day 24	Statistical Methods Used in Conducting Research...
Day 5	Social and Cultural Diversity	Day 15	Theories, Models, and Strategies for...	Day 25	Practice Questions
Day 6	Practice Questions	Day 16	Developmentally Relevant Treatment...	Day 26	Practice Test #1
Day 7	Human Growth and Development	Day 17	Developing a Personal Model of Counseling	Day 27	Answer Explanations #1
Day 8	Theories of Learning	Day 18	Group Counseling and Group Work	Day 28	Practice Test #2
Day 9	Theories and Etiology of Addictions...	Day 19	Practice Questions	Day 29	Answer Explanations #2
Day 10	Systemic and Environmental...	Day 20	Assessment and Testing	Day 30	Take Your Exam!

Build your prep plan online by visiting:
testprepbooks.com/prep

As you study for your test, we'd like to take the opportunity to remind you that you are capable of great things! With the right tools and dedication, you truly can do anything you set your mind to. The fact that you are holding this book right now shows how committed you are. In case no one has told you lately, you've got this! Our intention behind including this coloring page is to give you the chance to take some time to engage your creative side when you need a little brain-break from studying. As a company, we want to encourage people like you to achieve their dreams by providing good quality study materials for the tests and certifications that improve careers and change lives. As individuals, many of us have taken such tests in our careers, and we know how challenging this process can be. While we can't come alongside you and cheer you on personally, we can offer you the space to recall your purpose, reconnect with your passion, and refresh your brain through an artistic practice. We wish you every success, and happy studying!

Professional Counseling Orientation & Ethical Practice

Professional Roles and Functions of Counselors Across Specialty Areas

Roles of Counselors

A person who earns the title of professional counselor can fulfill many roles within the private and public sectors. The following categories are a sample of the general options available to professional counselors but should not be considered a comprehensive list. One of the appeals of becoming a professional counselor is that it offers significant opportunities to explore and seek employment in an incredible array of areas.

Nonprofit Organizations or State-Funded Mental Health Care

One of the largest sectors for employment for professional counselors includes the wide variety of **nonprofit human services organizations** around the country. Additionally, there are significant opportunities for employment as a professional counselor through **state-funded agencies**, sometimes referred to as Community Mental Health or Social/Human Services. These agencies and organizations exist as opportunities for people who are uninsured, underinsured, or on state insurance to more easily access health care with a mental health professional. Many aspects of employment as a professional counselor in the social services sector are unique. The counselor is often part of a multi-disciplinary team and participates in case staffing with psychiatrists, social workers, case managers, and other human services professionals that may be simultaneously working with the same client. Sometimes, the counselor collaborates with court systems and other state organizations such as Child Protective Services (CPS). The counselor is often assigned annual mandated training to keep up with state-set standards for mental health professionals. Nonprofit organizations, although independent from state-funded agencies, often contract with the state to service an overflow of clients. They also independently attract clients seeking mental health care. Caseload rates among state-funded and nonprofit agencies are generally high, given the demand for their services.

Outpatient Mental Health

Outside of nonprofit and community agencies, counselors may decide to work within an agency or business to provide outpatient counseling on a regular or contractual basis. A few different scenarios are outlined below that encompass the private practice options available to clinicians.

One option is **group practice**, in which you work in an agency with other therapists. You receive referrals directly from the agency, and in some cases, your schedule is managed by the agency as well. This means that a therapist working in this agency is not necessarily obligated to seek out clientele and market themselves. Rather, the agency handles marketing, receives referrals directly, and doles them out as appropriate to the professionals on their team. The agency often determines a set pay structure, including a percentage of the individual client rate that the agency takes in exchange for marketing and managing referrals on the therapist's behalf. There is often increased support within group practices like this, including supervision and group consultations in which the therapist can staff their client with other mental health professionals.

Another option is **private practice**, in which the counselor is running their own practice. The counselor oversees all elements of this practice: securing and funding an office space, marketing and branding their business, setting policies and procedures, attracting clientele, managing referrals, setting rates,

12

and so on. This option can be attractive to individuals who are seeking to exercise more control of their practice.

A third model is **independent group practice**, which functions as a unique blend of group and private practice. This entails a group of mental health professionals who run their own independent businesses within a group/communal setting. While each professional is responsible for managing their own individual practice and clientele, they benefit from having a chosen network of support among the larger group.

Inpatient and Hospital Mental Health Support

Ample career opportunities are available for professional counselors who provide inpatient and hospital mental health care. This may include working at a hospital's behavioral health or psychiatric program, a long-term residential program, or any other facility in which mental health is integrated into the standard of care. Psychiatric hospitals often seek to staff multiple mental health professionals to maintain a regular caseload of patients entering programming. General hospitals also have opportunities to contract or become a regularly staffed counselor to support grieving families of patients, assess patients seeking mental health care, and give care to patients experiencing a wide variety of different medical conditions that might warrant mental health support.

Substance Abuse Programs

There is a significant need for professional counselors within the field of **substance abuse recovery programs** in both private and public sectors. There are several programs that focus on recovery from substance abuse in which consistent and quality mental health treatment is a priority, including Social or Medical Detoxification, Residential/Inpatient Rehabilitation, Outpatient Rehabilitation, and Medication-Assisted Treatment (MAT) Programs.

Crisis Response and Community Outreach

As mental health becomes a growing societal focus, increased opportunities for mental health professionals, including professional counselors, are available to support individuals who are in crisis or experiencing an emergency. This can look like **on-the-ground intervention** with teams sometimes referred to as Mobile Crisis Response Units. Depending on availability and access within a community, access to these response teams can look different. These teams are sometimes organized to be accessed independently through a community mental health organization or a local crisis line. They can also be integrated into the local emergency response system and accessed through 911, with mental health professionals being deployed with first responders such as police and EMS. This can also look like **telephonic support**, through a local crisis line or the 988 service. 988 is a newly instated nationwide line that a person can call 24/7 from anywhere in the United States, to be connected with a mental health professional. Many mental health professionals find this work appealing, given the focus on short-term, solution-focused intervention and, often, the capacity to work from home.

Educational System

Counselors are often hired to provide services in both primary and secondary educational settings. Most often hired in middle and high school settings, professional counselors in pre-college education settings can fulfill a variety of roles. Some school counselors are responsible for working directly with students and their parents to support academic and behavioral challenges and to support planning for future education and professional goals. Other school counselors are hired by school districts or partnering entities as therapists to provide mental health support to students. This can look like regularly seeing students for therapy, or providing brief, solution-focused interventions to students in crisis.

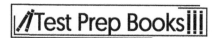

The client system can include not only the client, but those who are in the client's immediate environment, or who have an influential role in the client's life and treatment. A client system may also consist of an organization or community, which may involve many people. It is important to clarify and define the roles of each person involved in the client system, including the counselor, individual client, or the different members of the organization.

Client systems and counselors may initially have differing expectations of their roles in the helping relationship, so it is important that the roles and responsibilities of each are clarified as soon as possible. Although the client may have the expectation that the counselor will have the most active role in treatment, it is important for the client to also be fully engaged and proactive. While the counselor plays a supportive, helpful role, there should be a collaborative effort in which everyone in the client system is working together toward goals that have been set cooperatively. Clients must be actively involved in identifying areas of strengths and weaknesses, setting goals for treatment, choosing providers, and working towards the changes that are needed. In situations where the client system consists of many people, the counselor's role will be to maintain unity and cohesiveness so that goals can be achieved.

Purposes of Documentation

Accurate case recording is an integral part of counseling. Keeping accurate client records has many purposes, such as documenting the history and treatment of a client, getting insurance reimbursement, providing counselors a historical account of client sessions, and protecting confidentiality. There are numerous reasons for keeping thorough documentation throughout the counseling process:

- The information contained in a client record can be used to evaluate the effectiveness of services.

- Counseling records serve as a reference for reviewing the client's plan of care and measuring goal achievement. Throughout the course of therapy, counselors may need to refer back to the treatment plan to facilitate interventions. Client records, when combined with other evaluation tools (e.g., client satisfaction surveys, reactions to treatments, accomplishments of goals), can be an effective method of evaluating treatment progress.

- Counselors should record and review any notes pertaining to client behaviors that indicate any chance of clients becoming suicidal or homicidal. These clients will require crisis intervention from other professionals, and their records will need to be reviewed.

- Supervisors may review client records to evaluate the effectiveness of the treatment process, counselor performance, and client progress, or to ensure documentation is being completed accurately and on time.

- Counselors who decide to introduce new techniques, such as group or family counseling, will need to revisit the client's consent and revise the treatment modalities. Clients will need to consent to any amendments indicating a change in therapy techniques.

- Records also provide other counselors with information for continuity of care should the original counselor not be able to continue the sessions.

Litigation and Reimbursement

Accurate case recording is also required to protect the agency from possible legal ramifications and to ensure reimbursement from funders. Counselors must adhere to any state or federal legal requirements

related to storage, disclosure of information, release of client records, and confidential information. Client records should be kept up-to-date, objective, and completed as soon as possible to ensure accuracy of information. Counselors should assume it is always possible that records may be requested as part of legal proceedings. In litigation, the client records will be reviewed by lawyers, and any applicable information will be admitted as evidence during court. Treatment notes should always be clearly written and only include information necessary to the client's treatment to protect confidentiality as much as possible. Because client records are confidential, clients need to sign an informed consent form permitting the access of records by any third party.

Client Reports

Elements of client reports may include developmental history, family history, substance use information, medical history, the presenting problem, and recommendations. There are a variety of elements of client reports that may be required by the agency. With the advent of electronic records, client reports are often built into the software that the agency uses. Client reports may also be in **DAP** (data, assessment, plan) format or in the model of **SOAP notes** (subjective, objective, assessment, and plan). Reports are at the agency's discretion, and the counselor should use the format that is required by the agency to develop client reports.

Contracts

As part of the intake process, counselors may wish to develop and agree upon a contract with the client. **Contracts** outline goals and responsibilities of both parties and may help to alleviate potential miscommunication. Important components of a contract include an outline of the service being provided, a description of the counselor's qualifications, and any explanation of the scope of practice. A clause outlining client rights and confidentiality should be included. Lastly, the counselor may wish to include specifics about session time, fees, and consequences of a client being late, missing, or canceling sessions. Contracts can serve to empower clients by clarifying service and allowing clients to take an active role in their therapeutic care. They may also be flexible, allowing either party to modify the contract as needed.

Writing and Maintaining Client Records

Counselors must document their practice with the client. Counselors document sessions with clients as well as client legal mandates, such as visitation with minors in state custody. Documentation may be a combination of narrative and quantitative descriptions, depending on agency requirements. Records should be kept confidential either electronically or in a physical location. New laws require that all records be electronic, and they are called electronic health records. These records must be confidential as stated in the **Health Insurance Portability and Accountability Act of 1996 (HIPAA)**. It is crucial for the counselor to maintain accurate documentation.

Note-Taking Styles

During the assessment and treatment processes, the information from both the subjective and objective data is combined to formulate a concise, yet comprehensive, assessment for the client. In some note-taking practices, the identification of the subjective and objective data along with assessment formation is required. This style of documentation is known as the *SOAP method*, an acronym that stands for Subjective, Objective, Assessment, and Plan. Another note-taking style that focuses on the subjective and objective data is the BIRP documentation method. *BIRP* stands for Behavior, Intervention, Response, and Plan. It is not as commonly used as SOAP.

15

Organization and Storage of Client Information

Organization and storage of client information varies greatly depending on the counselor, the institution, and the requirements of any external funding sources. Information may be stored electronically in online systems or on paper. Important components of information in counseling include: intake forms; personal, medical, and demographic information; assessments and reviews; any diagnoses, intervention, and treatment outlines with measurable goals; and discharge plans or paperwork. Since this is all highly sensitive and confidential information, counselors should be mindful to keep all information updated, accurate, and stored securely.

Client's Rights and Responsibilities

When providing services, it is important to ensure that clients understand all aspects of the treatment they will receive. In addition to the plan of treatment, it is also necessary to ensure that clients understand the possible risks involved, the costs associated, the length of treatment, and any limitations to confidentiality that might exist due to both mandated reporting laws and third-party payers. Alternatives to the therapeutic plan may also be discussed with clients before beginning treatment. Clients need to be given the opportunity to ask questions and receive answers to ensure they completely comprehend what their therapies will entail. Informed consent should require that the client sign legal documentation stating that they fully understand what will be involved—including all the risks, limitations, and alternatives—prior to beginning treatment. This documentation should become a part of the client's chart.

There will be circumstances in which a person may be receiving treatment on an involuntary basis. In these situations, the counselor should fully explain the terms of the treatment as it pertains to the individual's situation, as well as any rights the person does have in regard to refusal. An example of this type of situation would be someone who is court mandated to receive treatment, such as drug and alcohol counseling, anger management, or other therapies.

Sometimes client information needs to be shared with other individuals such as the client's family or other professionals for referrals. In these situations, the client must agree to these disclosures, and consent for disclosure of information must be obtained.

Clients have a right to obtain their records. Counselors are permitted, however, by the Code of Ethics to withhold all or part of the client record from the client if the counselor determines there is a great risk of harm in releasing the information. In these cases, it is important to fully document the request, whether or not the records were released, and the rationale for either releasing or not releasing them.

Limits of Confidentiality

Counselors have a duty to protect confidential information of clients. Ethically, client information should not be discussed with anyone other than the client. Legally, a client has a right to keep their medical and therapeutic information confidential. The **Health Insurance Portability and Accountability Act of 1996 (HIPAA)** requires that medical information (including therapeutic and mental health information) be protected and kept confidential. However, there are certain limitations to confidentiality. These generally involve risk of harm to the individual being served, as well as others. Counselors are not as protected as some other professionals when it comes to confidentiality and often find themselves being called to testify in court cases related to their clients. There are also certain situations in which counselors may have to release confidential information to protect the client or satisfy the duty to warn.

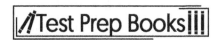

Minors

Providing services to minors can be challenging when it comes to confidentiality issues, especially since the legal rules and regulations vary from state to state. At times, there can be a conflict between the counselor's feeling of ethical responsibility to maintain the privacy of the minor and the legal right of parents to be informed of issues discussed. Adolescents in particular may discuss concerns with a counselor that they do not want their parents to be aware of, and it can be a violation of trust if these issues are subsequently revealed to parents. It is imperative that at the start of treatment, the expectations of the counselor's relationship with each person are discussed with the parents and minors, as well as the benefits and limits of confidentiality. Minors should never be promised confidentiality when the counselor cannot keep that promise, but the privacy and individuality of the minor should be maintained as much as possible. In cases where private information about the minor is going to be revealed, counselors should always inform the minor. This holds true regardless as to whether it is with the client's consent, mandated reporting, or due to the parent utilizing their right to information.

Groups

Confidentiality also becomes more complicated when a counselor is working with two or more people, either in a family or group session. All participants must agree that any information shared within the context of treatment will be kept confidential and not shared with others. However, the counselor should stress with clients that they cannot force other members to abide by the confidentiality agreement and that breach of confidentiality is a risk.

Mandated Reporting

It's important to note that counselors are considered mandated reporters in all states. This means there is a legal and ethical obligation to break confidentiality to report any signs and symptoms of child and elder abuse or neglect. In some cases, it will be impossible to know for sure if abuse or neglect is happening. Often the counselor will have only a small amount of information that may raise concerns but must make a report so that an investigation can occur. Any professional who has a suspicion of abuse or neglect of a child or a vulnerable adult must legally make a report to either Child Protective Services or Adult Protective Services, and they cannot be held liable for reports made in good faith.

Self-Harm

Some clients may disclose intent to harm themselves. It is necessary in these situations to fully assess suicidal intent and determine if the client is serious about carrying out a plan for self-harm. It might be sufficient, in cases where a client has considered self-harm but has no clear plan, to complete a safety plan with the client. The safety plan will outline what the client agrees to do should they begin to experience the desire to engage in self-harm. However, if the client has a clear plan of action and access to items necessary to carry out the plan, then confidentiality should be broken to protect the client. This would involve notifying police and having the client committed for observation for their own protection.

Duty to Warn

In addition to protecting clients from themselves, counselors also have a duty to warn third-party individuals if there is threat of harm. **Duty to warn** was established by the 1976 case Tarasoff vs. Regents of the University of California. In this case, a graduate student at the University of California-Berkeley had become obsessed with Tatiana Tarasoff. After significant distress, he sought psychological treatment and disclosed to his therapist that he had a plan to kill Tarasoff. Although the psychologist did have the student temporarily committed, he was ultimately released. He eventually stopped seeking

17

treatment and attacked and killed Tarasoff. Tarasoff's family sued the psychologist and various other individuals involved with the university. This case evolved into the duty to warn third parties of potential risk of harm. Satisfying the duty to warn can be done by notifying police or the individual who is the intended victim.

Because ethical dilemmas can involve legal situations, they may also have legal consequences for a counselor or necessitate involving the legal system. For example, a client may disclose that he frequently drinks large amounts of alcohol and then drives his children to school. Ethically, there is an obligation to keep what the client has said in confidence. However, the client's children are being placed in a situation in which they are in great danger of being injured or harmed. Due to laws protecting the welfare of children, the counselor would need to make a report to Child Protective Services. In some states, if someone has a good faith reason to believe that a child is being neglected or abused, and does not report the situation, that person may face a civil lawsuit and even criminal charges.

DETERMINING CLEARLY ESTABLISHED THREATS

One of the difficulties associated with breaking confidentiality to protect a third party is that the threat isn't always clearly established. If a client discloses during treatment that he is going to go home and stab his neighbor, this is clearly a plan of intended harm. However, what about an HIV-positive client who fails to warn sexual partners of her HIV status? What if the client fully understands the risk to her partners and has no intention of disclosing her status? This is a situation which would require thorough documentation, thoughtful debate, and possibly conferencing with colleagues to decide upon the best course of action.

Technology

With technology being utilized extensively by counselors, confidentiality of electronic information is another important issue. Counseling sessions are now being provided by telephone, video chat, and online simulation, and these media open new possibilities for information abuse. If a counselor provides a video therapy session, they should be aware that it is possible for the client to have someone else in the room, off-camera, without informing the counselor or other participants. The same could be true with electronic communication such as texting or email. There is no way to know if a client is forwarding electronic information to third parties without the counselor's knowledge.

Storage of Records

Other issues relating to confidentiality include the storage and maintenance of records and charts. All confidential material should be kept in a secure location and locked at all times. For example, if a counselor takes a clipboard into client rooms to make notes for later documentation, that clipboard should be locked in a drawer when not in use so that no one can turn it over and see confidential information when the counselor is away from their desk. With the use of electronics and computers, there should be policies in place to lock computers when away to avoid anyone seeing notes or other confidential information. Collaboration between colleagues in which clients may be discussed should be done behind closed doors to avoid anyone else hearing the conversation.

Sharing Client Information in Malpractice Lawsuits

There may be instances in which a counselor is sued for malpractice. In these cases, the Code of Ethics states that it is permissible for the counselor to share confidential client information to aid in self-defense, but only so far as is necessary to adequately defend oneself.

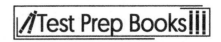

Legal and Ethical Issues Regarding Confidentiality

Disclosing Breaks in Confidentiality with Clients

Often when abuse or neglect is suspected, the concern about breaking confidentiality is at the forefront of the mind of the counselor. When disclosing information due to legal requirements, it is always important to discuss the situation with the client. It should be noted that the counselor should evaluate their own safety when discussing disclosure of confidential information with the client. If the counselor believes the situation to be unsafe if/when the client learns of the disclosure, then it is not necessary to alert the client prior to disclosing the confidential information. During informed consent, this requirement to report any signs of abuse or neglect should have been disclosed to the client. This is something that should be discussed in detail with clients during the informed consent process and throughout the relationship.

When such breaks in confidentiality occur, they can damage the relationship. In some cases, it may be necessary or appropriate to disclose to the client that a report is being made. For example, if a new mother has tested positive for cocaine and the infant has tested positive for cocaine while in the hospital, the infant will remain in the Neonatal Intensive Care Unit due to withdrawal. Disclosing to the mother that a report is being made, and why it's being made, could prepare her and create an opportunity to speak further with her about treatment options and other important considerations. It's important to note that counselors who fail to report suspected abuse or neglect can be subject to civil penalties and/or prosecution.

Relationships and Collaboration with Human Services and Behavioral Health Care Systems

Providing Information to Third Parties

Disclosure of client information will be necessary in certain instances. Some clients will require further medical treatment by a mental health provider. In order for a client to attain the best possible outcome, mental health providers will need to be informed of the assessments and interventions performed during the counseling sessions. Counseling services are often paid for by insurance companies. Basic information about the treatment, the client's diagnosis, and the frequency of counseling sessions will be necessary for billing purposes. In addition, clients may share with a counselor that they have a contagious communicable disease. If the disease is life-threatening, a counselor is justified in informing an identifiable third party of the situation. When court ordered, a counselor may reveal limited information about the client's counseling sessions that are relevant to the case. In the case of minors, each state has a minor-consent law that allows clients younger than 18 years of age to seek treatment without parental consent. Counselors should be knowledgeable about their state statutes related to counseling minors without parental knowledge. In any case where an outside agency or individual requests client records, the client must sign an informed consent agreeing to the release of their information.

Developing Reports for External Organizations

Counselors often receive requests to provide reports to the courts and other organizations that may be making decisions regarding the client's life and future. Reports must be written thoughtfully, in a professional and objective manner, and should be drawn from the counselor's notes and observations regarding the client. Reports for external organizations must provide detailed and relevant data and be clear and concise so they can be easily understood. Counselors do not need to provide information beyond what has been requested by a court order, and only in the case of a court order should

19

information be released without the client's prior consent. Even if information must be legally released, the client should be informed of the situation and be aware that the information is being submitted to the external organization. A helpful habit for counselors is to take regular, comprehensive progress notes about visits and interactions with clients. If client records are already available, it is easier to compile a summary report with factual observations and the counselor's professional opinion.

Providing Referral Sources

Counselors frequently encounter clients who need assistance beyond the scope of the agency/counselor from whom they seek help. During assessment or throughout services, a counselor may need to refer a client to another professional for assistance. Counselors should make referrals to those resources in alignment with the best interests of the client. Agencies may also have partnerships with other local organizations that their target population would frequently access. For example, a mental health agency may have an interagency agreement or partnership with a substance abuse provider. It is also essential to discuss with the client why a referral is recommended and ensure the client is comfortable with the decision and understands next steps. When making referrals and sharing information with other providers, counselors must always obtain client consent.

The counselor must be familiar with ethical guidelines surrounding referrals and not refer out simply due to discomfort with or dislike for a client. A counselor who refers out for such personal reasons risks clients feeling abandoned, and the ACA Code of Ethics states that the needs of the clients must be put before those of the counselor. In these situations, the counselor should seek supervision and consultation regarding their personal issues. If the counselor is unable to provide appropriate care, then the client should be referred out.

Professional Advocacy and Counseling Organizations

The **philosophy of counseling** includes the belief that counselors should encourage clients to advocate for their own needs. A counselor's duty is to intervene in the early stages of a client's problem to avoid a crisis situation in the future. Counselors may also assist clients with life's challenges, such as finances, job searches, and medical care, by facilitating phone calls or referrals to government assistance programs.

Counselors are often faced with limitations of resources and insufficient representation of the profession. Advocating for their profession involves joining organizations that can make a difference. There are various state and national organizations, such as the American Counseling Association (ACA), that encourage counselors to voice their concerns and advocate for change. Knowledge of public policy allows counselors to participate in committees that can produce changes in legislation.

Ethical Standards of Professional Counseling Organizations

ACA Code of Ethics
Purpose
In general, counselors follow basic ethical guidelines to do no physical or psychological harm to their clients or to society and to provide fair, honest, and compassionate service to their clients and society when making professional decisions. The **ACA Code of Ethics** exists as a resource to provide clear guidelines for counselors to practice by and as a resource for counselors to consult when facing an ethical decision that they're unsure of making. This Code supports the mission of the counseling profession as established by the ACA. The ACA keeps an updated copy of their Code of Ethics, as well as

other media and interactive resources relating to ethical practices, on their website at www.counseling.org.

Core Values
The foundation of the ACA Code of Ethics is defined by the following six core values:

Autonomy: Freedom to govern one's own choices for the future
Nonmaleficence: Causing the least amount of harm as possible
Beneficence: Promoting health and wellbeing for the good of the individual and society
Justice: Treating each individual with fairness and equality
Fidelity: Displaying trust in professional relationships and maintaining promises
Veracity: Making sure to provide the truth in all situations and contacts

Ethical Guidelines
The Code of Ethics is comprised of nine sections that cover ethical guidelines to uphold the core values:

- The Counseling Relationship: The counselor-client relationship is one that is built primarily on trust. Counselors have the obligation to make sure the confidentiality and privacy rights of their clients are protected and, therefore, should protect and maintain any documentation recorded during services. Additionally, clients have rights regarding informed consent. Open communication between the client and counselor is essential; in the beginning of the relationship, the counselor must provide the client with information on all services provided, with sensitivity to cultural and developmental diversity. Counselors should also pay special attention to clients who are incapacitated in their abilities to give consent and should seek a balance between the client's own capacities and their capacity to give consent to a more capable individual. Finally, with mandated clients, counselors should seek transparency in areas regarding information they share with other professionals.

- Confidentiality and Privacy: With trust as the cornerstone of the counselor-client relationship, counselors must ensure the confidentiality and privacy of their clients in regards to respecting client rights through multicultural considerations, disclosure of documentation to appropriate professionals, and speaking to their clients about limitations of privacy. Some exceptions to confidentiality include the potential for serious harm to other individuals, end-of-life decisions, information regarding life-threatening diseases, and court-ordered disclosure. Counselors are encouraged to notify clients when disclosing information when possible, with only the minimal amount of information shared.

- Professional Responsibility: Counselors have the obligation to facilitate clear communication when dealing with the public or other professionals. They should practice only within their knowledge of expertise and be careful not to apply or participate in work they are not qualified for. Continuing education is part of the counselor's development as a professional, and the counselor should always be aware of evolving information. It's important for counselors to also monitor their own health and wellness, making sure to refer clients to other competent professionals if they find themselves unable to practice due to health or retirement.

- Relationships with Other Professionals: Developing relationships with other professionals is important for counselors in order to provide their clients with the best possible resources. Being part of interdisciplinary teams is one way for counselors to provide the best, well-rounded services to clients. Counselors should always be respectful to other professionals with different

approaches, as long as those approaches are grounded in scientific research. It is important for counselors to develop and maintain relationships with other professionals.

- Evaluation, Assessment, and Interpretation: In order to effectively plan for a client's treatment, general assessments should be made at the beginning of the counselor-client relationship regarding education, mental health, psychology, and career. Clients have a right to know their results and should be informed of the testing and usage of results prior to assessment. Counselors must take into account the cultural background of clients when diagnosing mental disorders, as culture affects the way clients define their problems. Counselors should take care not to perform forensic evaluations on clients they are counseling and vice versa.

- Supervision, Training, and Teaching: It is important for counselors to foster appropriate relationships with their supervisees and students. A client's wellbeing is encouraged not only by counselors but everyone the counselor works with. For counselors who are involved in supervising others, continuing education is important in providing the students or trainees with correct information. Any sexual relationship with current supervisees or students is prohibited, as well as any personal relationship that affects the counselor's ability to be objective. Finally, counselors should be proactive in maintaining a diverse faculty and/or a diverse student body.

- Research and Publication: When conducting research, counselors must take care to make sure they adhere to federal, state, agency, and institutional policies in dealing with confidentiality. Counselors should keep in mind the rights of their participants and facilitate safe practices during research that do not harm the client's wellbeing. As with any objective research, counselors should take care not to exaggerate or manipulate their findings in any way, even if the outcome is unfavorable. Counselors should take care where the identity of participants is concerned. All parties involved in the research of case examples must be notified prior to publication and give consent after reviewing the publication themselves. It's important for researchers to give credit to all contributors in publication.

- Distance Counseling, Technology, and Social Media: The field of counseling is evolving to include electronic means of helping clients. Counselors should take into consideration the implications of privacy and confidentiality when treating clients online and take precautions in securing these, notifying the clients of any limitations to privacy. It's important to verify the client's identity when using electronic sources throughout the duration of treatment. In distance counseling, counselors must also be aware of the laws in their own state as well as the client's state.

- Resolving Ethical Issues: This section ensures that all counselors act in an ethical and legal manner when dealing with clients and other professionals. It's important for counselors to make known their allegiance to the ACA Code of Ethics and try to resolve ethical issues following this manner. If the conflict cannot be resolved this way, counselors may be obligated to solve the conflict through the appropriate legal and/or government authority.

Ethical Dilemmas

Ethical dilemmas occur when three different conditions are met in a situation. The first is that the counselor must make a decision. If the situation does not require that a decision be made, then there isn't an ethical dilemma. The second is that there are different decisions that could be made or different actions one could take. The third condition is that an ethical ideal will be conceded no matter what decision is made.

One type of ethical dilemma occurs when you have a situation in which two ethical principles are conflicting. This is a pure ethical dilemma because either choice of action involves conceding one of these principles, and there is no way to keep both principles intact. Another type of ethical dilemma occurs when ethical principles conflict with values and/or laws. In these types of situations, a counselor's values may conflict with an ethical principle, and a decision must be made.

Once you have determined which kind of ethical dilemma you are facing, there are steps to take in order to reach a conclusion and, ultimately, the resolution of the dilemma. The NASW lays out steps that should be taken when attempting to resolve an ethical dilemma.

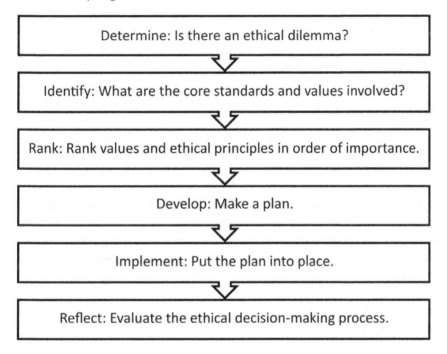

Ethical Issues

Ethical issues can present themselves in any field. In counseling, ethical issues often center on the confidentiality and anonymity of clients, client cases, and data collected about the client (especially in group or family settings). However, counselors are obligated to report any instances of abuse, self-harm that could lead to a fatality, or harm to others that could lead to fatalities. Counselors also need to ensure that clear personal and professional boundaries are maintained between themselves and their client. In all instances of counseling, counselors must exhibit respect and tolerance for individuals of all backgrounds, attitudes, opinions, and beliefs.

Testing

A variety of ethical issues must be considered before, during, and after any test or assessment is administered. To begin, the counselor must be adequately trained and earn any certifications and have the supervision necessary to administer and interpret the test. Tests must be appropriate for the needs of the specific client. Next, the client must provide informed consent, and they must understand the purpose and scope of any test. Test results must remain confidential, which includes access to any virtual information. Finally, tests must be validated for the specific client and be unbiased toward the race, ethnicity, and gender of the client.

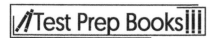

Dual Relationships

Dual relationships are clearly outlined in the NBCC Code of Ethics. The Code of Ethics states that counselors should not engage in dual relationships with clients or former clients in which exploitation of the client may occur. The Code of Ethics does recognize that there might be situations where dual relationships are unavoidable. For example, a counselor might have two jobs, one of which involves providing group therapy to survivors of sexual abuse. It is possible that a member of the aforementioned therapy group could become an employee or client at the counselor's second place of work. In these types of situations, the Code of Ethics suggests that the counselor establish clear boundaries that are sensitive to the client/former client.

Under no circumstances should a counselor ever become involved in a sexual relationship with a client. In addition, the Code of Ethics establishes that counselors must avoid sexual relationships with anyone who is related to or has a close personal relationship with a client or former client. The Code of Ethics also states that counselors should not become involved in sexual relationships with former clients because of the high risk of harm that may occur with such relationships. If, however, a counselor does become involved in a sexual relationship with a former client, the counselor is responsible for demonstrating that the former client entered into the relationship without manipulation or exploitation. The Code of Ethics also specifies that, due to the obvious risk of harm, a counselor should not provide professional services to anyone with whom the counselor has had a previous sexual relationship.

Situations called "**boundary crossings**" are when a counselor does not intend to create a dual relationship but inadvertently does so, as would be the case were a counselor to self-disclose personal information during a therapy session. This is distinguished from a boundary *violation*, which occurs when a dual relationship is established that is inherently coercive or manipulative and therefore harmful to the client. The following are some clues that a boundary crossing is unethical:

- It hinders the counselor's care.
- It prevents the counselor from being impartial.
- It exploits or manipulates the client or another person.
- It harms clients or colleagues.

Dual relationships are sometimes unavoidable in practice, particularly in small communities. However, it is possible to avoid dual relationships that involve boundary violations and ethical violations.

Professional Boundary Issues

Professional boundary issues occur when counselors have multiple types of relationships with a client. This may include a professional, business, or personal relationship. For example, it is permissible to see a client out in public at a restaurant, but not to invite a client to dinner for business or personal reasons. When encountering a client in public, the relationship with the client must be kept confidential.

However, if the client chooses to say hello, saying hello in return and quickly ending the encounter would be acceptable.

There are several boundary issues that come with working with clients. These issues are:

- **Intimate contact**: This refers to things such as hugging a client at the end of a working relationship or patting a client on the hand during a crying session. Sexual contact also falls into this category.

- **Personal gain**: This refers to instances in which a counselor engages in activity with a client that results in a monetary (or otherwise valuable) benefit to the counselor. This could involve situations such as referring a client to a business owned by the counselor or a friend/family member of the counselor, selling something to a client, or even asking a client for professional suggestions.

- **Emotional and dependency issues**: This refers to instances in which a counselor's own personal issues cause the counselor to have impaired judgment, possibly resulting in other boundary issues, such as a dual relationship with the client.

- **Altruistic instincts**: In some instances, a counselor's own good intentions and concerns for a client can result in boundary violations and confusion about the relationship between the counselor and the client. An example of this would be going to a client's bridal shower or retirement party.

Setting and Maintaining Professional Boundaries

Despite these difficulties, counselors must set and maintain boundaries with their clients and colleagues to ensure an effective practice. Counselors should consistently monitor how their professional boundaries enhance or harm relationships with clients, colleagues, supervisors, and administrators. They must also gauge the impact of their boundaries on the amount of time they devote to work, their ability to cope with stress at work, and the amount of time and energy that they spend on extraneous activities and relationships.

There are several strategies for building and maintaining appropriate professional boundaries and relationships. First, counselors should examine their motivations for giving extra time and attention to a client. If a counselor treats one client differently, this indicates that the boundary may be overextended. Counselors can manage this situation by determining whether the services provided are in line with the client's care plan, the organization's mission, the job description, and scope of practice.

Counselors should also avoid encouraging clients to contact them through personal channels. Clients should use the channels of communication set in place by the organization, such as work email, voicemail, cell phones, pagers, receptionists, on-call staff, and procedures for after-hours referrals to 911, emergency rooms, or mental health crisis centers. Extending the professional boundaries of the counselor role puts colleagues and the organization at risk for failure. It also sets an unfair expectation that other colleagues will extend their professional boundaries. If boundaries are inconsistent between colleagues and within the organization, then clients may become confused and distrust the entire organization.

A third strategy for building appropriate professional boundaries is establishing clear agreements with clients during the initial sessions about the role of a counselor and the dynamics of a client-counselor relationship. When warning signs indicate that healthy boundaries may be in jeopardy, counselors must

address the issues with the client clearly, quickly, and sensitively. This involves clarifying the roles and boundaries with the client and asking the client to restate these boundaries to ensure understanding.

A fourth strategy is limiting self-disclosure about the counselor's personal life to information directly related to the client's goals. If there is a dual relationship between the counselor and client, the counselor must preserve the client's confidentiality, physical security, and emotional well-being in social situations.

A fifth strategy is avoiding social media within professional practice. Counselors should not connect with clients on social media. This includes adding clients as friends on Facebook or following clients on Twitter. Counselors should use discretion and limit the amount of online information that is made available to the public or social network connections to prevent conflicts of interest. Counselors also shouldn't attempt to access online information about clients without prior informed consent. Finally, counselors shouldn't post negative information about colleagues or the organization online.

A sixth strategy is for counselors to foster strong work relationships with their colleagues at the organization. These connections will help counselors cope with stresses, think through questions of ethics and professional relationships, and help maintain a sense of humor. Counselors should be sensitive to signs of bullying in the workplace, as each counselor deserves respect and dignity to ensure social justice for others. It's important that counselors use appropriate channels of supervision and consultation to determine appropriate boundaries in difficult situations. Supervision can also be useful when trying to remedy concerns with existing organization procedures that address or inhibit client needs.

A final strategy for maintaining professional boundaries is ensuring appropriate self-care. This includes taking time for nurturing oneself throughout the workday, maintaining a regular work schedule, and taking time away from the office each day to refocus. Counselors should limit communication when they are away from work to ensure time for rejuvenation, especially during vacations or personal time. They must also be aware of how they handle work stress and monitor how often they take work home. This includes physical work, emotional strain, or hyper-vigilance about work situations. If a counselor consistently struggles to maintain professional relationships and work boundaries, they should seek supervision or outside mental health counseling.

Professional boundaries in counseling are clearly defined limits on the counselor-client relationship that provide a space for the creation of safe connections. Some helpful things to keep in mind include: the line between being friendly and being friends; being with the client versus becoming the client; and understanding the limits and responsibilities of the counselor role.

Mandates and Guidelines

The practice of professional counselors is guided by laws and policies. **Statutory law** is a body of mandates that is created and passed by U.S. Congress and state legislatures. Many of the laws are state-specific and may be more restrictive than federal legislation. Agencies such as schools or mental health facilities can also develop specific guidelines, procedures, and policies. In school systems, the local boards of education can rewrite policies and state regulations to meet the needs of their communities. For example, the ratio of students to counselors differs across the nation. In one state, the mandated ratio can be 1 counselor to 350 students, whereas in another state, the ratio may be 1 to 500. Other mandates may include the requirement of every school to provide comprehensive guidance and counseling programs, such as crisis assessment with referral, dropout prevention, and conflict resolution. Similarly, a large number of state laws require healthcare service plans and insurers to

provide some level of coverage for mental health services. Some outliers related to this mandate include copayments, deductibles, and limitations on the number of visits. It is important for a professional counselor to understand the difference between a mandate and a guideline.

A **mandate** is a set of rules and regulations set forth by governing bodies that must be followed when practicing counseling. **Guidelines** are suggestions on how to meet mandates. Ethical standards should guide the professional counselor when conflicting mandates arise. Documentation of the logical course of action is key in legal defense. Mandates that result from federal legislation or court cases will usually cover all counselors. Some of these mandates include child abuse or neglect laws. Counselors who have multiple credentials should know the mandates and regulations that apply to their work setting. School counselors rarely require informed consent to meet with students. However, a mental health counselor who works in a school but is employed by an outside agency would have to obtain an informed consent to see these same students.

Sharing Client Information with Third Parties

Because of legal and ethical issues surrounding privacy and informed consent, which are a means of maintaining a client's self-determination and dignity, it is critical that counselors always complete the appropriate forms when information is being shared about the client or decisions are being made on their behalf. Foundational to service provision is to first get written informed consent from the client to participate in services. Clients must fully understand the services being offered and agree to participate before treatment begins. Because it is often valuable for counselors to collaborate with other providers and professionals, it is important to obtain the Consent for Release of Information form before sharing any information with other providers. Clients must also be made fully aware of the reasons for this collaboration and information sharing and be told what information will be shared. Even if the client consents to having information released, the counselor should share only the relevant information with other providers, being careful to still maintain the client's confidentiality and privacy.

Impact of Agency Policy and Function on Service Delivery

Counselors may be employed in a variety of agencies. Some organizations, such as hospitals or government entities, employ diverse professionals. Other types of organizations, such as direct service non-profits or private practice agencies, maintain predominantly social services staff. Agency policies directly and significantly impact the working environment, the services provided, and as a result, the effectiveness of the care clients receive. All agencies should have a mission statement that gives the agency purpose and serves as an umbrella for the agency's smaller goals and objectives. Agency policies must be in the best interest of the client and must support the ethical guidelines to which counselors adhere. They must also be clearly written and available to counselors and clients where appropriate. Counselors and all those providing care to clients should be able to help shape policy development to ensure consistency with client and counselor needs and protection. Policies must address:

- Appropriate confidentiality, consent, and information protection.
- Case management and supervision.
- Cultural competency guidelines.
- Professional development and ongoing trainings.
- Anti-discriminatory/diversity practices.

Payment, Fees, and Insurance Benefits

A topic that must be discussed when obtaining informed consent from clients is payment and fees associated with the counseling services. Fees set by a counselor may be influenced by the standards of

living in the local area of practice. A clear outline of the payment policy and fees associated with each counseling session should be provided and explained to the client. One form of payment is termed **sliding fee scale** wherein fees are adjusted depending on the client's income. Professional counselors should consider that a sliding fee scale provides the same service to different clients for varying fees. Counselors who go through credentialing with insurance companies can become network providers.

A fee schedule will be discussed during the contracting phase with an insurance company. After providing counseling services to clients, counselors can bill the insurance. Claims will be reviewed and payment will be made to independent counselors directly. Government insurance options such as Medicare and Medicaid require the professional counselor to be within the network. Clients who do not have insurance or a health savings account can provide payment via private pay with cash or a credit card. The written agreement should include when payment is expected from the client or if the counselor plans to bill the client's insurance. The policy on missed appointments without notice should also be included in the disclosure along with a clear cancellation fee.

Obtaining Informed Consent

The majority of state counseling boards require professional counselors to obtain informed consent from clients prior to providing services. An **informed consent** form is a document signed by both parties agreeing to provide or receive a service. Some of the main topics included on an informed consent form are the qualifications and credentials of the counselor, risks and benefits of receiving the counseling service, goal expectations, and the provider's personal philosophy of counseling. The right to terminate counseling by either party and transfer service to another provider, if applicable, should also be discussed. Confidentiality is a prominent legal aspect of informed consent. The consent form should clearly outline situations in which confidentiality cannot be honored, such as in cases of neglect, intent to harm, and abuse of vulnerable populations. Additionally, informed consent documents should include clear expectations of fees, payment methods, and cancellation policies.

In this day and age, it is common for professionals to use electronic means of communication, such as email or text. It is important that the risks associated with using these avenues are fully disclosed. Depending on the nature of the professional relationship and the needs of the individual, a treatment may necessitate audio taping, videotaping, or observation by a third party. The informed consent of the client should be obtained before any recording takes place. Some counselors will have audio and videotaping as a part of the informed consent documentation when clients begin therapy, and others will have a separate form to be used if and when the need should arise. As long as the client has signed that they understand and give consent, either way will suffice.

Assessing Competency to Provide Informed Consent

In certain instances, a client may have difficulty in fully understanding the information being presented. This could be true especially if there is a language barrier or if the person receiving services either is not fully alert or is disoriented. Appropriate measures should be taken to ensure that the person receiving services fully understands the information provided to satisfy that informed consent has been achieved. This may require utilizing a translator or a third party, such as a durable power of attorney or family member, if the person is not able to make their own decisions. In the event that a client has a conservator or power of attorney acting on their behalf, it is also the role of the counselor to ensure that this person is making decisions that coincide with the wishes of the client.

Reviewing Client Records

While the privacy and confidentiality of the client must always be protected, with proper permission it can be beneficial for the counselor to access and view records from others who have played a significant role in the client's life and treatment. This helps to establish a more holistic view of the client and gives a comprehensive perspective of the client's strengths and difficulties. Medical records can provide information about some of the physical and medical reasons behind the client's behaviors, as well as information about the medications the client is taking. Educational and employment records can shed light on how the client functions within the milieus of school and work, providing insight into areas that may need to be addressed with the client. Employment information can also assist the counselor in determining the client's financial eligibility for services. Psychological assessments and psychiatric diagnoses can also help the counselor provide more efficient and knowledgeable treatment. Although the counselor should never depend primarily on secondhand reports, these records can provide a complete picture that may assist in effectively meeting the needs of the client.

When reviewing client records for evaluation, ethical standards must always be upheld. The NBCC Code of Ethics specifically addresses guidelines for using client information for evaluation, including:

- Protecting confidentiality to the fullest extent possible
- Accurately reporting information
- Protecting clients from harm
- Obtaining required client consent for all uses of their information (e.g., supervisory review, reimbursement)
- Making clients aware that the consent can be withdrawn without punishment

Credentialing, Licensure, and Public Policy

Accreditation

Accreditation refers to two different processes: **institutional accreditation** and **specialized accreditation**. Institutional accreditation refers to the institution itself being evaluated and found to have met set standards for an educational institution. Specialized accreditation, which is what this section discusses in detail, refers to the process in which colleges and universities voluntarily submit their programs for review under an organization that specializes in ensuring professional education programs meet the standard for their perspective professions. All academic accrediting bodies are overseen by the **Council on Higher Education Accreditation (CHEA).** In the counseling profession, there are three major organizations responsible for accrediting counseling programs in colleges and universities in the United States. These are the **Council for the Accreditation of Counseling and Related Educational Programs (CACREP), the Council on Rehabilitation Education (CORE),** and **the American Psychological Association (APA)**. Of these three organizations, CACREP is the accrediting agency for the largest number of master's and doctoral programs in the world. The CACREP has a comprehensive accreditation process that programs must submit to on a regularly scheduled timeline to ensure that they meet, and continue to meet, professional standards.

Licensure

Licensure as a professional counselor refers to the credentialing required, monitored, and regulated by the government. The **process for licensure** as a professional counselor in the United States depends on the state in which one is intending to practice. Each state has separate laws and regulations that govern the requirements you must meet to become a Licensed Professional Counselor, as well as continuing education and renewal procedures for ongoing licensure. There is a basic set of standards for most

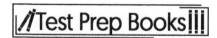

states issuing said licensure, which includes a master's degree from an accredited program, clinical supervision hours, a background check, and a passing score on a state-administered or state-recognized counselor exam. Several states hold **two licensure tiers**: one for fully licensed professional counselors (Licensed Professional Counselors (LPC) or the equivalent) and another for counselors who hold the required master's degree but have yet to complete clinical supervision hours (Limited License Professional Counselor (LLPC) or the equivalent).

The **National Board for Certified Counselors (NBCC)** oversees the National Counselor's Examination (NCE) and the National Clinical Mental Health Counseling Examination (NCMHCE). Although some states offer alternative exams, the NCE and the NCMHCE remain the two most widely used primary examinations in each of the 50 states and U.S. territories to become a Licensed Professional Counselor (LPC). Additionally, the NCE is the only exam you can take to become a Nationally Certified Professional Counselor, a title detailed in a subsequent section of this outline. The NCE and NCMHCE are administered twice per year during the months of April and October, exclusively by Pearson VUE. Recently, a virtual option to take this exam from home has become available through the OnVUE platform on one's computer. The NBCC also provides significant resources on its website that detail preparation for the exam, scheduling and exam locations, and exam sensitivity and bias review.

Certification

In the field of counseling, **certification** can refer to a few different things. It can sometimes refer to the process of voluntarily seeking additional training to become proficient in a specialized area. This process involves seeking coursework through independent professional certification organizations for counseling. Certification for a multitude of different specializations is available for professionals who seek to focus primarily on areas of service. Furthermore, certification provides recognition to the professional that they have acquired additional training surrounding a certain area, allowing them to present themselves to the public officially as having done so. Examples of popular voluntary certifications for counselors include Substance Abuse, Infant Mental Health, and Perinatal Counseling.

Additionally, certification can refer to the voluntary process of becoming nationally certified as a professional counselor through a respected organization. Two leading organizations for the counseling profession oversee certification: the previously mentioned **NBCC** and the **Commission on Rehabilitation Counselor Certification (CRCC)**. Achieving the designation of National Certified Counselor through the NBCC indicates that you have met set national standards for professional counseling. The CRCC offers certifications, including Certified Rehabilitation Counselor (CRC) and Certified Vocational Evaluation Specialists (CVE). The CRCC exists for counselors who seek additional training and certification surrounding working with individuals with disabilities.

Public Policy

The practice of professional counselors is guided by laws and policies. **Statutory law** is a body of mandates that is created and passed by U.S. Congress and state legislatures. Many of the laws are state-specific and may be more restrictive than federal legislation. Agencies such as schools or mental health facilities can also develop specific guidelines, procedures, and policies. In school systems, the local boards of education can rewrite policies and state regulations to meet the needs of their communities. For example, the ratio of students to counselors differs across the nation. In one state, the mandated ratio can be 1 counselor to 350 students, whereas in another state, the ratio may be 1 to 500. Other mandates may include the requirement of every school to provide comprehensive guidance and counseling programs, such as crisis assessment with referral, dropout prevention, and conflict resolution.

Similarly, a large number of state laws require healthcare service plans and insurers to provide some level of coverage for mental health services. Some outliers related to this mandate include copayments, deductibles, and limitations on the number of visits. It is important for a professional counselor to understand the difference between a mandate and a guideline. A **mandate** is a set of rules and regulations set forth by governing bodies that must be followed when practicing counseling. **Guidelines** are suggestions on how to meet mandates. Ethical standards should guide the professional counselor when conflicting mandates arise. Documentation of the logical course of action is key in legal defense. Mandates that result from federal legislation or court cases will usually cover all counselors. Some of these mandates include child abuse or neglect laws. Counselors who have multiple credentials should know the mandates and regulations that apply to their work setting. School counselors rarely require informed consent to meet with students. However, a mental health counselor who works in a school but is employed by an outside agency would have to obtain informed consent to see these same students.

Providing Adequate Accommodations for Clients with Disabilities

Enacted by Congress, the **Americans with Disabilities Act of 1990 (ADA)** is a comprehensive civil rights legislation designed to protect individuals with disabilities from discriminatory practices, such as refusal of employment or lack of access to buildings. Disabilities covered under the act include mental and physical impairments that may limit normal activities. An individual considered a viable candidate for employment is one who can perform the necessary activities with reasonable accommodation. Consequently, the ADA requires all workplace and public entities to provide the necessary accommodations and structures for access, unless doing so places an unreasonable burden on the entity. Counselors must abide by all ADA guidelines and provide appropriate accommodations for all clients with disabilities. Additionally, besides meeting the minimum requirements per the ADA, counselors should strive to make any and all additional accommodations for the comfort and ease of clients with disabilities.

Labor Market Influence on Counseling

Studies have shown that the demand for mental health professionals has increased overall. Though demand has been trending upward consistently for several years, it has skyrocketed over the last two to three years. This is in part due to the COVID-19 global pandemic, which caused the general population unparalleled stress, increased isolation from social supports, financial strain due to employment changes, and a host of other stressors that increased rates of anxiety and depression. In addition to an increased demand for treatment for anxiety and depression, mental health practitioners have seen an uptick in substance abuse related disorders as well as higher instances of patients seeking trauma-related care. Studies have shown young people and health care workers are seeking mental health care at disproportionately high rates.

Given the swell in demand for mental health services, the supply of mental health professionals has struggled to keep up. Many states report a shortage of mental health professionals, including professional counselors. This has created what many refer to as a mental health crisis, given the patient waitlists that exist at many practices around the country. As the push to educate and train more mental health professionals continues, employment for professional counselors, particularly mental health and substance abuse counselors, is projected to increase by 22 percent by 2031, which is far higher than the average for all other professions. Furthermore, an annual average of 43,000 additional openings for substance abuse and mental health counselors is predicted over the next decade.

Impact of Technology on Counseling

Counseling is traditionally done in a face-to-face format. With the innovations in technology, virtual counseling is becoming more convenient. Some of the benefits of using technology include the ability to provide services to clients who may live in remote areas, those who do not have access to reliable transportation, and clients who are more comfortable receiving services online versus in person. One of the biggest challenges of using technology is maintaining client confidentiality. Professional counselors should be educated on the use of encryption standards that prevent unauthorized access to counseling sessions. **Encryption** is a safeguard to protect information that is being transferred online. Some common encryption methods include **Transport Layer Security (TLS)** and **OpenPGP encryption.** **OpenPGP encryption** requires a password when accessing an e-mail or data that has been transferred to a recipient.

If a data breach occurs, counselors should be prepared to show the efforts taken to safeguard **electronic protected health information (ePHI)**. Counselors may choose to use e-mail services that provide a **Business Associate Agreement (BAA),** which places the responsibility on the service should a data breach occur. The informed consent should disclose the limitations of providing services via technology. Malfunctioning equipment or connectivity issues may arise and should be discussed with the client prior to providing services. Professional boundaries must also be established, and counselors should be cautious not to display any client information on social media. The **American Counseling Association (ACA)** Code of Ethics states that professional and personal presence in the virtual world should be kept separate.

Strategies for Personal and Professional Self-Evaluation

Evaluation is an important component of any field of study, as it allows counselors to understand which processes are working well and providing results. Evaluation also allows one to identify areas of opportunity and areas for improvement. The process often utilizes data and consumer feedback, and it focuses on processes in place and specific desired outcomes of the practice.

Counselors should continuously evaluate their practice. This evaluation begins with what exactly they would like to evaluate. An evaluation typically focuses on processes (such as clinical intake, client satisfaction, time spent with clients, frequency of sessions, type of intervention) and outcomes (such as were specific goals met for a client, how many clients return after being discharged). Many healthcare organizations provide evaluation tools for counselors, such as benchmark reports that provide client satisfaction responses or practice outcomes.

Self-Care Strategies for Counselors

Due to the highly emotional, interpersonal, and empathic demands of the counseling field, counselors must employ and sustain self-care practices to protect their personal health. Without self-care, counselors are highly susceptible to burnout and compassion fatigue—two risks that occur when working in a field that often provides exposure to disheartening humanitarian situations, abusive intrapersonal relationships, and cases that, for bureaucratic or personal reasons, take a long time to resolve. Unchecked, these experiences can lead the counselor to feel detached from work and hopeless toward cases or to consistently experience the ill effects of chronic stress.

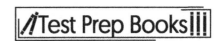

Burnout Symptoms

At times, counselors may experience a sense of disinterest or disengagement from their work, which may signal burnout. Symptoms of burnout can include physical symptoms, such as fatigue, headaches, insomnia, and decreased resistance to illness. Emotional symptoms can include depression, anxiety, boredom, lack of empathy, cynicism, and anger. **Burnout** may be a result of overworking and/or providing service to clients who are not progressing in therapy, thus causing counselors to feel incompetent and ineffective. It is important to know the warning signs of burnout and engage in self-care, which may involve taking a vacation; getting increased supervision or therapy; making changes to one's hours, fees, or practice; or seeking continuing education options.

Self-Care Practices

Self-care practices may include establishing boundaries between one's work and personal life, having a regular meditation practice or other mental exercises that are shown to soothe the nervous system, eating a healthy diet and engaging in regular physical exercise (as these behaviors decrease inflammation in the body and reduce stress hormones), and having a trustworthy support system of friends and colleagues. Introspective exercises, such as daily journaling, can provide the counselor with a better understanding of which activities bring stress to their lives and which activities bring peace. By knowing these, the counselor can bridge the gap to reduce stress in areas they can control, such as setting a clear cut-off time for answering emails or scheduling personal activities that bring them joy. They can adopt healthy coping mechanisms for the areas in which they are unable to control factors that might contribute to their stress, such as an emotional case or external funding issues.

Caseload Management

A **caseload** refers to the number of clients that are assigned to a particular counselor. Managing heavy caseloads can be a challenge for counselors, as it means balancing the needs of many clients with limited time and resources. This may result in poorer quality of services, which directly impacts the client system, and can lead to exhaustion and burnout for the counselor. When possible, a counselor's caseload should be minimized so that more comprehensive services are provided for each client. Unfortunately, there are various and complicated reasons that often contribute to higher caseloads in counselor organizations, such as financial restrictions, understaffing, and high numbers of clients. When large caseloads are unavoidable, then counselors must use other strategies to minimize stress and optimize services, including effective time management and more frequent referrals to other providers who can help meet the various needs of the clients. Additionally, it is important for counselors to prioritize client systems according to the complexity of their needs. Balanced and well-managed workloads, although difficult to achieve, can make a significant difference in the level of services provided to client systems and will result in better overall outcomes.

Impairment

Impairment is a professional issue that should be addressed swiftly. Impairment occurs when a counselor's personal problems (e.g., mental health conditions, difficult life circumstances, or alcohol/drug use) have an impact upon their practice. The Code of Ethics states that counselors should seek to rectify their impairment by consulting with colleagues or supervisors, seeking their own treatment, limiting work, and/or terminating client relationships until the impairment has been fully addressed.

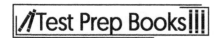

Counseling Supervision

Supervision takes place when a more experienced professional mentors or coaches an emerging professional counselor in fieldwork, practical application, or other service delivery settings. This requires strong interpersonal skills, a sense of respect, and open communication between both parties. The supervisor should be able to provide supportive instruction and guidance without arrogance and condescension; the supervisee should be receptive to instruction and have an honest desire for professional growth and learning. Some commonly used models of supervision in the counseling setting include individual-oriented types of supervision, in which the supervisor may ask the supervisee to reflect upon their interactions with different clients or their personal judgments and biases that may have arisen during a session. The supervisor may also present the supervisee with different forms of research and data and ask the supervisee to utilize the evidence to structure interventions. Finally, the supervisor may provide coaching related to the supervisee's development, by establishing small objectives that lead to larger professional goals.

In peer-oriented and group-oriented approaches, lateral-level colleagues (perhaps with the aid of one or two supervisors) learn from one another by sharing clinical experiences and lessons, new research and literature, or other professional development opportunities. This may take the form of team meetings at the beginning or end of the day, social events where work can be discussed, or conference settings. In some workplaces, individual, peer, and group models may be integrated to provide a more holistic sense of supervision.

Responsibility to Seek Supervision

Sometimes it may be necessary to seek supervision if the counselor experiences burnout, secondary trauma, compassion fatigue, countertransference or the inability to develop a trusting relationship with the client. Although the focus is often on the supervisor's role of ensuring that clients are provided with ethical services by training and evaluating the supervisee, the supervisee's role in supervision is not passive. The counselor should fully engage in the process of supervision and use this relationship to grow and improve. In order to do that, the supervisee must be willing to discuss areas of ethical or legal concern that have arisen in their interactions with clients. They must also be ready to honestly address their own struggles and identify their learning needs, and seek the help and advice of the supervisor. This can only happen effectively through genuine self-assessment, which flows from a desire to become a better counselor. The process of self-assessment in supervision can help them see any biases or weaknesses that may be holding them back from fully meeting their clients' needs. If the counselor is defensive or resistant to the supervisory relationship, then they will make little progress.

Factors to consider when receiving feedback during supervision/consultation:

- Counselors can benefit from feedback during supervision or consultation, especially with difficult clients/cases or at significant times in treatment, such as termination.

- When discussing cases, client confidentiality should be protected as much as possible, and client consent to release information should be acquired.

Practice Quiz

1. A human resources manager who only reviews applications from individuals that are between twenty-two and thirty years of age, regardless of any other credentials or experience, is demonstrating which of the following?
   a. Sexism
   b. Millennial-leaning bias
   c. Ageism
   d. Classism

2. A counselor tells her client, "I understand how the divorce has hurt you. It has caused you many years of pain and loneliness." The counselor is demonstrating which of the following?
   a. Empathy
   b. Selective attunement
   c. Congruence
   d. Sympathy

3. For which of the following reasons must a counselor refer a client to another counselor?
   a. The client is suicidal.
   b. The counselor has a sexual history with the client.
   c. The client is threatening to harm the counselor.
   d. The counselor is closing his practice.

4. When required by law to disclose confidential information about a client, the counselor should always discuss the disclosure with the client before the disclosure occurs. Is this true or false? Why?
   a. False. At the time of the informed consent, the client should have been told about legal requirements that cause the counselor to break confidentiality, and therefore, the counselor never needs to discuss a specific disclosure with the client.
   b. True. The counselor has to get the client to sign a new informed consent form stating that the client understands the disclosure will be made.
   c. False. The counselor should assess any threat to their personal safety, or the safety of others, and should only discuss the disclosure with the client if no one appears to be at risk of harm.
   d. True. The counselor has a duty to tell the client that a disclosure is being made and that confidentiality is being broken.

5. Which of the following is an example of a third-party entity that requires the release of limited client records?
   a. The client receiving treatment
   b. The primary counselor providing treatment
   c. A client involved in group therapy
   d. The client's insurance provider

See answers on next page

35

Answer Explanations

1. C: Ageism. Ageism is discrimination against someone because of his or her age. In this situation, the manager is automatically filtering out older applicants even if they bring appropriate skills and knowledge for the position, simply because of age. Choice *A*, sexism, is when prejudice or discrimination is shown against someone on the basis of sex. Choice *B*, millennial-leaning bias is not an actual term. Choice *D*, classism, is prejudice against someone because of a certain socioeconomic class.

2. A: The counselor demonstrates empathy by seeing the client's perspective of the situation and displaying understanding. The remaining choices are incorrect.

3. B: Choice *B* is correct. It is unethical for counselors to have sexual dual relationships with their clients. Choice *A* is incorrect. Suicidal clients should not be referred to another counselor but rather evaluated for possible hospitalization. Choice *C* is incorrect. A client who is threatening to harm the counselor should be reported to the police. Choice *D* is incorrect. Prior to closing a practice, counselors must prepare their clients for eventual termination. This may include referral to another counselor, but it is not mandatory.

4. C: False. A counselor should always assess their own personal safety, as well as the safety of others, when deciding if a confidential disclosure should be discussed with the client. For example, a counselor is working with someone who has a history of violence toward women, and he discloses that he has been contemplating harming his neighbor who has turned down his advances. In this instance, it would be safer if the counselor didn't discuss the disclosure with the client. Given his history of violence, discussing the disclosure might put both the counselor and the neighbor at risk.

5. D: Third-party payers such as insurance companies may request basic client information, diagnosis, and treatment for billing purposes. Choices *A* and *B* are not considered third parties. Choice *C* is incorrect because client confidentiality is limited in group therapy.

Social and Cultural Diversity

Cultural Awareness

Counselors must be adept at working with diverse populations. **Diversity** includes race, culture, gender, ethnicity, sexual orientation, socioeconomic status, religion, and age. As part of the profession, counselors will provide services to individuals and families with whom they have no cultural similarity. Thus, it is essential for counselors to develop and maintain a level of cultural competence. The first step is for them to engage in self-awareness and gain an understanding of their own identity, including their belief systems and biases. As part of the counseling process, counselors should be able to acknowledge differences and communicate to clients with trust and credibility while demonstrating mutual respect. They should engage in ongoing professional development to gain skills and awareness of differing cultural needs and, from an ethical standpoint, to ensure they are providing competent services. To maintain credibility and trust, counselors must clearly define issues and goals for counseling, taking into consideration cultural variations.

Counselors need to be culturally aware in their attitudes and beliefs. This requires a keen awareness of their own cultural background and gaining awareness of any personal biases, stereotypes, and values that they hold. Counselors should also accept different worldviews, be sensitive to differences, and refer minority clients to a counselor from the client's culture when it would benefit the client.

Counselors need to have the appropriate knowledge of different cultures. Specifically, counselors must understand the client's culture and should not jump to conclusions about the client's way of being. Throughout their careers, counselors should be willing to gain a greater depth of knowledge of various cultural groups and update this knowledge as necessary. This includes understanding how issues like racism, sexism, and homophobia can negatively affect minority clients. Counselors should understand how different therapeutic theories carry values that may be detrimental for some clients. Counselors should also understand how institutional barriers can affect the willingness of minority clients to use mental health services.

Techniques for Working with Clients from Diverse Backgrounds

When working with clients from diverse backgrounds, counselors should be able to shift their professional strategies. Below are techniques and strategies counselors should keep in mind when working with clients of different cultures:

- Have appropriate attitudes and beliefs, gain knowledge about the client's background, and learn new skills as needed.

- Encourage the client to speak in his or her native language and arrange for an interpreter when necessary.

- Assess the client's cultural identity and how important it is to the client.

- Check accuracy of any interpretations of the client's nonverbal cues.

- Make use of alternate modes of communication, such as writing, typing, translation services, and the use of art.

- Assess the impact of sociopolitical issues on the client.

- Encourage the client to bring culturally significant and personally relevant items.

- Vary the helping environment to make it conducive to effective work with the client.

The following strategies can be used when working with clients with various religious backgrounds:

- Determine the client's religious background in the beginning sessions.
- Check personal biases and gain information about the client's religion.
- Ask the client how important religion is in his or her life.
- Assess the client's level of faith development.
- Avoid making assumptions about the religion.
- Become familiar with the client's religious beliefs, important holidays, and faith traditions.
- Understand that religion can deeply affect the client unconsciously.

Cautions and Broad Statements Regarding Cultures

It is important not to use information about culture, race, and ethnicity in a stereotypical or overgeneralized manner. There are vast differences within groups. For example, group members holding a traditional viewpoint are likely to identify very strongly with their group and to reject the practices of other groups. In contrast, other individuals may be acculturated into a dominant group culture and may not identify with their culture of origin. With that caution in mind, some broad statements may be made to help counselors gain a better understanding of the ways in which race, culture, and/or ethnicity can influence behavior and attitude:

- Native Americans: Core values include sharing, honor, respect, interdependence, obligation to family, group cohesion, and co-existence with nature.

- Latinos: There is enormous variability among the various Latino groups due to the differences in their histories and cultural experiences. Values include family, avoidance of conflict, respect for others, religiosity, and patriarchy.

- Asian Americans: Great diversity among groups should be noted, as this is a very broad category. Typically shared values across Asian cultures include family honor, deference to authority and to elders, humility, and avoidance of confrontation.

- White Americans: Personal preferences or desires frequently supersede those of the family unit. Values may include capitalism, individuality, and freedom.

- African-Americans: Extended family is held as very important; women are viewed as the center and strength of the family unit. Church and the extended church community may play a large role in an individual or family's life. There is a distrust of government and authority figures.

- Pacific Islanders and Native Hawaiians: Values include the interconnectedness between all people, not just family, that is related by blood, community, and sharing. They are often polytheistic, with a belief that spirits exist in animals and in objects.

The Impact of Heritage, Attitudes, and Beliefs on an Individual's Self-Image and View of Others

Self-image has to do with how people view themselves. This concept includes *self-esteem*, whether a person has feelings of high or low worth. The concept of self evolves throughout the lifespan, but it always plays a significant role in how a person functions in life.

Impact of Cultural Heritage on Self-Image

Although personal factors play a large role, self-esteem is also based on how closely a person matches the dominant values of their culture. For example, Western society tends to value assertiveness, independence, and individuality. Living up to these values is seen as an important accomplishment, and thus, children receive messages about their personal competence and success based on whether or not they are living up to these ideals.

Children are more likely to develop a positive self-concept when they are able to exhibit behaviors that are valued in their family, home, and culture.

One study suggests that across cultures, self-esteem is based on one's control of life and choices, living up to one's "duties," benefiting others or society, and one's achievements. However, the degree to which one's culture values each of those factors has an impact on how the individual derives their self-esteem.

A widely cited example of the way that a culture can affect a person's self-image is in the portrayal of women's bodies in the media. In the United States, young women are exposed to underweight models and unrealistically drawn cartoon "heroines," which can lead to the development of unachievable expectations and significant negative perceptions about their bodies.

Impact of Race and Ethnicity on Self-Image

Culture, race, and ethnicity can greatly impact one's self-image, whether one is part of a majority population or a minority population. One's ethnic and racial background provides a sense of belonging and identity. Depending on a country's treatment of a particular group, self-image can be negatively impacted through racism and discrimination. As mentioned, non-whites are more likely to be arrested than whites and often receive harsher sentences for similar offenses. Racial jokes and racial slurs are common. Stereotypes abound, and some people judge entire racial groups based on the behavior of a few. Such treatment consistently impacts the self-esteem of minority groups. As children become aware of the environment and the culture in which they live, they inevitably notice a lack of prominent nonwhite politicians, entertainers, CEOs, or multi-millionaires. Non-white Americans who grew up in the fifties or earlier were denied access to restaurants, theaters, high schools, professions, universities, and recreational activities. Even within the last fifty to sixty years, African Americans who had achieved great status in the fields of music, sports, and entertainment were still denied access to certain clubs, hotels, or restaurants.

Every person must explore and come to terms with their own culture, ethnicity, and race. Sometimes, this even means rejecting cultural aspects with which he or she disagrees and embracing new and evolving cultural norms. This is a significant part of self-identity development among teenagers and young adults as they are part of a new generation that may be culturally different from their parents. Those who have more exposure to other cultures and backgrounds will have a more open perspective and are better able to evaluate their own culture and ethnicity objectively.

Gender, Gender Identity, and Sexual Orientation Concepts

The term **gender** refers to a range of physical, behavioral, psychological, or cultural characteristics that create the difference between masculinity and femininity. **Gender identity** is a person's understanding of their own gender, especially as it relates to being male or female. **Sexual orientation is a more complex concept as it refers to the type of sexual attraction one feels for others and how they identify sexually.** This is not to be confused with **sexual preference**, which refers to the specific types of sexual stimulation one most enjoys.

Types of Sexual Orientation

- **Heterosexual**: An individual who is sexually and emotionally attracted to members of the opposite gender, also known as "straight"

- **Homosexual**: An individual who is sexually and emotionally attracted to members of the same gender, sometimes referred to as "gay" or "lesbian"

- **Bisexual**: A male or female who is sexually attracted to both same and opposite gender sex partners

- **Asexual**: An individual who has a low level of interest in sexual interactions with others

Types of Gender Identity

- **Bi-gender**: An individual who fluctuates between the self-image of traditionally male and female stereotypes and identifies with both genders

- **Transgender**: A generalized term referring to a variety of sexual identities that do not fit under more traditional categories, a person who feels to be of a different gender than the one he or she is born with

- **Transsexual**: A person who identifies emotionally and psychologically with the gender other than that assigned at birth, lives as a person of the opposite gender

Those who are transgender or transsexual may be homosexual, heterosexual, or asexual.

Influence of Sexual Orientation on Behaviors, Attitudes, and Identity

Even with today's advances in technology, medicine, and genetics, scientists have not clearly established how sexual orientation develops. It is believed that sexual orientation is a complex interplay of environmental, hormonal, and genetic influences. According to the American Psychological Association, **sexual orientation** refers to an innate attraction to either or both sexes, as well as the person's identity in relation to their attraction. As such, the Association opposes psychiatric treatments such as **conversion therapy**—a form of treatment designed to help homosexuals become heterosexuals through therapy and, sometimes, medical interventions.

Research indicates that family composition may play a role in sexual orientation. For example, homosexual males are more likely to have older male siblings than homosexual women. For men, other factors include being the youngest child, having older mothers, absent fathers, or divorced parents. In women, examples include being an only child, youngest child, being the only girl in the sibling group, or the death of a mother during adolescence. Setting and culture also influence homosexual behavior, i.e., urban areas vs. rural areas.

Impact of Transgender and Transitioning Process on Behaviors, Attitudes, Identity, and Relationships

Being **transgender** can be defined as identifying as a gender other than the gender one was born with. Publicly sharing that one is transgender can be difficult for some individuals. Transgender individuals may live in a community where their identity is not positively accepted or is misunderstood, and they may feel shamed or ridiculed. It may be a difficult experience for close family members to understand the perspective of a transgender individual, which can affect the cohesiveness of family relationships and the family unit. Transgender individuals may also feel a lack of acknowledgement when others fail to use the correct pronouns or respect other identity wishes.

Some transgender individuals choose to medically transition to the gender they identify as. This is a procedure that requires physical, emotional, and psychological support. Individuals not receiving support during their transition can experience extreme feelings of sadness, isolation, and lack of belonging. Medically transitioning individuals also undergo hormonal changes in addition to surgical procedures, and these can cause unexpected feelings and reactions in the individual. There are also medical risks that go along with both the surgical and hormonal procedures of transitioning that the individual has to be aware of and manage. Finally, after the transition is complete, individuals may struggle with living as someone who is relatively unfamiliar to their friends, family members, and colleagues. The transgender person may or may not experience support and acceptance in these groups and relationships, and some group members may even act aggressively toward the transgender person. If this is the case, it may be helpful to find support groups where transgender individuals can find not only friendship and community, but also guidance on how to navigate their new life, society, friends and relationships, and medical recovery.

The Impact of Spiritual Beliefs on Clients' and Counselors' Worldviews

Religious and Spiritual Values

Religion is a potentially influential component of counseling that should be explored in the first sessions. A client's behaviors and values may be based on religious beliefs. Depending on the client's religion, their beliefs could either assist the client in creating change or they could hinder the process. Religion can be a valuable tool to help clients cope with stressful situations or to recover from lifechanging circumstances. Encouraging prayer or attendance to worship services as part of treatment can be beneficial for clients who find strength through their faith. It can be a reminder of the morals and values of their religion, which can motivate clients to commit to change. Although religion can be useful in counseling, it can also be part of the client's presenting problem. Exploring a client's religious beliefs and having knowledge of different religions can be crucial in developing a plan for treatment. For instance, if a client is struggling with an identity issue that is seen as a sin in their religion, an understanding of those beliefs will play a significant part in the counseling process. Respecting a client's religious beliefs and incorporating them into treatment will also help to build the therapeutic relationship.

Spiritual development refers to the way a person grows and changes spiritually, particularly regarding the purpose for their existence, over the course of their life. This process may have conscious or unconscious origins, and it may be affected by other growth and development factors. Spiritual development is often linked to the stages of cognitive development, but evidence-based research pertaining strictly to spiritual development is limited. Theories often focus on the influence of psychosocial constructs (such as morality), cognitive beliefs, and religious or faith-based influences.

Jean Piaget (1896–1980) is renowned for his work in the field of cognitive development. He examined social, biological, and psychological constructs that influence cognitive development and intellect. He theorized four stages of cognitive development, from birth through adulthood. He believed that a multitude of constructs influences a person's moral beliefs and values, and this leads to their ultimate perspective on themselves and the environment.

Lawrence Kohlberg (1927–1987) studied moral psychology and development, and he developed a theory of the stages of moral reasoning. He theorized that individuals model behavior around them and behavior patterns to develop concepts of right and wrong as they progress through life. The more aware a person becomes of the effects of their thoughts, actions, and decisions, the more capacity they have for moral decision making. This may be connected to what shapes an individual's spiritual beliefs.

James Fowler (1940–2015), a theologian and university professor, contributed his "stages of faith" development, which breaks spiritual evolution down into six stages. He believed in the importance of safety and nurturing in the early years, which lead individuals to feel they are in touch with a greater good. Comparatively, individuals who feel unsafe or do not feel nurtured in their younger years are less likely to focus on spiritual aspects of life. Fowler made connections between his stages of faith and the developmental stages of Piaget and Kohlberg.

Spirituality is sometimes mistaken for religion, but in fact, they are quite different terms. Religion is an organized system of beliefs that generally contain a code of conduct and often involve specific devotional or ritual observations. Spirituality is more abstract and includes participation in spiritual activities such as meditation, chanting, or prayer. A spiritual person may or may not belong to a religious organization. Spirituality places emphasis on the growth and well-being of the mind, body, and spirit.

Studies have shown that persons who embrace spirituality tend to live both longer and happier lives. Several benefits of being a spiritual person include the following:

- Individuals are encouraged to strive towards being a better person.
- There is an increased likelihood of connections with others.
- It offers hope to the hopeless through strong faith.
- It provides a path to heal from emotional pain
- It helps reduce anxiety through meditation and other spiritual activities
- It leads to greater life commitment via the optimism spiritual persons tend to have

Intentional and Unintentional Oppression and Discrimination

Making unjust distinctions between people or groups based on characteristics such as race, sex, age, religion, disability, or sexual orientation is **discrimination**. Discriminatory treatment and practices must be consciously combatted in the counseling profession to ensure that all clients receive appropriate care. Counselors should be aware of the various forms of discrimination and their effects, including those defined below.

Direct discrimination refers to unfair treatment based on someone's characteristics. An example would be refusing to hire someone because of their ethnicity.

Indirect discrimination refers to situations in which a policy applies the same to everyone, but a person or group of people are negatively impacted due to certain characteristics. For example, a company might require that everyone help unload shipments that come to the office. The policy is the same for

everyone, but it's discriminatory towards any disabled employees. In a workplace environment, indirect discrimination can sometimes be allowed if there's a compelling reason for the requirement. For example, firefighters have to meet certain physical criteria due to the nature of their work.

Another form of discrimination is **harassment**. This involves unwanted bullying or humiliation intentionally directed to another person. **Secondary victimization** refers to the unfair treatment received when a person reports discrimination and is not supported by authorities.

Effects of discrimination on the individual may include depression, anxiety, and other mental health issues; and medical/health-related problems caused by lack of access to health resources. Effects of discrimination on society include diminished resources (e.g., employment, educational opportunities, healthcare) and a culture characterized by fear, anger, or apathy.

Systemic (institutionalized) discrimination refers to discrimination taking place within a society or other institution (e.g., a religion or educational system). Such discrimination can be either intentional or unintentional and results from the majority of people within the institution holding stereotypical beliefs and engaging in discriminatory practices.

Systemic discrimination is often reflected in the laws, policies, or practices of the institution. Systemic discrimination creates or maintains a disadvantage to a group of people by way of patterns of behavior; it can have wide-reaching effects within a region, profession, or specific institution.

The following are example of systemic discrimination:

- Hiring practices that create barriers or result in lower wages for certain groups

U.S. Supreme Court case, *Plessy vs. Ferguson* (1896) – "separate but equal" public facilities for African-Americans

- Oppression of women in certain countries (e.g., being unable to vote, obtain education, or hold jobs)

Practice Quiz

1. Which of Erikson's stages of development is associated with school-aged children?
   a. Autonomy vs. shame and doubt
   b. Intimacy vs. isolation
   c. Industry vs. inferiority
   d. Trust vs. mistrust

2. A woman tells her therapist that she is worried about her seven-year-old son. She caught the boy talking to himself, and he explained that he was talking to his imaginary friend. The woman is afraid that this means her son is mentally ill. What should the therapist tell the woman?
   a. This behavior suggests that the boy is being neglected or abused.
   b. This behavior indicates that the boy is experiencing psychosis.
   c. This behavior is normal for very young children but is concerning at age seven.
   d. This behavior is normal for the boy's age and development.

3. According to Piaget's theory of cognitive development, people reach the formal operations stage at age eleven. The formal operations stage is characterized by all of the following EXCEPT:
   a. Magical thinking
   b. High-level abstract thinking
   c. Planning for the future
   d. Hypothetical thinking

4. According to Kohlberg's theory, at which level of moral development do people conform to established rules and laws of society?
   a. Preconventional
   b. Conventional
   c. Postconventional
   d. Adult

5. A child refuses to do his homework, so his mother takes away his phone as a consequence. What type of operant technique is this?
   a. Positive reinforcement
   b. Positive punishment
   c. Negative reinforcement
   d. Negative punishment

See answers on next page

Answer Explanations

1. C: Industry vs. inferiority is the developmental stage that children go through during their school years, from age six until puberty. This is when children learn to initiate projects, follow through with them, and feel proud of their accomplishments. To complete this stage successfully, children must be encouraged and supported in their endeavors. On the other hand, if their attempts to take initiative are criticized or restricted, children will doubt themselves and feel inferior to their peers. Choice *A* is incorrect because autonomy vs. shame and doubt is the stage from age one to three when children start to become independent from their primary caregiver. Choice *B* is incorrect because intimacy vs. isolation takes place during young adulthood when people develop committed intimate relationships outside of their family of origin. Choice *D* is incorrect because trust vs. mistrust is the stage from birth to age one when babies develop the ability to trust others if their needs are met by their caregivers.

2. D: The therapist should reassure the woman that her son's behavior is normal for his age and developmental level. Many children develop imaginary friends around this time, and it does not indicate the presence of a disorder or problem. Although children talk to and play with their imaginary friends, they usually understand that they are not actually real people. The behavior can be distressing for parents, and therapists can help by providing empathy and psychoeducation. In the absence of other concerning symptoms, a seven-year-old having an imaginary friend is not an indicator of abuse/neglect (Choice *A*), psychosis (Choice *B*), or abnormal development (Choice *C*).

3. A: Magical thinking is associated with the preoperational stage of cognitive development, which occurs between ages two and seven. Magical thinking involves believing events are connected when they are not. Because young children are egocentric, they often believe that they have more influence over the events around them then they actually do. For example, a child calls his sister a name. The sister gets sick. The child believes his sister got sick because he called her a name. As children develop cognitively, magical thinking is replaced by more logical thinking and a better understanding of cause and effect. The formal operations stage is the final stage of Piaget's model. It represents the most mature thinking processes. People who have reached this stage are able to think abstractly at a high level (Choice *B*), effectively plan for the future (Choice *C*), and think hypothetically (Choice *D*). This level of cognitive development allows people to take on adult roles and responsibilities.

4. B: Kohlberg theorized that people go through three main levels of moral development, subdivided into six stages. The second level (stages three and four) is conventional morality. At this level of moral development, people conform to the rules of society. They follow the rules both to be seen as a good person by others and because they believe that rules are important to society. Choice *A* is incorrect because the preconventional level is the first level of moral development and lasts until age nine. At this level, children are focused on avoiding punishment and seeking rewards. Choice *C* is incorrect because the final level of moral development is postconventional. At this level, people are motivated by concern for the general welfare of others and develop their own set of principles based on a broad understanding of ethics. Choice *D* is incorrect because adults can be at either the conventional or postconventional level; many adults do not make it past conventional morality.

5. D: Operant conditioning describes how people learn through consequences. Negative punishment involves taking away a desirable stimulus (the phone) after an undesirable behavior (refusing to do homework). Choice *A* is incorrect because positive reinforcement involves rewarding a desirable behavior. For example, if the child does his homework, he is allowed extra video game time. Choice *B* is

45

incorrect because positive punishment involves providing an undesirable stimulus in response to an undesirable behavior. For example, the boy refuses to do his homework, so his mother yells at him. Choice *C* is incorrect because negative reinforcement involves removing an undesirable stimulus in response to a desirable behavior. For example, the child does his homework, so his mother will stop hassling him.

Human Growth and Development

Theories of Individual and Family Development Across the Lifespan

There are a number of theories on human growth and development. The most important theories are addressed in this section.

Freud's Model of Development

Freud is known for his research on stages of human development and his assertion that there were five stages of psychosexual development:

Oral Stage (birth to 18 months)
- An infant's focus of gratification involves the mouth.
- The primary need is security.
- Security needs are met when caretakers provide baby with essentials, such as food, shelter, warmth, and cleanliness.

Anal Stage (18 months to age 3)
- A child's focus of gratification involves the anus and the bladder.
- These organs represent sensual satisfaction.
- Internal conflict arises when the child begins the process of toilet training.

Phallic Stage (age 3 to age 6)
- The child engages in exploration of their body with greater interest in genitals.
- Oedipus and Electra complexes may occur.
- There is a pseudo-sexual attraction to the parent of the opposite gender.
- Conflict arises when the child realizes he/she has failed to win control over the parents' bond with one another.

Latent Stage (age 6 to puberty)
- The child's sexual interests become subdued or dormant.
- Energy is focused on school, hobbies, athletics, and mastering social skills.

Genital Stage (puberty until death)
- The teen becomes aware of physical changes and onset of sexual feelings.
- The individual is less egocentric and more compassionate.
- There's a motivation to seek relationships that are emotionally and sexually satisfying.
- Success in this stage lays groundwork for future relationships that are healthy and long lasting.

Erikson's Model of Development

Erikson devised eight stages of psychosocial development. He emphasized the importance of social context, asserting that family and environment are major contributors to child development.

Trust vs. Mistrust (birth to 18 months)
- The primary goal is to learn to trust others.
- Trust occurs when a caretaker appropriately responds to a need in a timely, caring manner.

- Mistrust occurs when caretakers fail to meet the infant's basic needs.

Autonomy vs. Shame and Doubt (18 months to age 3)
- The primary goal is the development of self-control without loss of self-esteem.
- The toddler develops cooperation and self-expression skills.
- Failure to reach this goal leads to defiance, anger, and social problems.

Initiative vs. Guilt (age 3 to age 6)
- Initiative means confidently devising a plan and following it through to completion.
- Guilt is generated by fear that actions taken will result in disapproval.
- Failure to achieve initiative can lead to anxiety and fearfulness in new situations.

Industry vs. Inferiority (age 6 to age 11)
- Industry refers to purposeful, meaningful behavior.
- Inferiority refers to having a sense of unworthiness or uselessness.
- The child focuses on learning skills, such as making friends and self-care activities—e.g., dressing or bathing.
- Failure in this stage could lead to negative social or academic performance and the lack of self-confidence.

Identity vs. Role Confusion (age 12 to age 18)
- This stage involves the desire to fit in and to figure out one's own unique identity.
- Self-assessment of sexual identity, talents, and vocational direction occurs.
- Role confusion is the result of juggling multiple physical changes, increased responsibility, academic demands, and a need to understand how one fits into the greater picture.

Intimacy vs. Isolation (age 18 to age 40)
- This stage pertains to an ability to take risks by entering the workforce, finding a long term relation, and possibly becoming a parent.
- Failure to navigate this stage leads to isolation, loneliness, and depression.

Generativity vs. Stagnation (age 40 to age 60)
- This stage involves developing stability in areas of finance, career, and relationships, as well as a sense that one is contributing something valuable to society.
- Failure to achieve these objectives leads to unhappiness with one's status and feeling unimportant.

Ego Integrity vs. Despair (mid sixties to death)
- Important life tasks, such as child rearing and career, are being completed.
- Reviewing and evaluating how one's life was spent occurs.
- Success in this stage provides a sense of fulfillment.
- Failure emerges if one is dissatisfied with accomplishments, which leads to depression or despair.

Erikson's Psychosocial Stages of Development

Stage	Age	Psychosocial Crisis	Basic Virtue
1	Infancy (0 to 1½)	Trust vs. mistrust	Hope
2	Early Childhood (1½ to 3)	Autonomy vs. shame	Will
3	Play Age (3 to 5)	Initiative vs. guilt	Purpose
4	School Age (5 to 12)	Industry vs. inferiority	Competency
5	Adolescence (12 to 18)	Ego identity vs. role confusion	Fidelity
6	Young Adult (18 to 40)	Intimacy vs. isolation	Love
7	Adult hood (40 to 65)	Generativity vs. stagnation	Care
8	Maturity (65+)	Ego integrity vs. despair	Wisdom

Seasons of Life Theory (Levinson)

This theory of adult development is classified by development stages, with each stage defined by different, yet meaningful and developmentally necessary, tasks. There are transition periods where stages overlap.

The *pre-adulthood stage* ends at age twenty-two. Beginning at birth, this is the stage when a person develops and prepares for adulthood. It is a time of major growth and transition where the individual develops a state of independence.

The *early adulthood transition* is roughly age seventeen to twenty-two. Pre-adulthood is ending, and early adulthood is beginning, but the time of transition is actually part of both periods. Physical development is completed, but this time of transition can be compared to the infancy of a new period of development. During this stage, adolescence ends, and the individual begins to make decisions about adult life. He or she further develops independence and separates from the family of origin.

Early adulthood stage is roughly age seventeen to forty-five. This stage begins with the early adult transition. From a biological perspective, an individual's twenties and thirties are at the peak of the life cycle. This stage can be the time at which individuals have their greatest energy, but are also experiencing the greatest amount of stress as they try to establish families and careers simultaneously.

Midlife transition is roughly age forty to forty-five. This is a time of transition that bridges the end of early adulthood and the beginning of middle adulthood. At this time of life, people tend to become more reflective and compassionate and less concerned with external demands. Values may change, and it is possibly a time where crisis is experienced due to limited time to reach goals. Individuals become aware of death and leaving a legacy.

Middle adulthood stage is roughly age forty to sixty-five. There is a diminishment of biological capacities, but only minimally. Most individuals are able to continue to lead fulfilling and relatively energetic lives.

Many take on a mentoring role and responsibility for the further development of young adults. Choices must be made about livelihood and retirement.

Late adulthood is at roughly age sixty. A transition period occurs from around sixty to sixty-five. Late adulthood is a time of reflection on other stages and on accomplishments. During this stage, retirement takes place, and the individual gives up their role in the workplace. Crisis occurs at this stage due to declining power and less accolades of work performed.

Social Clock Theory (Bernice Neugarten)

Neugarten proposed that every society has a *social clock*: an understood expectation for when certain life events should happen (e.g., getting married, buying a home, having children). When individuals do not adhere to this timeframe, they often experience stress, the sense of disappointing others, or the experience of an internal "clock ticking" and reminding them that time is running out.

Family Dynamics and Functioning

Family dynamics are the interactions between family members in a family system. As discussed previously, under "Family Theories," each family is a unique system; however, there are some common patterns of family dynamics.

Common influences on family dynamics:

- The type and quality of relationship that the parents have
- An absent parent
- A parent who is either extremely strict or extremely lenient
- The mix of personalities in the family
- A sick or disabled family member
- External events, particularly traumatic ones that have affected family members
- Family dynamics in previous generations or the current extended family

Common roles in the family that may result from particular family dynamics:

- **The problem child**: child with problematic behavior, which may serve as a distraction from other problems that the family, particularly the parents, do not want to face

- **Scapegoat**: the family member to whom others unjustly attribute problems, often viewed as "bad," while other family members are viewed as "good"

- **Peacekeeper**: a family member who serves to mediate relationships and reduce family stress

The Effects of Family Dynamics on Individuals

There are many ways in which the family influences the individual socially, emotionally, and psychologically. All family systems have their own unique characteristics, with both good and bad functional tendencies. The family interactions are among the earliest and most formative relationships that a person has, so they define the relational patterns that the individual develops and utilizes with all subsequent relationships. Parenting styles, conflict resolution methods, beliefs and values, and coping mechanisms are just a few things that a person learns from their family of origin. It is also within the family that a person first develops an image of self and identity, often having to do with the role that they are given within the family system and the messages communicated by parents. If a child has a

50

secure and healthy relationship with the family members, this will likely lead to overall well-being and emotional stability as an adult.

When it comes to physical or mental illness, the role that the family plays is critical in lowering risk factors and minimizing symptoms. A strongly supportive family will help a person function at the highest level possible. Oftentimes, family members can serve as caregivers or play less formal—but still critical—roles in supporting a person's health.

Parenting Skills and Capacities

Good parenting practices are essential for raising emotionally healthy children. Child psychologists vary on what types of parenting styles are most effective, but there are four generally recognized styles of parenting.

Authoritarian parenting style: This style of parenting reinforces the role of parent as controller and decision maker. Children are rarely given input into decisions impacting their lives, and the parent takes on a dictatorial role. Children raised by this kind of parent are often obedient and tend to be proficient. The drawback is that they do not rank high on the happiness scale.

Authoritative parenting style: This style of parenting allows for a greater sense of democracy in which children are given some degree of input into issues that impact their lives. There is a healthy balance between firmness and affection. Children raised in this environment tend to be capable, successful, and happy individuals.

Permissive parenting style: This type of parenting allows children to be more expressive and freer with both feelings and actions; they are allowed to behave in whatever manner they please. There are very few rules, and no consequences will be given, even if a rule is violated. These children are more likely to experience problems in school and relationships with others. In the long run, they are often unhappy with their lives.

Uninvolved parenting style: This form of parenting often occurs in dysfunctional families in which parents are emotionally or physically unavailable. They may be remiss in setting clear expectations, yet they may overreact when the child misbehaves or fails to understand what is expected. This is often seen in families where poverty is extreme or addictions or mental illnesses are present.

The authoritative style of parenting is considered to be the most effective form of parenting, yet much depends on the individual child or parent and the economic situation or cultural setting. One rule of thumb is that whatever style one chooses, it is helpful to remain consistent. A parent who is permissive one day and authoritarian the next sends mixed and confusing messages to the child. It is also important that the child is completely aware of rules, expectations, and consequences that may follow if the rules are broken. Communicating a sense that children are loved, wanted, and accepted is one of the most important parts of parenting.

Family Life Cycle

Family life cycle theories assume that, as members of a family unit, individuals pass through different stages of life. Although various theories will break down the stages somewhat differently, the following is a common conceptualization of the stages:

Unattached Young Adult

The primary tasks for this stage are selecting a lifestyle and a life partner. Focus is on establishing independence as an adult and independence from one's family of origin.

Newly-Married Couple

The focus in this stage is on establishing the marital system. Two families are joined together, and relationships must be realigned.

Family with Young Children

The focus in this stage is on accepting new family members and transitioning from a marital system to a family system. The couple takes on a parenting role. Relationships must again be realigned with the extended family (e.g., grandparents).

Family with Adolescents

The focus here is on accommodating the emerging independence of the adolescents in the family. The parent-child relationship experiences changes, and the parents may also begin to take on caregiving roles with regard to their own parents.

Launching Family

The focus in this stage is on accepting the new independent role of an adult child and transitioning through the separation. Parents also must face their own transition into middle or older age.

Family in Later Years

In this stage, spousal roles must be re-examined and re-defined. One focus may be the development of interests and activities outside of work and family. Another focus is on navigation of the aging process and losses that may occur.

The basic family life cycle can vary significantly as a result of cultural influences, expectations, and particular family circumstances (e.g., single-parent family, blended family, multi-generational family).

Family Life Education in Counseling

Family life education is an important aspect of counseling in the psychoeducational realm of treatment. Families sometimes need to be educated concerning their biopsychosocial structure and other kinds of family structures. Family life models have changed in recent years and continue to change at a rapid pace with the advent of the legalization of gay marriage and the increase in extended and blended families. Family life has become very diverse, and counselors need to be educated on these models so they can further educate clients.

Aging Parents on Adult Children

There are about 10 million Americans over the age of fifty who are caring for aging parents. In the last fifteen years, thanks to modern medicine, the adult population has begun living longer. As a result, the number of adult children between the ages of fifty and seventy who provide care to aging parents has tripled. This amounts to about 25 percent of adult children who provide either personal or economic assistance.

Research indicates that becoming a personal caregiver to a parent increases the rates of depression, substance abuse, and heart disease. These adult children sometimes take significant financial blows in the form of lost income, earlier than planned retirement, and reduced pension plans, due to leaving the

workforce earlier. At the same time, these adult children are assisting their own children as they move towards independence. Those in the youngest generation may still be in college or in the early stages of starting a career and still look to parents for some financial assistance. From a different perspective, the positives of this situation are that children are able to form deeper bonds with grandparents, and the longevity of life in loved ones can have a very positive impact on all involved.

Theories of Learning

Piaget's Model of Development

Piaget is best known for his concept that children's minds are not just smaller versions of adult minds, but that they also grow and develop in different ways. His work has been influential within academic settings and has helped educators better determine what and how children can learn at various stages of their educational process. The following are the key ideas related to his research into the way cognition develops in children:

- Assimilation: A process by which a person accepts and organizes information then incorporates new material into existing knowledge

- Accommodation: A process by which old ideas must be changed or replaced due to obtaining new information from the environment

- Schemas: A set of thoughts, ideas, or perceptions that fit together and are constantly challenged by gaining new information and creating change through knowledge

Piaget also recognized and defined the following *four stages of cognitive development*:

Stage 1: Sensorimotor Stage (birth to age 2)
- The infant becomes aware of being an entity separate from the environment.
- Object permanence occurs as the baby realizes that people or objects still exist, even if they are out of sight.
- Object permanence builds a sense of security as the baby learns that though mommy has left the room, she will still return.
- This reduces fear of abandonment and increases their confidence about the environment.

Stage 2: Pre-operational Stage (age 2 to age 7)
- The child moves from being barely verbal to using language to describe people, places, and things.
- The child remains egocentric and unable to clearly understand the viewpoint of others.
- The process of quantifying and qualifying emerges, and the child can sort, categorize, and analyze in a rough, unpolished form.

Stage 3: Concrete Operational Stage (age 7 to age 11)
- The ability to problem solve and reach logical conclusions evolves.
- By age 10 or 11, children begin to doubt magical stories, such as the Tooth Fairy or the Easter Bunny.
- Previously-held beliefs are questioned.

Stage 4: Formal Operational Stage (age 12 through remaining lifetime)
- More complex processes can now be assimilated.
- Egocentrism diminishes.
- One assimilates and accommodates beliefs that others have needs and feelings too.
- New schemas are created.
- The individual seeks their niche in life in terms of talents, goals, and preferences.

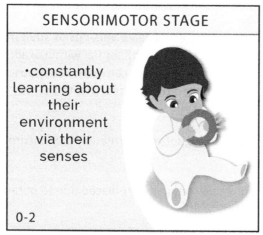

SENSORIMOTOR STAGE

- constantly learning about their environment via their senses

0-2

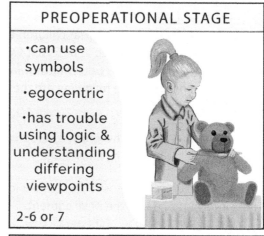

PREOPERATIONAL STAGE

- can use symbols
- egocentric
- has trouble using logic & understanding differing viewpoints

2-6 or 7

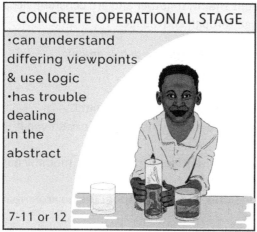

CONCRETE OPERATIONAL STAGE

- can understand differing viewpoints & use logic
- has trouble dealing in the abstract

7-11 or 12

FORMAL OPERATIONAL STAGE

- can think in the abstract
- can solve problems systematically

12 - Adulthood

Ivan Pavlov (Classical Conditioning)

Another important concept of development has to do with learning and the way in which humans learn new behaviors. A famous psychologist, Ivan Pavlov, conducted research with dogs that proved to be ground-breaking in the field of classical conditioning. In his experiment, a ringing bell was paired with the presentation of food, which produced salivation in the dog. The ringing sound eventually produced salivation from the dog even in the absence of food. Salivation then became the conditioned response to hearing a bell, and thus, the theory of classical conditioning was developed. The important finding of this research is that we learn by association.

B.F. Skinner (Operant Conditioning)

Skinner also did important research in the field of learning, specifically operant conditioning. Operant conditioning theory focuses on behavioral changes that can be seen or measured. The basic concept is

that behavior that is reinforced will increase, and behavior that is punished will decrease. There are several key concepts integral to an understanding of this form of learning:

- **Positive Reinforcement:** Anything that serves as a form of reward, including food, money, praise, or attention

- **Negative reinforcement:** An unpleasant stimulus that is removed when behavior is elicited, such as a man finally cutting the grass to stop his wife from nagging him about it

- **Punishment:** An unpleasant response from the environment—e.g., a slap, an unkind word, or a speeding ticket—that when encountered, increases the likelihood that a behavior will cease. Two problems arise with using punishment. Once the negative stimulus is removed, the behavior is likely to continue. Punishment can also cause humiliation, anger, resentment, and aggression.

- **Superstition:** An incorrect perception that one stimulus is connected to another. Skinner found that when teaching a rat to press a lever for food, if the rat chases its tail before pressing the lever, it will mistakenly believe that the tail chase is required and will do both behaviors each time it wants food.

- **Shaping:** The process of changing behavior gradually by rewarding approximations of the desired behavior, e.g., first rewarding a rat for moving closer to the lever

Skinner found that there are different schedules of reinforcement and that some work better than others. These include the following:

- Continuous rate: Person or animal is rewarded every time a behavior is demonstrated
- Fixed ratio: Reward is given after a fixed number of attempts
- Variable ratio: Reward is forthcoming at unpredictable rates, like a slot machine
- Fixed interval: Reward is given only after a specific amount of time has passed
- Variable interval: Reward is given after an unpredictable amount of time has passed
- Extinction: Occurs when a behavior disappears or is extinguished because it is no longer being reinforced. To stop tantrum behavior in toddlers, ignoring the behavior will decrease or stop the tantrum if the desired reward is parental attention or parental aggravation.

Role Theories

Different role theories have culminated in the social role theory, which emphasizes that people's behaviors are motivated by the roles they are given within society. These roles can include aspects of race, gender, employment, position in the family, etc. When a person assumes a particular role, they tend to adopt the expectations of that role as governed by social norms and conventions. Some roles, such as gender, may affect many domains of life, while others—like being a student—may be confined to a particular situation or environment. The roles that a person adopts can strongly impact self-image and behaviors. **Philip Zimbardo** illustrated this role dynamic when he conducted the Stanford Prison Experiment, in which individuals given the roles of prisoners and guards assumed their positions so completely that the experiment became dangerous. The guards became violent and aggressive, and the prisoners became overly submissive and afraid.

Social roles can both negatively and positively impact the individual. While the smooth functioning of society is dependent on different people fulfilling different roles and responsibilities, certain role

expectations can limit a person's individuality and self-determination. For example, typical gender roles may cause a woman to feel that her role in society is restricted by the expectations placed upon her.

Feminist Theory

Feminist theory is the study of relations between the sexes, especially in the context of inequality. Discussions often include the topics of gender roles, gender in work-life contexts, societal norms for the genders, and cultural perceptions of gender. Feminist theory also focuses on gender relations and certain power relationships. Feminist pioneers have fought for equal political and social rights for men and women (such as the right to vote or the ability to work outside the home), for making previously male-oriented terms gender neutral (such as using "firefighter" instead of "fireman), for female body positivity and acceptance, for sexual and reproductive rights and protection, and for encouraging supportive relationships between the genders. Feminist theories also support equality for men in such areas as paternity leave, stay at home parenting for fathers, and a redefined masculinity that includes heightened emotional intelligence, awareness, and expression. Feminist theory researchers have been striving to reinvigorate feminist studies, believing that prior theories formed by primarily male researchers should be reexamined.

Influential Feminist Theorists

A number of American female psychologists, psychiatrists, and psychoanalysts have been influential in shaping psychological research that pertains to development in women and in serving as leaders in feminist theory.

- **Anna Freud** (1895–1982) made significant contributions to the field of psychoanalysis, especially regarding the ego and child development. She was the youngest daughter of Sigmund Freud. Some of her works include *Introduction to Psychoanalysis: Lectures for Child Analysts and Teachers* and *Ego and the Mechanisms of Defense*.

- **Jean Baker Miller** (1927–2006) is best known for authoring the revered text *Toward a New Psychology of Women* (1976). She is also known for her work with **relational-cultural theory**, which focuses on how culture affects relationships and how healthy connections with others are an integral part of psychological health and personal growth. These ideas often played a role in diagnosing and treating depression in women.

- **Carol Tavris** (1944–) promotes critical thinking and evidence-based research in psychology, focusing on cognitive dissonance. She believes many of women's so-called psychological issues are actually social beliefs about women's limitations, and that these social beliefs are not backed by science.

- **Nancy Chodorow** (1944–) authored the renowned text *Psychoanalysis and the Sociology of Gender* (1978). Her research focuses on mothering, gender systems, how the family influences female roles in society, and gender identity formation.

- **Harriet Lerner** (1944–) is best known for her work regarding gender roles in marriage, cultural gender norms, and how women can balance self-care with other competing priorities in their lives.

- **Carol Gilligan** (1936–) was a research assistant to **Lawrence Kohlberg**. She argues that his theories of moral development are male-focused and do not apply to women. Her research focuses on the development of morals and ethics in women. She initially published her findings as *In a Different Voice* in 1982.

Gail Sheehy (1937–2020) was an author and journalist who wrote Passages (1976), which supports many of the beliefs and ideas of feminist psychologists. This book covers the different periods of life that women progress through and the emotions they experience in each one. The Library of Congress honored Passages as one of the top ten most influential books of its time.

Communication Theories and Styles

One of the main names associated with communication theory is **Niklas Luhmann**, a sociologist and systems theorist. In **Luhmann's theory**, it is the communication *between* people and not the people themselves that makes up a social system.

Luhmann uses the term **autopoiesis** to define social systems as self-creating. By this he means the social system has the ability to produce itself and maintain itself. Luhmann believed that communications make up the system, and communications create other communications. The meaning of a communication is the response it generates.

The **Shannon and Weaver model of communication**, though its origins are mathematical and technical, is cited as one of the primary communication models. This model was the first to conceptualize the activity of the sender and the receiver. For communication to occur in this model, the sending entity has to prepare and actively deliver information, and the receiver has to wait and actively accept information. The **Berlo model of communication** added that all communication also needed a channel over which to travel.

There are four primary communication styles. **Passive communication** refers to senders who avoid full, direct, and clear verbal or written expression to send a message. Rather, their body language and behaviors may provide a large chunk of the intended message. **Passive communicators** tend to avoid direct communication; they are unassertive, quiet, and anxious. **Aggressive communicators** are overly direct senders, so much so that their communications may harm those who are listening to them. Aggressive communicators are characterized as dominating, impulsive, and critical. **Passive-aggressive communication** refers to senders who outwardly show mildly expressive communication but inwardly feel aggression that is manifested in body language or behavior. **Passive-aggressive communicators** often have a difficult time with confrontation, expressing powerful feelings, and understanding anger. **Assertive communication** refers to senders who are clear and firm yet considerate when stating their message. Assertive communicators tend to speak clearly, feel in control, and respect themselves and others.

Theories of Conflict

Conflict theories center on the premise that all human interactions involve some degree of power struggle, and this struggle may be exacerbated by differences in ideologies, acquisition of resources, culture and class differences, or other variables. Eventually, some groups end up controlling resources and decision-making, therefore limiting opportunities for more submissive or resource-constrained groups. These dynamics eventually shape the culture and interpersonal relationships of a group, whether it is a small team or a country's entire society.

Karl Marx (1818–1883) contributed one of the most widely recognized social conflict theories, **Marxism**, which sees conflict between socio-economic classes as the driver of history. Marx saw capitalist societies as necessarily entangled in conflicts between the working class and the ruling class over resources and opportunities. As privileged groups leave wealth and other resources to their descendants, those descendants have more opportunities, compared to groups who possess lesser quantities and quality of resources. Marx also believed these class conflicts would eventually unseat the ruling class.

Ludwig Gumplowicz (1838–1909) focused on conflicts that arise between different cultures. They arise as one group's desired way of living is threatened by a group with vastly different ideals, especially if one group tries to force its cultural and ethnic norms, beliefs, and systems on another group. These norms may encompass religious views, social views, financial views, family views, and racial views.

C. Wright Mills (1916–1952) developed conflict theories that focus on class structures and political parties. Inspired by Karl Marx, Mills focused his theories on ruling classes in societies and how their behaviors influence the larger group. He states that those in authority shape a society's culture and beliefs; however, the majority of the society does not have the same resources to uphold these behaviors. This is likely to eventually lead to conflict.

Theories of Normal and Abnormal Personality Development

Typical and Atypical Physical Growth and Development
It is important to understand normal developmental milestones. Not all children progress at the same rate, but there are some guidelines that help determine whether the child has any developmental delays that might prevent them from reaching goals by a certain age.

Infancy Through Age Five
During the first year of life, abundant changes occur. The child learns basic, but important, skills. The child is learning to manipulate objects, hold their head without support, crawl, and pull up into a standing position. The toddler should be able to walk without assistance by eighteen months. By age two, the child should be running and able to climb steps one stair at a time. By age three, the child should be curious and full of questions about how the world works or why people behave in certain ways. The child should have the balance and coordination to climb stairs using only one foot per stair. By age four, the child is increasingly independent, demonstrating skills like attending to toilet needs and dressing with some adult assistance.

School Age to Adolescence
By age five, speech is becoming more fluent, and the ability to draw simple figures improves. Dressing without help is achieved. By age six, speech should be fluent and motor skills are strengthened. The youth is now able to navigate playground equipment and kick or throw a ball. Social skills, such as teamwork or friendship development, are evolving. The child must learn to deal with failure or frustration and find ways to be accepted by peers. They become more proficient in reading, math, and writing skills. Towards the end of this phase, around age twelve, secondary sexual characteristics, such as darker body hair or breast development, may occur.

Adolescence
This is a period of extraordinary change. The process of *individuation* is occurring. The teen views themself as someone who will someday live independently of parents. More time is spent with peers

and less with family. Identity formation arises, and the teen experiments with different kinds of clothing, music, and hairstyles to see what feels comfortable and what supports their view of the world. Sexuality is explored, and determinations are being made about sexual preferences and orientation. Sexual experimentation is common, and some teens actually form long-term intimate relationships, although others are satisfied to make shorter-term intimate connections. There is often a period of experimentation with drugs or alcohol. As the thinking process matures, there may be a questioning of rules and expectations of those in authority. Moodiness is common, and troubled teens are likely to "act out" their emotions, sometimes in harmful ways.

Typical and Atypical Cognitive Growth and Development

Cognitive development refers to development of a child's capacity for perception, thought, learning, information processing, and other mental processes. The *nature vs. nurture* debate questions whether cognitive development is primarily influenced by genetics or upbringing. Evidence indicates that the interaction between nature and nurture determines the path of development.

Some commonly recognized milestones in early cognitive development:

- One to three months: focuses on faces and moving objects, differentiates between different types of tastes, sees all colors in the spectrum

- Three to six months: recognizes familiar faces and sounds, imitates expressions

- Six to twelve months: begins to determine how far away something is, understands that things still exist when they are not seen (object permanence)

- One to two years: recognizes similar objects, understands and responds to some words

- Two to three years: sorts objects into appropriate categories, responds to directions, names objects

- Three to four years: Demonstrates increased attention span of five to fifteen minutes, shows curiosity and seeks answers to questions, organizes objects by characteristics

- Four to five years: Draws human shapes, counts to five or higher, uses rhyming words

The *Zone of proximal development* is the range of tasks that a child can carry out with assistance, but not independently. Parents and educators can advance a child's learning by providing opportunities within the zone of proximal development, allowing the child to develop the ability to accomplish those actions gradually without assistance.

Typical and Atypical Social Growth, Development, and the Socialization Process

Social development refers to the development of the skills that allow individuals to have effective interpersonal relationships and to contribute in a positive manner to the world around them.

Social learning is taught directly by caregivers and educators, but it is also learned indirectly by the experience of various social relationships.

Social development is commonly influenced by extended family, communities, religious institutions, schools, and sports teams or social groups. Positive social development is supported when caregivers do the following:

- Attune to a child's needs and feelings
- Demonstrate respect for others
- Teach children how to handle conflict and solve problems encountered during social experiences
- Help children learn to take the perspective of another person and develop empathy
- Encourage discussion of morals and values and listen to the child's opinions on those topics
- Explain rules and encourage fair treatment of others
- Encourage cooperation, rather than competition

Social development begins from birth as a child learns to attach to their mother and other caregivers. During adolescence, social development focuses on peer relationships and self-identity. In adulthood, social relationships are also important, but the goal is to establish secure and long-term relationships with family and friends.

Social institutions, such as family, church, and school, which assist people in realizing their full potential, also contribute to social development. Lev Vygotsky was a pioneer in this field with his concept of cultural mediation. This theory emphasizes that one's feelings, thoughts, and behaviors are significantly influenced by others in their environment.

Typical and Atypical Emotional Growth and Development

Emotional development encompasses the development of the following abilities:

- Identifying and understanding the feelings that one experiences
- Identifying and understanding the feelings of others
- Emotional and behavioral regulation
- Empathy
- Establishing relationships with others

Caregivers who are nurturing and responsive enable children to learn to regulate emotions and feel safe in the environment around them.

- By age two to three months, infants express delight and distress, begin smiling, and may be able to be soothed by rocking.

- By three to four months, infants communicate via crying and begin to express interest and surprise.

- Between four to nine months, infants respond differently to strangers in comparison to known individuals, solicit attention, show a particular attachment for a primary caregiver, and have an expanded range of expressed emotions that include anger, fear, and shyness.

- At ten to twelve months, babies show an increase in exploration and curiosity, demonstrate affection, and display a sense of humor.

- Children at age twelve to twenty-four months often demonstrate anger via aggression, laugh in social situations, recognize themselves in a mirror, engage in symbolic play, and have a complete range of emotional expression.

- Around age two, children begin using different facial expressions to show their emotions, begin to play cooperatively, and may transition from being calm and affectionate to temperamental and easily frustrated.

- At age three, children engage in more social and imaginative play, show interest in the feelings of others, begin to learn to manage frustration, and are often inconsistent and stubborn.

- Children at age four show improved cooperation, express sympathy, and may exhibit lying and/or guilty behavior.

- At age five, children can play rule-based games, often want to do what is expected of them, express emotion easily, and choose friends for themselves.

- Children at age six typically describe themselves in terms of their external attributes, have a difficult time coping with challenges and criticism, prefer routines, and show inconsistent self-control.

- Around age seven, children can typically describe causes and outcomes of emotions and show better regulation of emotions in most situations.

- From ages eight to ten, children have an increased need for independence, want to be viewed as intelligent, experience and better understand emotional subtleties, and may be defiant.

- During adolescence, children begin to master emotional skills to manage stress, increase self-awareness, develop identity, show increased ability for empathy, and learn to manage conflict.

Normal versus abnormal behavior is difficult to distinguish because each person is unique, so creating a standard of normal can be challenging. Though labeling behaviors as normal or abnormal can be problematic, it is important to have some standard by which it is possible to identify those behaviors that are indicative of an underlying psychological condition. Notwithstanding the challenges, it is possible and helpful to have general definitions of normal and abnormal behavior.

Normal behaviors are those that are common to the majority of the population, as related to emotional functioning, social interactions, and mental capacity. *Abnormal behavior* is generally considered that which is maladaptive, dysfunctional, and disruptive to life. These behaviors may be an exaggeration of a normal behavior or even an absence of a typical response. They do not conform to the accepted patterns or common behaviors of society. Sadness over the death of a loved one is considered normal, but disabling depression that interferes with school and work responsibilities is not. The *DSM-5-TR* is the current standard for determining the diagnostic criteria that distinguishes abnormal behavior from normal.

Typical and Atypical Sexual Growth and Development
While not everyone develops sexually on exactly the same timeline, there are certain expectations that define healthy and unhealthy sexual development. These expectations differ based on age. During the early stage of life, from birth until age two, the child is focused on developing a relationship of trust with caregivers. Eventually, children become aware of their genitals and explore these through self-touch. By

ages two to five, they begin to develop the ability to name and describe genitalia. They understand that male and female bodies are different. They have little inhibition about nudity.

As children enter middle childhood (ages six to eight or nine), they begin to understand the concept of puberty and what to expect about future body changes. They have a more sophisticated knowledge of reproduction, and may become more inhibited about nudity.

By the age of nine or ten, some children show signs of puberty, although the typical age of onset is eleven for girls and thirteen for boys. During puberty, there is a dramatic development in both primary and secondary sex characteristics. Children at this age show an increased interest in sex and may have questions about sexual orientation, sexual practices, or how the opposite sex behaves. By age twelve or thirteen, they begin to understand the consequences of sexual behavior, such as pregnancy or STDs. As they enter later adolescence, they may form longer relationships with their love interests, but many prefer casual dating. They are beginning to form an identity in terms of sexual orientation, preferences, and values.

It is important to understand red flags that may be signs of unhealthy sexual development. These may be brought on by abuse or by exposure to sexually explicit scenes. Children who are preoccupied with sexuality at an early age and whose behaviors differ from peers their own age may be at risk. Other indicators include attempting adult-like sexual interactions. These behaviors may include oral to genital contact or some form of penetration of another person's body.

These issues should raise concerns:

- A child overly preoccupied with sexual thoughts, language, or behaviors, rather than in more age-appropriate play
- A child engaging in sex play with children who are much older or much younger
- A child using sexual behavior to harm others
- A child involved in sexual play with animals
- A child uses explicit sexual language that is not age appropriate

A sexually-reactive child refers to one who is exposed to sexual stimuli prior to being sexually mature enough to understand the implications. The child becomes overly preoccupied with sexual matters and often acts out what they witnessed or experienced.

Theories and Etiology of Addictions and Addictive Behaviors

Addiction Theories

Addiction is a complex process involving biological, social, cultural, and genetic factors. There is some disagreement in the addiction treatment community about the causes and best treatments for substance abuse disorders. There are several models of addiction.

The earliest theory of addiction is called the **Moral Model**. This model implies that the person abuses substances because they are morally weak. The addict is viewed as a sinner or criminal and one who does not have the intestinal fortitude to change negative behaviors, therefore choosing to wallow in the misery of their sins.

The **disease model** or **medical model** of addiction, upon which the twelve-step program of Alcoholics Anonymous (AA) is based, specifies that the addict suffers from an illness that will never be cured and is

progressive in its development. Even if the individual ceases alcohol intake, the disease remains. AA literature indicates that when one relapses, even after years of sobriety, the addict picks up, not where he left off, but where the disease would have taken him if the drinking had continued. It is seen as a medical disorder and, at times, referred to in the Big Book of AA as having an allergy, with alcohol as the identified allergen. This theory is accepted and understood by many successful AA participants who have maintained sobriety throughout this program for years and who have shared their experience of strength and hope to help others struggling with addiction.

The **bio-psychosocial model** of addiction focuses on the role of the environment. Cultural and social factors influence one's beliefs and attitudes about substance use. In certain religions, it is unacceptable to use alcohol. In others, it may be encouraged—such as the huge sale and consumption of beer at Catholic picnics and fish fries. An addict's observation of others and their patterns of alcohol ingestion influences their attraction to drug or alcohol use as a means for tension relief or a form of celebration. Exposure to family or community members who use large quantities of intoxicants may serve to normalize dysfunctional patterns of use. Some youth observing parents consuming a quart of vodka each night may believe their family members are just normal drinkers, whereas other youth are raised in environments where alcohol is unacceptable or served only on rare occasions.

The **learning theory** of addiction is based on concepts related to positive reinforcement. The assumption underpinning this model is that addiction is a learned behavior through operant conditioning, classical conditioning, and social learning. Social learning takes place through observation. Learning theory posits that the interplay between these three factors contribute to the initiation, maintenance, and relapse of addictive behaviors. The intoxicant serves as an immediate reinforcement in the form of increased euphoria or relaxation. In some cases, it also deters withdrawal symptoms. Both of these forms of reinforcement increase the likelihood that the behavior will be repeated in an effort to recreate the sensation of feeling better.

Genetic theory is based on research indicating that biological children of parents who struggle with addiction or alcoholics are more prone to addiction than children of non-alcoholics. According to genetic therapy, this genetic predisposition towards addiction accounts for about half of one's susceptibility to becoming an addict. Theorists of this model agree that other factors, such as social experiences, have an impact upon the formation of an addiction.

Effects of Addiction and Substance Abuse

The repercussions of the addict's behavior can affect many significant aspects of life. The impact of addictions is felt not only by the addict, but also by everyone in that person's family and circle of social support. Those most powerfully affected are the immediate family members—particularly those who live under the same roof as the addict. Friends, extended family, co-workers, and employers also experience fallout from the addict's behaviors.

The spouses or partners of people who struggle with addiction often feel depressed, anxious, and angry. Persons in the throes of addiction often lie and steal to maintain their habit. It is not uncommon for people who struggle with addiction to steal from friends, family, or employers. Families must deal with the anxiety of not knowing when their loved one will come home or what mood or condition the person may demonstrate upon arriving home. Some families must deal with the shame of seeing their loved one arrested or knowing that this person harmed others while under the influence. Others simply become embarrassed by behaviors that loved ones exhibit in public or their failure to show up for an important event, such as a graduation.

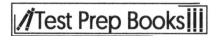

Children of parents who struggle with addiction experience embarrassment, fear, anxiety, and sadness. They are more likely to be abused or neglected, especially in single parent homes. Children may suffer when money intended for basic needs is spent on drugs or alcohol instead. When abuse and/or neglect are reported to CPS, these children may be taken from parents and placed in a series of group or foster homes. In some cases, custody is completely severed. Such experiences may lead to deep psychological scars for those closest to the addict.

Indicators of Addiction and Substance Abuse

Substance abuse and addiction problems come in many forms. These problems are often undetected or incorrectly attributed to other causes. Indicators include:

- Problems at work or school
- Friction with romantic partners, friends, or colleagues
- Neglect of household responsibilities, self-care, or hygiene
- Reckless behavior leading to legal trouble or financial problems
- Violence
- Tolerance of the substance/behavior over time
- Inability to stop using the substance/engaging in the behavior
- No longer engaging in normal activities in order to spend time/resources on the substance or behavior

Co-occurring disorders may also be known as **dual disorders** or **dual diagnoses**. Co-occurring disorders are more prevalent in clients who have substance use history (or presently use substances). Substance use is diagnosed when the use of the substance interferes with normal functioning at work, school, home, in relationships, or exacerbates a medical condition. A substance use diagnosis is often made in conjunction with a mood or anxiety related disorder, resulting in a dual diagnosis.

Co-occurring disorders or dual diagnoses may be difficult to diagnose due to the nature of symptom presentation. Some symptoms of addiction or substance abuse may appear to be related to another mental health disorder; conversely, some symptoms of mental health disorder may appear to be related to substance use. On the contrary, there are some signs that a co-occurring disorder is present:

Mental health symptoms worsening while undergoing treatment: For example, a client suffering from depression may be prescribed anti-depressants to address depressive symptoms. However, if the client is using substances, he or she may mix other medications with anti-depressants. This can be dangerous in itself, but it may also create a prolonged false sense of well-being while under the influence. Once this feeling fades, it can be confusing for the client to realize whether the prescribed medications are working. Even worse, the client may increase recreational substance use, leading to worse overall mental health symptoms over time.

Persistent substance use problems with treatment: There are some substance use treatment centers that transition clients off of one medication and place them on another, for example, methadone. This may result in a transfer of dependence and ongoing substance use while the client is receiving treatment for mental health disorders.

Another scenario is that a client may seek treatment from a substance use treatment center with clinicians that are not equipped to provide adequate mental health treatment for the client. As the mental health problems persist or worsen while undergoing withdrawal, the client may continue to

64

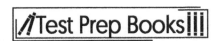
engage in substance use as a coping skill, therefore making the substance use problem appear resistant to treatment.

It is important for co-occurring disorders or dual diagnoses to be treated together because they occur simultaneously. This may be done utilizing a multidisciplinary team approach in an outpatient or inpatient setting. Treatment of dual diagnoses or co-occurring disorders at the same time in the same setting by the same treatment team is also known as an **integrated treatment** approach.

Biological, Neurological, and Physiological Factors That Affect Human Development, Functioning, and Behavior

Sigmund Freud's Psychosexual Stages of Development

Sigmund Freud was an Austrian neurologist who is considered the father of psychoanalysis. Freud developed important concepts in Western psychology such as the id, ego, and super ego, and wrote literature focusing on what he called the *unconscious* and the repression and expression that stems from it.

Freud also focused on human development, especially relating to sexuality. Freud theorized that each stage of human development is characterized by a sexual focus on a different bodily area (*erogenous zone*), which can serve as a source of either pleasure or frustration. He believed that *libido* (psychosexual energy) is the determinant of behavior during each of five fixed stages, and that if a developing child experiences frustration during one of these stages, a resulting fixation (or lingering focus) on that stage will occur.

To understand Freud's developmental stages fully, one must also understand his conceptualization of the human personality.

Freud describes three levels of the mind as follows:

- Consciousness: the part of the mind that holds accessible and current thoughts
- Pre-consciousness: the area that holds thoughts that can be accessed by memory
- Unconscious: where the mind motivates behavior and contains thoughts, feelings, and impulses that are not easily accessible

Freud believed that the personality, or psyche, consists of three parts called the Psychic Apparatus, each of which develops at a different time.

Id

The id is the most basic and primitive part of the human psyche, based on instincts and all of the biological aspects of a person's being. An infant's personality consists only of the id, as the other aspects have not yet developed. The id is entirely unconscious and operates on the pleasure principle, seeking immediate gratification of every urge. It has two instincts: a death instinct called *thanatos* and a survival instinct called *eros*. The energy from eros is called the libido.

Ego

The ego is the second personality component that begins to develop over the first few years of life. The ego is responsible for meeting the needs of id in a socially acceptable, realistic manner. Unlike the id, the ego operates on the reality principle, which allows it to consider pros and cons, to have awareness that other people have feelings, and to delay gratification when necessary.

65

Super Ego

The super ego is the final personality component, developed by about age five. The super ego is essentially a person's internal moral system or sense of right and wrong. The super ego suppresses the instincts and urges of the id, but also attempts to convince the ego to act idealistically, rather than realistically.

In a healthy personality, there is balance between the three personality components. The individual has *ego strength*—the ability to function well in the world despite the conflicting pressures that the id and super ego place upon the ego.

Five Stages of Psychosexual Development

Oral Stage (Birth to Eighteen Months)

The infant satisfies its libido by feeding and by exploring the environment, primarily by putting objects in its mouth. The id dominates the oral stage of development, and every action an infant undertakes is guided by the pleasure principle. The key task of this phase is weaning from the breast, which also results in the infant's first experience of loss. Too much or too little focus on oral gratification at this stage was theorized to lead to an oral fixation and an immature personality. Examples of an oral fixation were believed to be excessive eating, drinking, or smoking.

Anal Stage (Eighteen Months to Three Years)

The key task of this stage is toilet training, which causes a conflict between the id (which wants immediate gratification of the urge to eliminate waste) and the ego (which requires delay of gratification necessary to use the toilet). A positive experience with toilet training was believed to lead to a sense of competence that continues into adulthood. Anal-retentive personality results from overly-strict toilet training, characterized by rigid and obsessive thinking. Likewise, anal-expulsive personality results from a lax approach to toilet training, characterized by disorganization and messiness.

Phallic Stage (Three to Six Years)

The libidinal focus during this stage is on the genital area, and it is during this stage that children learn to differentiate between males and females. The Oedipus Complex develops during this stage; Freud believed that a young boy views his father as a rival for his mother's attention and wants to eliminate his father in order to take his place. Similar to the Oedipus Complex, the Electra Complex says that a young girl may view her mother as her rival. Freud also believed that girls experience penis envy. The key task of this stage is identification with the same-sex parent.

Latency (Six years to Puberty)

During this period, libidinal energy is still present, but the child is able to direct that energy toward school, friendships, and activities.

Genital Stage (Puberty to Adulthood)

The libidinal focus is once again on the genital area (as it is during the phallic stage), but at this point, the psyche is more developed. During the genital stage, an individual achieves sexual maturation, becomes independent of their parents, resolves any remaining conflict from the earlier stages, and is able to function as a responsible adult in terms of both work and relationships.

Impact of Age on Self-Image

Aging is an inevitable phase of human development, and the impact is physical, psychological, social, and economic. Self-image is the perception of oneself, but the perception is influenced by societal

values. Some cultures revere the elderly and look to them for wisdom and strength. These cultures include the Native Americans, Chinese, Koreans, and Indians. In the United States, there is a different perception of aging. Many elderly Americans feel less valuable or important once they enter retirement. At the same time, they are coping with undesirable body changes and learning to accept that, physically, they can no longer do what they once did. In the U.S., youth and physical attractiveness are highly valued. The elderly are seldom seen as important social figures. They are also less connected with families today, with only 3.7% of homes reporting multigenerational households, per Census Bureau reports. Currently, family support and family contact are less available. However, for some segments of the population, technology has allowed relatives to visit regularly with grandchildren and even participate in family meals or get-togethers.

- Infancy: The ego is in charge. The baby thinks primarily of basic needs, such as food or warmth.

- Childhood: In early to middle childhood, children tend to rate themselves higher than peers in terms of talents and intellect. As middle school approaches, there is a decline in self-evaluations. This could be related to feeling unattractive due to physical changes or being teased or bullied by peers in that age group.

Adolescence: In the early stage of adolescence (ages 9 to 13), another drop in self-esteem occurs. This is thought to be related to the need to let go of childish pleasures, such as a beloved toy or previous interests and step up to the plate of becoming a more responsible person. This can be a painful sacrifice for some youth. The next drop in self-worth occurs at the end of adolescence and beginning of young adulthood (ages 18 to 23). It is during this period that young adults realize that they truly are responsible for their own lives, yet they have not yet achieved a sense of mastery in the academic or vocational world. They are fearful and full of doubt about the ability to be successful as an independent adult.

Adulthood: Studies indicate a small but steady increase in self-image by mid-twenties. In general, during this period, men tend to have higher self-esteem than women. Persons who live in poor socioeconomic conditions tend to have lower self-esteem than their more financially stable peers. As later adulthood nears (the 70s), women tend to catch up with men in terms of how they evaluate themselves. Women in their eighties tend to have a more positive self-image than male counterparts. As a general rule, for both genders, there is a gradual increase in one's sense of self-worth throughout the life span until late middle age. Research shows that most adults' self-image peaks at around age 60.

Impacts of Disability on Self-Image

Disabilities impact self-image regardless of age; however, an individual who is born with a disability tends to fare better than one who acquires one later in life. Responses vary based upon severity of impairments. Some later-life medical conditions cause the individual to give up independence as the person is forced to retire the car keys or move to an institutional setting. Less severe acquired disabilities that still allow the person to maintain much of their previous lifestyle are painful but easier to accept. An individual's personality make-up and resilience to coping with change are also important factors. It is not uncommon for older adults to lapse into depression. This is often generated by a combination of losses. As one enters the later stages of life, loss of friends and family members is common. There may be declines in status, earning capacity, or physical abilities, all of which contribute to depression and negatively impact self-image.

Body Image

Body image refers to the thoughts and feelings about the appearance of one's body as well as thoughts and feelings about how one's body is perceived by others. Body image is shaped by the messages that we receive from the people around us, the culture we live in, and the media.

Persistent negative body image can be associated with these factors:

- Low self-esteem
- Depression and/or anxiety
- Sexual risk-taking
- Impaired relationship satisfaction
- Withdrawal from activities where one's body may be visible to others (e.g., exercise, sexual activity, swimming, seeking medical care)
- Development of eating disorders

Systemic and Environmental Factors That Affect Human Development, Functioning, and Behavior

The interplay of an individual's biological, psychological, social, and spiritual factors is an indicator of overall health and happiness. If one or more of these factors are imbalanced, the individual is unlikely to feel as though they are at their highest level of well-being or personal fulfillment (even if a clinically diagnosed disease is not present). This framework is often utilized in counseling settings where mental or emotional health appears to be compromised. Practitioners address the issue in the client's life by examining their physical and physiological health, medical history, personal history, moods, reactions to events, environment, family life, home life, cultural beliefs, personal relationships, faith or belief system, spirituality, personal desires, and other factors to provide holistic drivers for any necessary interventions.

A number of these factors strongly influence each other. For example, a client who feels tremendous stress daily at work may find themselves constantly falling sick with colds, as stress negatively affects the immune system's ability to perform. Clients with clinically diagnosed mood disorders may have a more difficult time coping with major stressors, such as a divorce. Clients who report having some level of faith or spiritual belief system often appear to have higher levels of positivity and healthier coping mechanisms in the face of adverse personal events. As practitioners intervene in such scenarios, they must address not only the individual client, but all the systems in which the client exists and interacts. Practitioners may also need to work with the client's families, in communities, or in other group settings in order to effectively create balance between biological, psychological, social, and spiritual factors.

Basic Human Needs

Abraham Maslow is the most notable researcher in the area of basic human needs. Maslow theorized that human needs could be described in the form of a pyramid, with the base of the pyramid representing the most basic needs and the higher layers representing loftier goals and needs. Unless the basic needs are met, a person cannot move on to higher needs. For example, a homeless woman living under a bridge will need food, shelter, and safety before she can consider dealing with her alcoholism.

The foundational layer in Maslow's hierarchy is physiological needs, and the final layer at the pinnacle of the pyramid is self-transcendence.

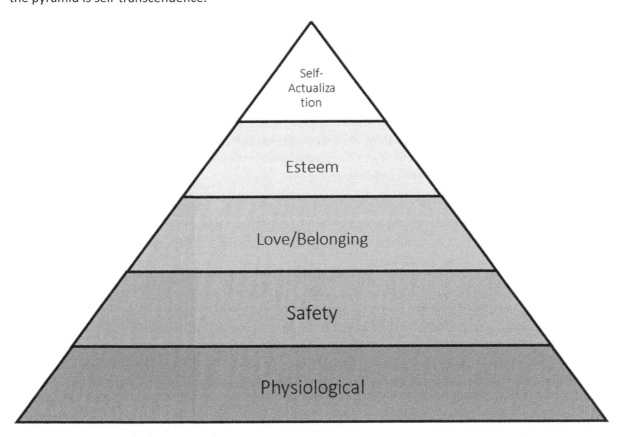

Maslow's Hierarchy of Needs

Physiological Needs: These needs, which pertain to what humans need to survive, must be met first. These needs include the basics, such as food, water, clothing, and housing.

Safety Needs: Once primary needs are met, the person may now focus on safety issues. This would include safety from abuse and neglect, natural disaster, or war.

Love and Belonging: Once the first levels of need have been satisfied, people are next driven to find a sense of acceptance and belonging within social groups, such as family, community, or religious organizations. Maslow suggests that humans have a basic need for love, affection, and sexual intimacy. Failure to achieve this level can lead to difficulty in forming and maintaining close relationships with others.

Esteem: The need for esteem is driven by a desire for recognition, respect, and acceptance within a social context.

Self-Actualization: The U.S. Army slogan, "Be All You Can Be," expresses this layer of need. Reaching one's highest potential is the focus. According to Maslow, this cannot be achieved until all the others are mastered.

Self-Transcendence: Devised by Maslow in his later years, he felt self-actualization did not completely satisfy his image of a person reaching their highest potential. To achieve self-transcendence, one must

69

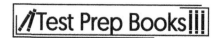

commit to a goal that is outside of one's self, such as practicing altruism or finding a deeper level of spirituality.

Attachment and Bonding

It has become more important than ever to understand attachment and bonding, especially in relation to changes within the U.S. culture's attitudes about child welfare over the last fifty years. Child Protective Service Teams have become more active in every city. The medical profession, the educational system, and the mental health profession are more informed about children at risk. As a result, more children are being taken from parents, sometimes as early as the day of birth. An older child victim may travel from relative to relative, back to the mother, then into foster or group homes. These children do not have an opportunity to form attachments with their caregivers, nor do caregivers have the opportunity to bond with the children.

Bonding refers to a mother's initial connection to her baby. This generally occurs within the first hours or days of the birth. Mothers who are able and willing to hold their child close to them shortly after birth generally have more positive relationships with the child. When a mother fails to bond, the child is at greater risk for having behavioral problems.

Attachment, on the other hand, refers to a more gradual development of the baby's relationship with their caretaker. A secure attachment naturally grows out of a positive, loving relationship in which there is soothing physical contact, emotional and physical safety, and responsiveness to the child's needs. The baby who has a secure attachment will venture out from their safe base, but immediately seek their mother when fearful or anxious, having learned that mommy will be there to protect him or her. This type of secure relationship becomes impossible if the child is moved from home to home or has experienced abuse or neglect.

A child whose needs have not been met or who has learned through mistreatment that the world is unfriendly and hostile may develop an avoidant attachment or ambivalent attachment. An *avoidant attachment* is characterized by a detached relationship in which the child does not seek out the caregiver when distressed, but acts independently. A child with *ambivalent attachment* shows inconsistency toward the caregiver; sometimes the child clings to him or her, but at other times, the child resists their comfort. Establishing a secure, positive attachment with a caregiver is crucial to a child's life-long emotional and social success. The development of attachment disorder is often present in foster children or those adopted later in life and can create much frustration and heartache as the more stable parents step in and attempt to bond with them.

Effect of Poverty

Poverty is often the foundation of a number of other socioeconomic and health problems faced by individuals, families, and communities. Without resources such as money, transportation, or housing, it becomes difficult to buy healthy food, access medical care, drive to work, have quality childcare, or live in a safe area. For adults in poverty, the extreme level of stress that arises from trying to pay bills, provide basic necessities for themselves and their families, and manage multiple jobs often leads to a number of mental, physical, and emotional problems.

These can include substance abuse, domestic violence, inability to maintain family units and romantic relationships, hopelessness, depression, and desperation. Children who live and grow up in poverty are prone to traumatic and catastrophic health risk factors, such as experiencing or witnessing violence, chronic malnutrition, higher rates of illness, and mood disorders. Experiencing such adverse events in childhood is associated with high levels of stress, impaired functioning, and impaired cognitive ability

that can be irreparable. Individuals experiencing poverty are more likely to visit the emergency room for health problems (and often be unable to pay), require government assistance, and commit crimes (often in order to obtain necessary resources). These outcomes create a financial burden on the community and local economy.

Effect of Aging on Biopsychosocial Functioning

Biological Aging

Biological aging is based on physical changes that have an impact on the performance of the body's organs and systems.

Psychological Aging

Psychological aging is based on changes in personality, cognitive ability, adaptive ability, and perception. Basic personality traits appear to be relatively stable through the lifespan, as does an individual's self-image. One aspect that does tend to change, however, is the tendency to become more inwardly focused, which may also result in reduced impulsivity and increased caution.

Studies have shown that a pattern of age-related changes in intelligence can typically be observed after age sixty, although changes vary widely across individuals. Furthermore, the somewhat poorer testing results are reflected in fluid intelligence (i.e., reasoning, problem-solving, and abstract thinking unrelated to experience or learned information), but not in crystallized intelligence (i.e., knowledge based on skills, learning, and experience). Normal age-related changes in memory typically involve acquisition of new information and retrieval of information from memory storage. *Sensory decline* is also a common experience for aging individuals.

Social Aging

Social aging is based on changes in one's relationships with family, friends, acquaintances, systems, and organizations. Most older persons experience a narrowing of their social networks. However, they are more likely to have more positive interactions within those networks, and they are more likely to experience more positive feelings about family members than younger persons do.

Disengagement theory states that it is natural and inevitable for older adults to withdraw from their social systems and to reduce interactions with others. This theory has been highly criticized and is incompatible with other well-known psychosocial aging theories. *Activity theory* proposes that social activity serves as a buffer to aging; successful aging occurs among those who maintain their social connections and activity levels. *Continuity theory* proposes that with age, individuals attempt to maintain activities and relationships that were typical for them as younger adults.

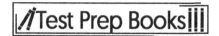

Gerontology

Gerontology is the study of biological, cognitive, and psychological features of the aging process. It includes the study of the impact of an aging population on social and economic trends. Gerontologists practice in the fields of medicine, psychology, physical and occupational therapy, as well as counseling. Geriatric counseling refers to a range of services provided to the population of those over age 60.

Personality Theories

There are several noted theories as to how personality is formed. In 400 B.C.E., Hippocrates attempted to identify personalities based on four temperaments. He called these *humors*, and these were associated with body fluid presence, such as phlegm or bile.

In the 1940s, William Sheldon came up with his body type theories that include the *endomorph*, an overweight individual with an easy-going personality; the *mesomorph*, a muscular person with an aggressive personality; and the *ectomorph*, a thin individual with an artistic or intellectual personality. Gordon Allport developed the trait theory of personality development. He believed that certain personalities were comprised of clusters of traits and that these traits could be categorized into cardinal, central, and secondary traits.

Freud believed the personality was composed of the id, the ego and superego. The *id* refers to a person's unconscious, with its suppressed desires and unresolved conflicts, whereas the *ego* and *superego* are more influenced by the conscious mind. He believed that these three components were often in conflict with one another and that how one resolved these conflicts determined personality. He also stressed the importance of childhood experience in personality development.

Carl Rogers was a proponent of the humanistic theory of personality development. This approach emphasized self-perception and a desire for striving to become the best person one can become. His theory was based on the basic goodness and potential of each person.

The behavioral theories of B.F. Skinner and others related to personality development imply that one's persona is developed as a result of classical or operant conditioning. Reinforcement and punishment guide behavioral choices.

Effects of Crisis, Disasters, and Trauma on Diverse Individuals Across the Lifespan

Phases of a Crisis Period

- In 1964, psychiatry professor **Gerald Caplan** defined the recognizable phases of a crisis:

- Phase 1. This first phase consists of the initial threat or event, which triggers a response. The individual may be able to employ coping skills or defense mechanisms to avoid a crisis. The individual may experience denial.

- Phase 2. This second phase is the escalation, during which initial attempts to manage the crisis are ineffective and the individual begins to experience increased distress. The individual may employ higher-level coping skills to alleviate the increasing stress levels.

- Phase 3. The third phase is the acute crisis phase, during which anxiety continues and may intensify to panic or a fight-or-flight response. As stressful feelings continue to escalate, the individual experiences major emotional turmoil, possible feelings of hopelessness, depression,

and anxiety. There are still attempts to problem-solve during this phase, and new tactics may be used.

- Phase 4. This final phase is marked by complete psychological and emotional collapse, or the individual finds a method to resolve the situation. the individual may experience personality disorganization and become severely depressed, violent, and possibly suicidal. There may be remaining emotional and psychological dysfunction or impairment if the coping mechanisms used were maladaptive.

- Caplan theorized that individuals need to maintain homeostasis or remain in balance with their environment. A crisis is caused by an individual's reaction to a situation, not by an actual incident.

Crisis Intervention

Crisis intervention is typically a short-term treatment usually lasting four to six weeks and is implemented when a client enters treatment following some type of traumatic event that causes significant distress. This event causes a state of disequilibrium when a client is out of balance and can no longer function effectively. Counselors can either use generic crisis intervention models for varied types of crises or can create an individualized plan for assisting the client. The main goal of crisis intervention should be to help clients develop and use adaptive coping skills to return to the level of functioning prior to the crisis.

A crisis situation requires swift action and specially trained mental health personnel and can occur at any time in any setting. Albert Roberts proposed a seven-stage model to deal with a crisis and provide effective intervention and support. Roberts's stages are as follows:

- Stage 1. Conduct thorough biopsychosocial assessments of client functioning and identify any imminent danger to self or others.

- Stage 2. Make contact, and quickly establish rapport; it is important that the counselor is accepting, nonjudgmental, flexible, and supportive.

- Stage 3. Identify specific problems and the possible cause of crisis; begin to prioritize the specific aspect of the problem most in need of a solution.

- Stage 4. Provide counseling in an attempt to understand the emotional content of the situation.

- Stage 5. Work on coping strategies and alternative solutions, which can be very challenging for an individual in crisis.

- Stage 6. Implement an action plan for treatment, which could include therapy, the 12-step program, hospitalization, or social services support.

- Stage 7. Follow up and continue to evaluate status; ensure that the treatment plan is effective and make adjustments as needed.

Effects of Trauma on Self-image

Trauma can have a significant impact on self-image as a person's entire identity becomes intertwined with the traumatic event and the subsequent emotions. Some victims of trauma report a sense of isolation from others, feeling that they are not good enough or that they are less competent or less

attractive than their peers. This generates feelings of shame and unworthiness, which, in turn, can lead to depression or anxiety. Some trauma survivors—especially victims of child or domestic abuse—feel a deep sense of betrayal and label the world and people as unsafe. They have trouble trusting others, and they may perform poorly in major areas of functioning, such as work or relationships. Some abuse survivors describe themselves as "damaged goods." Some individuals may engage in self-harm behaviors or may feel so depressed that suicide is seen as the only solution. These persons are prone to substance abuse as a means to numb the emotional pain. Addictive behavior can also negatively impact one's self-esteem. The more resilient will use their painful experiences as a tool for self-growth and may eventually learn to help others who have been through similar experiences.

Understanding Differing Abilities and Strategies for Differentiated Interventions

Approximately 7 percent of U.S. children have some type of disability. The most common physical disabilities that impact development are cerebral palsy, hearing issues, and visual issues. Learning disabilities are also common—these could be Down's syndrome or other developmental delays. Common psychiatric disabilities are ADHD and autism spectrum disorders. Others include mood disorders, oppositional disorders, anxiety disorders, and, in rare cases, schizophrenia. The impact upon the child and family corresponds to the family's ability to adapt to the condition and their ability to connect to community resources.

How the individual develops and copes with the disability depends greatly upon the social context and the child's own personal attributes. Raising a disabled child puts tremendous stress on parents and siblings. There are issues of stigma, financial burden, missed days of work for parents, and the time and energy needed to seek useful resources. Siblings may be called upon to take roles of parenting to help out. These siblings may be bullied by peers who make fun of their disabled family member. They may feel neglected by their parents. Additionally, there may be a need for special housing and special schools. Low-income families may face barriers to accessing services such as transportation, medical specialists, or assistance with childcare.

The impact of disabilities on development depends largely on (1) the extent of the disability and (2) whether that disability is experienced across the lifespan or for a limited amount of time. Positive coping skills and sufficient social support may lessen the impact of a disability. Although the tendency is to focus on negative impact, disabilities may also leave a positive impact in terms of the strengthening of relationships or the development of skills that an individual may not have otherwise acquired.

Promoting Resilience and Wellness Across the Life Span

Rather than focusing on problems and pathology, the **strengths perspective** (or **strengths-based approach**) in counseling encourages counselors to focus on a client's strengths or assets and to build upon the client's inherent resiliency and positive characteristics. Outcome studies regarding use of the "strengths" perspective are limited; however, it is posited that a strengths-based approach could help to remove some of the stigma attached to groups or conditions (e.g., mental illness, poverty).

Resilience theories account for risk factors that may threaten an individual's ability to cope with adverse events. **Risk factors** include lack of support, diagnosis of mental health disorders, and resource constraints. **Protective factors** support high levels of resiliency and can include the ability to think positively about situations, the ability to feel hope, strong confidence in one's self-reliance, problem-solving abilities, and competence. Developing resilience should be treated as a preventative approach, rather than a reactive approach.

Strengths- and resilience-based approaches allow individuals to feel empowered and maintain a sense of self-efficacy, both of which are crucial components for lasting behavior change and resolution. Additionally, they minimize client's self-identification with a problem or issue, which can cause the client to fall into a self-fulfilling prophecy. It is important to note that clients can build the capacity to be resilient as a healthy method of coping. This type of skill building can often serve as a crucial component of an intervention. Exercises may include reframing perspectives, journaling, learning new abilities (such as problem-solving skills), practicing flexibility when unexpected changes arise, and examining public stories of strength and resiliency with the client. Finally, practitioners can support clients by providing positive reinforcement and feedback when the client displays strong and resilient behaviors.

Practice Quiz

1. As an elementary school counselor, you are interacting with an eight-year-old child who is unable to speak clearly or coherently, who sometimes has issues with bladder control, and who cannot yet tie his own shoes. The child should receive further assessment for which of the following?
    a. Developmental Delays
    b. Conduct Disorder
    c. Genetic Deficiencies
    d. Oppositional Defiant Disorder

2. Most researchers divide adult development into three sections of life following the end of adolescence. What are these three sections called?
    a. Early adulthood (ages eighteen to forty), middle adulthood (ages forty to sixty-five), and late adulthood (age sixty-five until death)
    b. Post adolescence (ages eighteen to twenty-four), middle adulthood (ages twenty-five to forty), and mature adulthood (age forty until death)
    c. Initial adulthood (ages eighteen to thirty-five), middle adulthood (ages thirty-six to sixty) and later life stage (age sixty until death)
    d. Stage one adulthood (ages eighteen to twenty-eight), stage two adulthood (ages twenty-nine to fifty-eight), and stage three adulthood (age fifty-nine until death)

3. Biological, psychological, and social factors all interact together as an individual transitions through various life stages. As a clinician evaluating biological factors that may contribute to the person's current psychological issues, the areas to review should include which of the following?
    a. A parental history of psychiatric illness and/or addiction
    b. Family income and social status
    c. Years of education completed
    d. Employment history

4. For therapists working primarily with adolescents, it is helpful to share which of the following with clients?
    a. Sexual Identity and preferences will probably never change throughout one's lifetime.
    b. It is important to offer a diagnosis to the adolescent of their sexual orientation so that they can be reassured of where they stand.
    c. Disclosure of oneself or others' sexual orientation to help the client feel empowered to share their own experience.
    d. Sexual development is a unique and individual process, and not everyone reaches sexual milestones at the same time.

5. Gerontology is the study of what?
    a. The biological aspects of aging, economic trends of the aging, population, and the impact of aging on social trends.
    b. Economic trends of youth, consumer spending as it pertains to children, and the focus on youth in the media.
    c. The impact of social trends on schools, how schools function in the technology age, and the evolution of administration within schools.
    d. The biological aspects of mental illness, and how substance abuse is viewed within social trends.

76

Answer Explanations

1. A: While some children who are oppositional and defiant may refuse to conform to certain standards as a means to establish control, the child described in this scenario is more likely experiencing developmental delays due to the deficits in a number of areas. At one time, the state of Illinois required children to be able to tie their own shoes before being admitted to kindergarten. Although this is a crude measure of academic readiness, it probably served as a red flag, based on the fact that the vast majority of children can perform this task by age 5.

Pre-schools generally require that a three-year-old must be fully potty-trained before they will admit him or her to their program, again using a standard that the majority of children can achieve by that age. Language issues may have other causes, such as physiological symptoms, but being unable to meet these three standards is an indicator that the child is lagging behind others in attaining developmental milestones. Choices *B* and *D* refer to behavioral disorders of childhood that include symptoms of disregard/disrespect for others and sometimes include criminal behavior. Genetic deficiencies, Choice *C*, may contribute to a developmental delay, yet they could also be associated with physical issues passed genetically, such as deafness or dwarfism.

2. A: This description of states of adulthood is most commonly used in psychology and medicine. While some may question that early adulthood extends until age forty, with life spans increasing, this is a reasonable standard and is generally an acceptable conception in the fields of psychology and medicine as to how a lifetime is divided.

3. A: Parental history of mental illness is a biological feature and should serve as a red flag because some psychiatric conditions do have a genetic link, including—but not limited to—addictions and mood disorders. In addition, being raised by a parent impaired by mental illness or addictions often causes deep emotional scars that should be addressed in therapy. Income, education, and employment history are not considered biological factors; therefore, they are incorrect responses. The issues mentioned in *B*, *C*, and *D* can certainly have a biological impact, such as a scenario in which the child is deprived of good nutrition or medical care.

4. D: Sexual development is different for each person, and there is a wide range of variations in terms of achieving physical and emotional maturation. Sexuality is a very fluid and continuously changing process for most. The sexual practices one finds gratifying at age 16 may no longer be pursued at age 40. Some people do not seem to access their true sense of sexuality until mid-life. Others switch gears frequently throughout life when it comes to sexual preferences. This explains why *A* and *B* are incorrect. Choice *C* is also incorrect; in some cases, it may be helpful to share one's own experience with sexual orientation, but disclosing others' sexual orientation is inappropriate.

5. A: Gerontology covers a wide range of issues related to biological, social, and psychiatric features of aging. The study of gerontology is essential as the population ages and lives longer, healthier lives. How a population ages impacts the field of economics, psychology, medicine, even architecture. For example, a two-story apartment complex in the middle of Iowa will probably not have an elevator. In Florida, where there is a large senior population, almost every apartment complex has an elevator to accommodate those in wheelchairs or those who have difficulty climbing steps.

Career Development

Theories and Models of Career Development, Counseling, and Decision-Making

Counseling Process

Professional relationships with clients develop in six stages. In the first stage, counselors focus their efforts on building rapport and trust with clients. This involves the development of a comfortable and trusting working relationship using listening skills, empathic understanding, cultural sensitivity, and good social skills. In the second stage, the counselor identifies the problem(s) that led the client to seek the assistance of a counselor. Together, the counselor and client identify the initial problems that will be addressed, check the understanding of each issue through a conversation, and make appropriate changes as necessary. The third stage involves the counselor using skills that allow him or her to understand the client in deeper ways. The counselor begins to make inferences based on their theoretical orientation about the underlying themes in the client's history. Once these inferences are made, then goals can be established based on these overarching themes.

The fourth stage of professional relationship development involves working on the issues that were identified and agreed upon between the counselor and client. The client takes responsibility for and actively works on the identified issues and themes during and between sessions. As the client successfully works through issues, it becomes increasingly clear that there is little reason for the meetings to continue. Therefore, in stage five, the end of sessions is discussed, and both the client and the counselor work through feelings of loss. The sixth stage occurs after the relationship has ended if clients return with new issues, if they want to revisit old ones, or if they want to delve deeper into their self-understanding. This stage is the post-interview stage and occurs with many—but not all—clients.

Counseling Procedures, Risks, and Benefits

Counseling can provide individuals with the opportunity to learn about themselves with the guidance of a trained professional. It can be a time of self-discovery during which one's strengths and weakness are explored, inventoried, and modified. Counselors are bound by confidentiality, so the counseling environment is a safe one in which clients are free to open up and explore areas of themselves they might not feel comfortable doing otherwise. In addition to working with individuals, counselors are also able to help families and couples create healthier home environments by working on things like conflict resolution, communication skills, and parenting techniques. Individuals can also benefit from group counseling during which they can explore a variety of issues with others who are experiencing the same stressors or problems. Counseling also provides tools that can help to address various mental disorders such as depression, anxiety, bipolar disorder, etc. Counselors are trained to recognize when clients might need medication to help them successfully navigate their emotional issues. They can make referrals to appropriate medical professionals when necessary.

Although there are many benefits to counseling, there are also risks. Counseling can be unsettling for clients since the process explores potentially uncomfortable areas. Old images and memories may surface during and after counseling sessions that may leave clients feeling emotionally dysregulated. Some of the homework assignments may be difficult to complete and may even induce fear (for example, when clients are asked to face frightening situations or objects to overcome phobias). These assignments can be difficult because they challenge the way clients are accustomed to behaving and

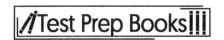

thinking. For these reasons, all potential clients should be apprised of the risks associated with counseling during the initial assessment and in the informed consent paperwork.

Relationship Phases

At the onset of the process, the counselor and client will progress through the relationship phase, which has four specific phases. These phases may be completed at a varying pace, depending on both parties. Some phases can be completed quickly, while others may take several sessions.

- Phase 1. **Initiation**, or **entry phase**: This is the introduction to the counseling process, which sets the stage for the development of the client/counselor relationship.

- Phase 2. **Clarification phase**: This phase defines the problem and need for the therapeutic relationship.

- Phase 3. **Structure phase**: The counselor defines the specifics of the relationship, its intended outcomes, and responsibilities of both parties.

- Phase 4. **Relationship phase**: The client and counselor have developed a relationship and will work toward mutually agreed-upon goals.

Advancement of Therapeutic Relationship and Reaching Goals

Once a working relationship is established, the client and counselor will need to develop and maintain positive interactions to ensure the effectiveness of counseling. Positive interactions ensure the therapeutic relationship advances and supports clients in meeting their goals. The counseling relationship has four stages.

- Stage 1. **Exploration of feelings and definition of problem**: Counselors will use rapport-building skills, define the structure of the counseling process and relationship, and work with their clients on goal setting.

- Stage 2. **Consolidation**: This is the process of the clients integrating the information and guidance from the counselor, allowing them to gain additional coping skills and identify alternate ways to solve problems.

- Stage 3. **Planning**: During this phase, clients can begin employing techniques learned in counseling and prepare to manage on their own.

- Stage 4. **Termination**: This is the ending of the therapeutic relationship, when clients feel equipped to manage problems independently and have fully integrated techniques learned in counseling.

Assessing Abilities, Interests, Values, Personality, and Other Factors That Contribute to Career Development

The process of acquiring values is important for counselors to keep in mind when working to understand where their own values and their clients' values originated. Counselors should be aware of their own moral codes, values, biases, and prejudices to avoid conflict with the treatment they are providing to clients. The process of acknowledging and controlling personal values in counseling practice is called *value suspension*. **Self-awareness** is a vital part of ensuring that one's personal values and beliefs do not

intrude on the counselor/client relationship. It may be necessary to seek consultation from a supervisor or colleague in situations where one's personal values or beliefs conflict with those of the client and when those feelings cannot be resolved. In extreme cases where consultation and self-reflection cannot remedy the conflict, termination of the counselor/client relationship and referral to another therapist may be necessary.

Professional Boundary Issues

Conflicting values occur when the counselor's values and knowledge about best practices are at odds with the client's values, history, relationships, or lifestyle. **Vicarious trauma** may happen when a counselor experiences symptoms of trauma after listening to a client's experience. These symptoms may arise due to the counselor sharing a similar history of trauma. Boundaries may be difficult to maintain if the counselor feels that they need to rescue the client due to an unhealthy attachment to positive results in practice. This is termed the **rescuer role**. Professional boundaries may also be difficult to set and maintain if there is poor teamwork between colleagues in the counseling organization. This is evident when counselors assume the roles of other team members because they believe they are not fulfilling their responsibilities to the client.

Motives for Helping Others Through Counseling

Just as clients are motivated to seek counseling to resolve issues and/or improve their lives, counselors exhibit motivation to help others. Counseling, as a profession, allows an opportunity to positively impact the lives of individuals and help improve society. It is important as part of professional development for counselors to explore their motivation to join the profession. Some graduate programs may require individuals to receive counseling as part of their education to ensure they have adequately addressed their own issues and prevent using the clients to get their own needs met. In some specific areas of counseling, such as addictions, it is more common for counselors to have experienced addiction and recovered, thus motivating them to assist others.

Genuineness and Congruence

The term **congruence** is associated with the person-centered work of Carl Rogers. Congruence can be defined as genuineness on the part of counselors, in that there is agreement on their words and actions. Counselors display congruence when their body language, affect, and words correspond to demonstrate genuine concern for the client. Lack of congruence is revealed when counselors express concern but at the same time seem bored, disinterested, or use language that does not indicate a true understanding of the client. Counselors who are nonreactive or act as a blank screen for clients are not expressing congruence. Rogers considered congruence to be essential for effective counseling.

Counselors need to be congruent—in agreement and harmony—with client feedback and encourage clients' self-direction. Counselors and clients begin treatment by enhancing congruence in communication so that mutually agreed upon goals may be developed for the client. The counselor should be invested in the therapeutic relationship and able to participate in a way that assists the client in becoming more self-aware. If a counselor is not congruent with the client, then treatment progress may be hindered and the client should be referred to another counselor who is a more appropriate fit.

Knowledge of and Sensitivity to Gender Orientation and Gender Issues

The term *gender* refers to a range of physical, behavioral, psychological, or cultural characteristics that create the difference between masculinity and femininity. *Gender identity* is a person's understanding of his or her own gender, especially as it relates to being male or female. *Sexual orientation* is a more complex concept as it refers to the type of sexual attraction one feels for others. This is not to be

80

confused with **sexual preference**, which refers to the specific types of sexual stimulation one most enjoys.

Types of Sexual Orientation
- **Heterosexual**: An individual who is sexually and emotionally attracted to members of the opposite gender, also known as "straight"

- **Homosexual**: An individual who is sexually and emotionally attracted to members of the same gender, sometimes referred to as "gay" or "lesbian"

- **Bisexual**: A male or female who is sexually attracted to both same and opposite gender sex partners

- **Asexual**: An individual who has a low level of interest in sexual interactions with others

Types of Gender Identity
- **Bi-gender**: An individual who fluctuates between the self-image of traditionally male and female stereotypes and identifies with both genders

- **Transgender**: A generalized term referring to a variety of sexual identities that do not fit under more traditional categories, a person who feels to be of a different gender than the one he or she is born with

- **Transsexual**: A person who identifies emotionally and psychologically with the gender other than that assigned at birth, lives as a person of the opposite gender

Those who are transgender or transsexual may be homosexual, heterosexual, or asexual. Being transgender can be defined as identifying as a gender other than the gender one was assigned at birth. Publicly sharing that one is transgender can be difficult for some individuals. Transgender individuals may live in a community where their identity is not positively accepted or is misunderstood, and they may feel shamed or ridiculed. It may be a difficult experience for close family members to understand the perspective of a transgender individual, which can affect the cohesiveness of family relationships and the family unit. Transgender individuals may also feel a lack of acknowledgement when others fail to use the correct pronouns or respect other identity wishes.

Some transgender individuals choose to medically transition to the gender they identify as. This is a procedure that requires physical, emotional, and psychological support. Individuals not receiving support during their transition can experience extreme feelings of sadness, isolation, and lack of belonging. Medically transitioning individuals also undergo hormonal changes in addition to surgical procedures, and these can cause unexpected feelings and reactions in the individual. There are also medical risks that go along with both the surgical and hormonal procedures of transitioning that the individual has to be aware of and manage. Finally, after the transition is complete, individuals may struggle with living as someone who is relatively unfamiliar to their friends, family members, and colleagues. The transgender person may or may not experience support and acceptance in these groups and relationships, and some group members may even act aggressively toward the transgender person. If this is the case, it may be helpful to find support groups where transgender individuals can find not only friendship and community, but also guidance on how to navigate their new life, society, friends and relationships, and medical recovery.

Communication

Being educated on diverse populations is crucial to increase understanding and avoid discrimination. While education can be helpful in learning to communicate effectively, it is also important to ask questions and clarify anything that may be confusing when communicating with someone from another culture. Counselors also should be aware and observant when communicating with a client to make sure that communication on both sides is fully understood.

Counselors should have basic understanding of the ways in which communication norms can vary across cultures. Counselors should exhibit cultural competence with regard to communication as demonstrated by the following:

- Their awareness of both nonverbal and verbal communication differences
- Their ability to use language that is appropriate and respectful to different cultures
- Their recognition of personal strengths and limitations in communication
- Their willingness to actively remove barriers that may inhibit effective communication with individuals from different cultures

Nonverbal communication can be a common source of misunderstanding in cross-cultural communication. Different cultures place different emphasis on these aspects of nonverbal communication:

- Levels of appropriate assertiveness
- Use of facial expressions and physical gestures
- Appropriateness of physical touch in communication
- Personal space and seating arrangements

There are cultural differences with regard to conflict as well:

- In the U.S., participants in a conflict are typically encouraged to resolve the conflict directly.
- In other cultures, conflict is viewed as an embarrassment that should be dealt with as privately and quietly as possible.

Disclosure of personal information and openness with regard to feelings are uncomfortable in some cultures, and it may be considered inappropriate to ask direct questions with regard to these topics.

Decision-making styles also vary across cultures:

- Delegating vs. making decisions
- Majority rule vs. consensus

Sometimes there will be communication difficulties between the counselor and client, most notably with language or cultural differences that hinder straightforward communication. It is ethically imperative that all clients have access to adequate language assistance, including the option of a translator, so that those with limited English proficiency are still receiving the same level of care. The optimal situation is for clients to have a counselor who can speak to them directly in their first language, and this should be arranged whenever possible. However, this is not always feasible and a translator must be used. In cases where interpreters are necessary or are requested by the client, they should be professional and trained interpreters, rather than family members or non-professionals. They must also understand and agree to the rules of privacy and confidentiality. Counselors should make sure their

communication is simple and easy to understand and also make sure to clarify what the client is saying if there is any confusion. Counselors should also familiarize themselves with the cultural backgrounds of the clients they work with to better understand their unique perspective and to minimize misunderstandings.

Uses and Limits of Social Media

Social media has become a huge part of life for most people, so counselors must be aware of the appropriate uses of social media as well as its limitations. Some counselors may choose to promote their practices through social media. As long as their page is professional, this is a convenient and acceptable tool for marketing. For communication, it is best to provide a phone number and email address on the page rather than allowing messages through the social media page. This helps maintain confidentiality of current or future client information. Counselors may also use social media to connect with other counselors and discuss professional issues. In these instances, it is important that no personal information is shared that could reveal the identities of clients. Aliases should be used to keep specific information about cases that are being discussed from being connected to the counselor or clients. When sharing, commenting, or liking posts on social media, counselors should always be aware that clients might come across anything that is shared publicly. It is crucial to be conscious of whether these interactions and displays on social media could be harmful to clients.

Besides using social media professionally, it is likely that counselors have personal social media accounts. Some clients will want to connect with their counselors through social media, so it is best to address this during the first session. It should be explained that the policy is to never accept friend requests from clients. If this isn't explained up front, the rejection of a friend request could be detrimental to the therapeutic relationship and to clients who are emotionally fragile. By establishing and maintaining this policy, boundaries regarding dual relationships remain intact.

Conflict Tolerance and Resolution

Helping clients deal with conflict requires resolution of negative emotions that result when individuals do not agree on a topic. **Emotional detours**, such as dominating or avoiding a situation, the inability to make decisions, and overaccommodating, can lead to emotional disturbances, including anger, anxiety, compulsions, and depression. Clients should be encouraged to express their initial positions, explore their underlying core concerns, and create a mutually agreed-upon plan that meets the expectations of all people involved. Conflict resolution is dependent on good communication. Obstacles such as threats, forceful opinions, and unsolicited advice can block effective communication. Counselors should also assess patterns of interaction, mediate effective dialogue, and block negative communication. The conflict resolution process begins with identifying concerns and establishing the importance of the confrontation. Taking turns defining the problem and acknowledging others' opinions can help build alternative solutions that satisfy conflicting ideals.

Empathic Attunement

Empathy is being able to relate to client circumstances and direction without the counselor actually experiencing it themselves. Sympathy differs from empathy in that sympathy is compassion for the client without having experienced the client's state of being. Empathy involves "being with" the client in their time and frame of mind. It involves connecting to the client on a visceral level while still maintaining some objectivity. Attunement occurs through listening to and watching the client. By tuning in to the client's words and body language, the counselor begins to experience empathy. The client's body language may reveal emotions that aren't being verbally communicated.

83

These emotions are usually subconscious, but sometimes they are emotions that the client doesn't feel safe sharing. Attunement to these unarticulated emotions, when expressed back to the client, can be a powerful way of showing the client they are in a place of safety and understanding. While working with a client, it is important to stay attuned to the changes in emotion and to pick up on the degree of comfort that the client has with moving forward and examining the emotions. In addition to feeling what the client is feeling, attunement can help the counselor guide the client through therapy at the rate that is most comfortable and effective for the client. Because empathy is the framework on which the counseling practice is built, it is imperative that counselors be empathetic with their clients. Those who cannot be empathetic should seek additional supervision or counsel in order to do their work effectively or refer the client to another counselor.

Empathic Responding

One of the most effective skills for encouraging clients to share and explore their emotions in counseling is **empathic responding**. The goals of empathic responding are for the client to know that the counselor understands exactly how they feel and to ultimately uncover the real significance and roots of their emotions. The counselor must have a deep sense of self-awareness in order to recall their own emotions from past experiences that enable the empathic response. Empathic responding is more than the counselor merely hearing the client and feeling pity for them, letting them know that they feel bad or happy for them, or telling them how awful, confusing, or stressful a situation must be. Empathic responding involves reflecting the emotions that the client expressed back to them and explaining the reasons for those feelings in a way that shows that the counselor can imagine being in the client's place.

It is crucial for the counselor to use words that describe precisely what the client is experiencing. This is not a time for problem-solving or judging the client's emotions. This is a time for the counselor to step away from their own perception of the client's problems and to step into the client's frame of reference and feel the same thing the client is feeling. When a counselor can show that they are simultaneously feeling the same emotions as the client without any judgment, the client should have no fear of being correct or incorrect in their expression of emotions. In this environment of true understanding and acceptance, the client will be more open to sharing their feelings. As the client's emotions are labeled accurately, the counselor and the client can deeply analyze and pinpoint the origins of the emotions and begin therapeutic change.

Facilitating Client Skill Development for Career, Educational, and Life-Work Planning and Management

Providing Education Resources

Counselors often don multiple roles in their profession, one of which includes providing information and assisting with access to educational services. When providing educational services, the counselor must determine what skills, information, or knowledge needs to be acquired, as well as the capabilities of the client and the amount of time available for the development of new skills. The provision of education may be done in individual, family, or small group classes, or large group forums. Counselors may also recommend resources such as books, articles, or websites that may help clients acquire new information.

Clients with substance addiction issues can benefit from resources that provide education on common addictions, locate rehabilitation centers near their area, or provide intervention hotlines in case of a crisis. Websites such as addictionresource.com and drugabuse.gov provide an array of information for clients seeking education and additional resources. Clients who experience depression can benefit from

84

outside engagement when counseling sessions do not occur. These clients are at a high risk of suicide and may require multiple resources. Organizations such as the **National Alliance on Mental Illness (NAMI)** provide support groups, advocacy, and educational articles to bring awareness and help clients experiencing emotional distress. Clients whose safety is at risk due to domestic violence also require a vast amount of resources. The **National Domestic Violence Hotline** offers pathways to creating a safety plan, education on recognizing the signs of domestic violence, and a list of regional organizations to help those in need.

Providing Psychoeducation for Clients and Groups

Psychoeducation refers to any form of training or instruction that is provided to clients and the client system as a part of understanding mental health or psychological issues and treatments. Its goal is to support clients experiencing mental illnesses, their families, and their networks while eliminating the stigma that has been associated with mental health issues for decades. Psychoeducation methods include explaining potential causes for specific mental health issues, understanding the challenges of specific mental health issues, explaining how support systems can acknowledge and cope with not only a client's mental health condition but also their own caregiving stress, and teaching coping skills, building resiliency, and overcoming obstacles in ways that are accessible. This form of education can occur in group settings, seminars or webinars, and in individual or family sessions. It can also be presented through newsletters, other media, and formal courses.

It may be offered in-home, online, in hospitals or other healthcare facilities, in community centers, or at conference venues. It is not considered treatment, but it is a beneficial complement to clinical care. It promotes positive and inclusive language, eliminates shame and fear around mental illnesses, creates educational value, fosters network support and understanding, and acknowledges a variety of feelings and responses to mental health conditions. Psychoeducation techniques are associated with reduced inpatient and hospitalization rates for clients with mental health conditions. Psychoeducation is correlated with clients' self-reported feelings of acceptance and increased family support. Family and friends self-report a better understanding of their loved one who may have a mental health condition, a better understanding of their role in providing positive support and care, the ability to draw healthy boundaries for themselves, and relief from learning and utilizing self-care techniques that reduce caregiver stress.

Practice Quiz

1. Reflection is a practice where counselors acknowledge the meaning behind a client's words. Why do counselors use reflection in sessions?
    a. To help clients understand underlying emotions
    b. To provide advice
    c. To set goals for sessions
    d. To allow for silence

2. Carl Rogers believed three core conditions must exist for effective counseling. What are those conditions?
    a. Trust, empathy, and kindness
    b. Empathy, positive regard, and kindness
    c. Genuineness, trust, and congruence
    d. Empathy, positive regard, and congruence

3. Group counselors need strong interpersonal skills in order to lead groups. Which skill is NOT required for a group counselor?
    a. Encouragement
    b. Support
    c. Confrontation
    d. Crisis intervention training

4. When a counselor "steps into a client's shoes" to see their view of life, which of the following techniques is the counselor using?
    a. Reframing
    b. Restructuring
    c. Empathizing
    d. Grounding

5. Which of the following is NOT true about a client's relationship with their counselor?
    a. Transference is possible.
    b. The counselor is in a position of authority to the client.
    c. The counselor can educate the client.
    d. It is appropriate for the counselor and client to become friends during the therapeutic relationship.

See answers on next page

Answer Explanations

1. A: To help clients understand underlying emotions. Reflection is also referred to as "reflection of feeling" and is used for counselors to indicate that they both hear and understand the meanings and emotions behind a client's words. Counselors do not provide advice during reflection, but let the client know they are being heard, so Choice *B* is incorrect. There is also no goal setting during this time, because it's important for the client to know their emotions are being validated, making Choice *C* incorrect. When reflection happens, the counselor provides communication to the client, so silence has less to do with it than Choice *A*, making Choice *D* incorrect.

2. D: Carl Rogers developed the person-centered approach to counseling, which stressed the important of the counseling relationship, as well as the need to evaluate therapy for effectiveness. Carl Rogers's three core conditions for effective counseling were empathy, positive regard, and congruence (genuineness).

3. D: Crisis intervention training is not needed for a group counselor, but the ability to encourage, support, and confront are necessary skills. A group counselor needs to have all the skills and training that an individual counselor would require. Encouraging group members, being supportive, and the ability to confront behavior are all skills needed and utilized by counselors.

4. C: Empathizing is when counselors try to understand the client's point of view by considering who they are and their life experiences that contribute to their perspectives. The remaining choices are incorrect.

5. D: Choice *D* is correct because it would be considered a dual relationship and would therefore be an ethical violation. Choice *A* is incorrect because it is possible for a client to have a reaction to their counselor based on earlier relationships. Choice *B* and *C* are also true.

Counseling and Helping Relationships

Theories and Models of Counseling

Individual

Individual therapy can be an appropriate option for many reasons. A few considerations for choosing this modality would be if the client needs individualized treatment, requires scheduling flexibility, or prefers the privacy of individual counseling. Issues addressed in individual counseling are numerous and can include the same issues that would be focused on in family or group counseling, but in individual counseling the client is the priority. The counselor can decide with the client whether the client's goals and needs would best be met through individual therapy. Interventions such as exposure therapy and psychodynamic therapy work well in individual therapy as these interventions are unique to the client and allow them to progress and open up emotionally at their own pace in an intimate and safe setting.

Family Practice Approaches

One of the main goals of **family therapy** is to allow each family member to function at their best while maintaining the functionality of the family unit. When working with families, the counselor must:

- Examine and consider all systems affecting a family and each individual member to determine problems, solutions, and strengths, and also consider the functionality of the family subsystems.

- Respect cultural, socio-economic, and non-traditional family systems and not automatically define those systems as dysfunctional if they are not the norm. The overall and individual family functioning should be accounted for.

- Work to engage the family in the treatment, while considering the specific traits of the family (i.e., culture, history, family structure, race, dynamics, etc.).

- Assist in identifying and changing dysfunctional patterns, boundaries, and family problems.

The following are important concepts in family therapy:

- **Boundaries**: Healthy boundaries around and within the family must exist for families to function effectively. The boundaries must be clear and appropriate.

- **Emotional Proximity and Distance**: These are the type of boundaries that exist within a family system.

- **Enmeshed**: Boundaries are unclear and pliable. Families that have very open boundaries within the family unit may have very fixed boundaries between outside forces and the family.

- **Disengaged**: Boundaries are rigid with little interaction and emotional engagement. Families that are disengaged within the family system tend to have very open boundaries around the family unit.

- **Family Hierarchy**: The power structure within the family. For families to function effectively, there must be a clear delineation of authority. There must be an individual or individuals who

88

hold the power and authority in a family system. In a traditional family, this should ideally be located within the parental system.

- **Homeostasis**: Family systems should maintain homeostasis or remain regular and stable. When life events become too stressful and the family can no longer function as it normally would, the state of homeostasis is threatened. This is usually when many families seek help.

- **Alliances**: Partnerships or collaborations between certain members of a family. When alliances exist between some members of a family, it can lead to dysfunction (i.e., parent and child have an alliance that undermines the parental subsystem).

Couples Intervention/Treatment Approaches

Many couples enter treatment after experiencing long-standing problems and may seek help because all other options have failed. One of the goals of couples' therapy is to help clients develop effective communication and problem-solving skills so they can solve problems throughout and after treatment. Other goals include helping the couple form a more objective view of their relationship, modifying dysfunctional behavior/patterns, increasing emotional expression, and recognizing strengths. Counselors should create an environment to help the couple understand treatment goals, feel safe in expressing their feelings, and reconnect by developing trust in each other. Interventions for couples are often centered on goals geared toward preventing conflicting verbal communication and improving empathy, respect, and intimacy in a relationship. Therapeutic interventions, along with exercises, are designed to help couples learn to treat each other as partners and not rivals. **Cognitive Behavioral** Therapy is also used when working with couples. It uses cognitive techniques to help change distorted thinking and modify behavior.

Group Work

Individuals seeking counseling may benefit from group work in addition to, or in place of, individual counseling. **Group work** can be defined as a goal-directed intervention with small groups of people. Groups focus on nonpathological issues, such as personal, physical/medical, social, or vocational, and act to support and encourage growth. Groups are popular for addictions, eating disorders or weight loss, grief, anxiety, and parenting. They can be homogenous and share demographic information and goals or can be heterogeneous and diverse with multifaceted goals. Group members benefit from the process through sharing and the ability to learn new ways to react and cope with difficulties. It is essential that groups have a trained leader to help create structure, boundaries, and rules and keep the group on track.

The intention of group work is to improve the socioemotional and psychoeducation needs of the individual members of the group through the group process. There are several types of treatment groups, including support, educational, and therapy groups. Groups can also be long-term or short-term, depending on the type and purpose.

Groups can be open or closed. **Open groups** are ongoing and allow for new members to enter at any time. Open groups are typically used for support and life transitions. There are challenges to this type of group, since the members are at different stages in the group process. The frequently changing membership can be disruptive to the group process because members may not feel as emotionally safe to share with others. **Closed groups** are time-limited, and new members can only join during the beginning stage. The advantages to this type of group are more engagement and better trust by the

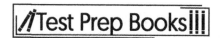

members, since the group process is more stable. A disadvantage is that if several members leave the group, the group process may not be as effective.

Using A Systems Approach

Systemic patterns of interaction are based on the belief that multiple factors impact the relationship between individuals. A client's social, familial, political, and cultural beliefs are all environmental factors that influence a current state of mind. This belief is part of the **systems theory**, which aims to conceptualize a client's issue based on their surroundings. The theory focuses on viewing individuals as their own system whose behaviors, thoughts, and emotions affect everyone in connection with them. In order to create a system that works for all members involved, counselors must help clients identify each person's expectations, behaviors, and desires. Using a systemic approach, insight into each member's role can help determine how that role affects the functionality of an entire group.

For example, a woman can be a nurturing mother at home, a disciplinary leader at work, and an encouraging friend within her social circle. All of these roles help to fulfill the overall system of interaction. Alternatively, there are negative interaction patterns that can strain communication and cause conflict among individuals. An example is individuals who rapidly escalate an argument with minimal provocation and have low frustration tolerance. This pattern is usually directed at another person who does not engage in shouting and will remain silent. Other individuals will attempt to control a situation by verbalizing threats of exposure, abandonment, or harm. Effective communication and constructive dialogue can help attain positive relationships and encourage clients to become an active participant within a system.

Components of a Family History

Family history can provide insight into an individual's influences. The family unit is the most immediate system to which an individual belongs, so understanding it can provide invaluable perspective.

Counselors often use a genogram to understand the individual's family dynamic. A genogram is a visual chart that depicts an individual's familial relationships over a specified period of time by collecting relationship dynamics, attachments, interactions, and behavioral patterns. It can also aid clients with self-understanding and help the counselor choose appropriate assessments.

Inquiries about family history may explore:

- Ethnic and cultural background.

- Immigration status and experiences.

- Family composition (i.e., nuclear, blended, fostered or adopted children, divorced parents, co-parenting status).

- Socioeconomic status.

- Educational levels of family members.

- Employment status of family members.

- Personal and occupational goals and ambitions of family members.

- Achievements of family members.

- Traumas or loss experienced by any family members.

- Medical, financial, or domestic problems.

- Values held by each family member and the priority of each value.

- Any perceived favoritism experienced to certain children or adults.

- Roles held within the family.

Some of these topics may be sensitive to discuss and should be approached empathetically.

Family Theories and Dynamics

Family systems theory is an iteration of the basic systems theory. When seeking to explain the behavior of an individual, one must look also at the interrelationships of the individual's family. The assumptions of this theory are as follows:

- A family is a unique unit and is unlike any other family.

- A family is interactional, and its parts vary in their resistance to change.

- Healthy family development depends upon the family's ability to meet the needs of the family and the individuals comprising the family.

- The family undergoes changes that cause differing amounts of stress to each family member.

External Boundaries

External boundaries define the family and distinguish it from individuals and systems outside of the family. Boundaries in systems theory are not physical or tangible, but can be observed, in a sense, via a family's attitudes, rules, and use of space. Some families have **closed boundaries**. Families that use closed boundaries are characterized by having many rules about associating with non-family, physical barriers used to limit access to the family, rigid rules and values, few connections with others, and are traditional and wary of change. Families that have **open boundaries** are characterized by having many connections to individuals outside the family, fluid rules, spontaneous decision-making skills, and minimal privacy. Uniqueness is valued more than tradition, and there is no fear of change. Open boundaries may lead to the family experiencing more chaos.

Internal Boundaries

Internal boundaries are rules that develop and define the relationships between the subsystems of the family. A **subsystem** might include the parents, the males of the household, or members of the family who share the same hobby. **Role organization** within a family is influenced by the size of the family, its culture and history, lifestyle, and values. In a healthy, well-functioning family, roles should be both clear and flexible.

As a family grows, rules develop that define how family members relate both to each other and to the world around them. Rules may be explicitly stated or implicitly understood. Families vary greatly in the type of rules that they have, as well as regarding whether rules can be easily discussed or modified.

Distribution of power in a reliable manner is important to the functioning of a family, though this distribution may change over time in response to changing needs of family members. Effective communication is also necessary for the family system. Roles, behaviors, and rules are all established through some type of communication. Communication can be open (clear and easy to understand) or closed (confusing and unclear).

Family Composition and Cultural Considerations

In the United States, a long-standing definition of the family unit has been the nuclear family, which consists of a single man and a single woman (typically married to one another) and their immediate children. However, there are other concepts of family reflected in other cultures that can encompass alternate dynamics.

Families can consist of any small group of individuals that are related by blood or choose to share their lives together. These can consist of heterosexual or homosexual couples with or without children, single parent households, childfree households, homes with extended family all living under one roof, blended families involving step-children and step-parents, or lifelong partners that choose not to marry legally.

Culture and ethnicity play a large role in defining a family unit. For example, many Eastern cultures value living with extended family and consider everyone in the physical household to be a member of the immediate family unit.

American psychiatrist **Murray Bowen (1913–1990)** first established the family systems theory, which later served as the basis for family, or systems-focused, counseling. The **family systems theory** seeks to explain the high level of emotional interdependence that family members have with one another and how this interdependence individually affects each member of the family system. This theory states that the unique and complex cohesiveness that is found in family systems promotes positive behaviors like teamwork and taking care of one another; however, it can also cause negative behaviors, like anxiety or addictions, to diffuse from one person into the entire system.

The family systems theory is made up of eight distinct concepts:

- **Triangles**: refers to three-person systems, considered to be the smallest system that can still be stable. A third person adds extra support to manage intense emotions, tension, or conflict. The theory states that a two-person system cannot usually weather high levels of emotion, tension, or conflict over time.

- **Differentiation** of Self: how much an individual's personal beliefs differ from that of his or her group's beliefs. It is an important function of developing one's self. A strong self usually correlates with confidence and pragmatism, while a weak self usually correlates with an unhealthy need for approval from others.

- **Nuclear Family Emotional System**: referring to four different relationship patterns in this system. The patterns are marital conflict, dysfunction in one spouse, impairment in one or more children, and emotional distance, which refers to the fact that it occurs and how it affects the way problems are handled within the family.

- **Family Projection Process**: how parents project emotional conflict onto their children. The process can lead to pathologies in the child's psyche.

92

This material is provided for exam preparation purposes only and does not indicate an endorsement of any specific scientific, political, or religious point of view. © TPB Publishing. You have been licensed one copy of this document for personal use only. Any other reproduction or redistribution is strictly prohibited. All rights reserved.

- **Multigenerational Transmission Process**: regarding the variance in differentiation of self between generations. The differentiation of self between parents and children over time leads to a widespread difference in beliefs between the oldest generation and the youngest generation of the family.

- **Emotional Cutoff**: regarding issue resolution. The act of failing to resolve issues between family members by reducing or eliminating contact with one another is emotional cut-off.

- **Sibling Position**: the importance of birth order and its influence on someone's functioning. It incorporates not only the birth order as it relates to how that person will function in workplaces and relationships, but also focuses on the birth order of each of the individual's parents and the influences those have on parenting styles.

- **Societal Emotional Process**: how the previous seven concepts hold true for any society. All families and societies will have progressive and regressive periods of development over time.

Important Terms

Affectional Orientation—a term used to describe one's romantic orientation toward a specific sex; an alternative term to *sexual orientation*

Alternative Family—any group of people that considers themselves a family unit but does not fall into the definition of a nuclear family

Emic—being aware of a client's culture and using counseling approaches accordingly

Empty Nest Syndrome—feelings of isolation, depression, or purposelessness that some parents may feel when their children move out of the family home

Ethnocentrism—a belief that one's culture is superior to another's

Ethnocide—purposely destroying another's ethnicity or culture

Ethnology—a branch of anthropology that systematically studies and compares the similarities and differences between cultures

Etic—an objective, universal viewpoint of clients

Gender Schema Theory—a theory by **Sandra Bem** in 1981 that describes how people in a society become gendered, especially through categories of information such as schemata

Heterogeneous Society—a society that is diverse in characteristics, cultural values, and language

High Context Culture—information is implicit and communicated through unspoken messages, with a focus on personal relationships and with fewer rules

Homogenous Society—a society that primarily consists of people with the same characteristics, cultural values, and language

Low Context Culture—information exchanged with little hidden meaning, with clear, explicit rules and standards, and relationships deemed less important than tasks

Modal Behavior—statistically, the most common and normative behaviors of a society

93

Nuclear Family—a family unit that consists of a married man and woman and their immediate children

Nuclear Family of Orientation—the family one is born into

Nuclear Family of Procreation—a family created by marriage and childbearing

Reciprocity—a social norm that says people should pay back what has been provided to them. This type of exchange relationship is used to build continuing relationships with others.

Sexual Orientation—an individual's sexual preference toward a specific gender

Stereotype—a preconceived notion about a group of people, not necessarily based in fact

Tripartite—awareness, knowledge, and skills of multicultural counseling

Facilitating Systemic Change

Counselors can apply the principles of systems theory to create change when working with families. An important concept of this theory is the idea that one part of a family system affects and changes other parts of the system.

Homeostasis is a concept that refers to families' resistance to change and their pressure to maintain balance and the status quo. Counselors must use techniques to disrupt the homeostasis of a family in which problematic behaviors exist. For example, in a family with a parentified male child, a counselor might physically move the boy away from his mother and father and place him across the room, while placing the mother and father next to each other. This maneuver has the potential to disrupt the system. It is designed to help the married couple create stronger boundaries around their marriage, thereby excluding the child from the husband-wife dyad.

Counselors can also facilitate systemic change by having clients draw genograms to show generational patterns. These diagrams visually depict family patterns of marriage, substance abuse, violence, divorce, etc. across multiple generations. They are designed to show families' negative and positive patterns and may give them motivation to begin intentionally creating new patterns.

Theories, Models, and Strategies for Establishing and Maintaining Counseling Relationships

Establishing a Therapeutic Alliance

An important element of the counseling relationship is the establishment of a **therapeutic alliance**, or collaborative effort between the counselor and the client, that will predict the success of the counseling experience. The relationship between the counselor and the client or client system is influenced by a number of components. These include the type of emotion that is shown by the parties during sessions, the general attitude toward the working relationship (e.g., positive, supportive), and the value each party places on the working relationship. The counselor should ensure that empathy, sympathy, and acceptance of the client and client system are shown during sessions to help foster a positive relationship. These aspects can be further supported by the counselor's initiative to build rapport with the client, such as through allowing the client to openly express feelings, work at a pace that feels comfortable, and encouraging them to shape and make decisions related to the intervention.

Generally, counselors who are inviting and interpersonally sensitive will be able to form a positive therapeutic alliance with the client. The working alliance can be assessed using a couple of tools. The

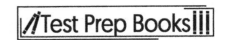

Working Alliance Inventory is a self-reporting Likert questionnaire that explores how well the client's and counselor's thoughts about therapy are aligned. Both the counselor and the client answer more than thirty questions pertaining to counseling goals, first impressions, and the effectiveness of counseling sessions. The Barrett-Lennard Relationship Inventory is another tool used to measure congruence, regard, and empathy of a relationship. It is important for the therapeutic alliance to be established in the early counseling sessions to ensure the development of a positive working relationship.

When working with non-voluntary or involuntary clients who are mandated legally to seek treatment, the counselor must help the client overcome any negative feelings of anger or mistrust about treatment. With all clients, appropriate relationship building between the counselor and client is a necessary part of engagement and motivation. Clients must feel they are in a safe, empathetic environment. They also should experience a sufficient level of trust for the counselor in order for treatment to be effective. To create an effective treatment relationship, the counselor must project an attitude free of judgment, recognize the client's individual attributes, strengths, and abilities, and encourage the client's right to be an active participant in their own treatment.

Monitoring the Therapeutic Relationship and Building Trust as Needed

Rapport building begins during the initial contact the counselor has with the client, a crucial time for establishing trust and harmony. After building rapport, the client and the counselor can begin working on client issues and continue developing the relationship on deeper levels. The relationship that the client has with the counselor is representative of the relationships the client has in other areas of life; the counselor needs to engage with the client within this framework to effect the greatest change. As the principal conduit for client change and acceptance, the counselor/client relationship is primary to the problem solving and therapy process.

A common occurrence in counseling is **transference**. Without realizing it, the client misdirects feelings about another person onto the counselor. If transference isn't recognized or the counselor doesn't explain the transference to the client, the therapeutic relationship could be damaged if the emotions that the client is feeling are negative. Being mindful of transference and working on these feelings with the client can help to maintain the therapeutic relationship and assist the client in developing appropriate approaches for interactions outside of counseling.

If the counselor cannot develop a positive relationship with the client, the change process is hindered. The counselor/client relationship should be based on trust, empathy, and acceptance by both parties in order to facilitate growth. Some clients may have difficulty building trust with the counselor, and the counselor may need to be patient with the client in order to make treatment goal progress. If the counselor cannot develop an appropriate trusting, empathetic, and accepting relationship with the client, the counselor should seek supervision.

In some cases, the counselor will need to transfer the client because it will be very challenging for the client to make progress if trust does not exist. Counselors should also be alert for countertransference issues in the relationship with the client and address these issues promptly if they occur.

Non-Judgmental Stance

When interviewing a client, a counselor must be careful to eliminate all personal bias from their language. This relates to all subtle negative phrasing related to race, ethnicity, socioeconomic status, gender, gender identity, life choices, disability, or psychological disorders. The job of the counselor is to support the client without bias, always promoting the client's self-identity. Phrases or expressions that

demean or stereotype a particular group of people should never be used. Similarly, labeling someone can be hurtful, especially in cases where that label has a negative connotation or stigma attached to it. Sometimes it may even be appropriate for the counselor to ask the client how they wish to be identified or addressed. Inclusive and affirming language should be used when talking about all groups of people and especially when talking to or about the client. Terms that are known to be offensive or degrading should always be avoided.

Counselors should treat all clients of all backgrounds with open-mindedness, without judgment, and with the client's desired intervention outcomes at the center of all interactions. Counselors may work with clients of different cultures, and counselors should respect the opinions and boundaries that these differences bring to treatment.

Counselors can communicate support and a nonjudgmental attitude through an open posture and eye gaze that shows interest but not intimidation.

Importance of Nonjudgmental Support

Support is a broad term for the way in which a counselor provides assistance and care to clients. Nonjudgmental support helps clients to open up, identify issues and the need for counseling, and set personal goals. A counselor can support a client by providing reassurance, acting as a sounding board, and simply listening without reaction. For the client, support from the counselor can allow a sense of being temporarily unburdened, which can facilitate healing. Support groups allow for peers or individuals experiencing similar issues (such as single parents and those struggling with addiction or eating disorders) to provide companionship and comfort through shared experiences.

Positive Regard

Carl Rogers believed that clients can begin to make changes independently once they experience positive regard from the counselor. **Positive regard** means that the counselor puts aside any judgment and embraces the client as a person of worth, not defining the client by their actions or expressions of emotions or beliefs. Counselors can show positive regard by allowing clients to speak freely about their behaviors, feelings, or thoughts without responding critically to what the client has said. The counselor should be able to communicate an understanding that the client is behaving or experiencing emotions to the best of their ability. This freedom from judgment then allows the client to be more accepting of themselves and more confident in their decisions to create change.

Respect and Acceptance for Diversity

Clients may come from all backgrounds. It is important that counselors do not make any prior negative judgments regarding the personality or life of any client. Each individual has worth. It is essential for counselors to be mindful of any personal prejudices or biases and employ empathy and sensitivity when working with the client.

The client must be allowed to disclose details of a situation to determine influences from his or her culture. This can be done by conducting an interview with the client about his or her background, customs, personal beliefs, values, and relationships. Appropriate group interviews with key members in the client's life can also provide additional verbal and nonverbal information.

It is recommended that in order to be effective, counselors engage in ongoing professional development to gain skills and awareness of differing cultural needs and ethical standpoints and to ensure they are providing competent services. To maintain credibility and trust, counselors must honor the client's motives and goals for the session, taking into consideration cultural variations.

Active Listening and Observation

Active listening is crucial to the relationship- and rapport-building stage with clients. Counselors must be fully engaged in the listening process and not distracted by thoughts of what will come next or intervention planning. The counselor must not only hear the audible language the client is offering but must also look at the nonverbal behaviors and the underlying meaning in the words and expressions of the client. Nonverbal behaviors include body language, facial expressions, voice quality, and physical reactions of the client. Using certain facial expressions, body language, and postures shows that the counselor is engaged and listening to the client.

Counselors should display eye contact and natural but engaged body movements and gestures. An example would be sitting slightly forward with a non-rigid posture. As with all communication techniques, counselors should be aware of cultural differences in what is appropriate, especially related to direct eye contact and posturing. Other aspects of active listening include head nodding, eye contact, and using phrases of understanding and clarity (e.g., "What I hear you saying is ..." and "You (may) wish to ...") Counselors may verify they understand the client's message by paraphrasing and asking for validation that it is correct (e.g., "What I hear you saying is ...").

Identifying the Underlying Meaning of Communication

Clients use both verbal and nonverbal communication during treatment. Counselors must develop the ability to interpret communication congruency or develop the ability to assess both types of expressions simultaneously to understand client messaging accurately. Clients may use facial expressions, gesturing, eye contact, tone of voice, or other ways to express feelings nonverbally. Counselors must notice whether the nonverbal communication reinforces or conflicts with verbal messaging.

Silence

Silence can be an effective skill in therapy but must be used carefully, especially in the early stages of the process. Initially, clients may be silent due to many factors, such as fear, resistance, discomfort with opening up, or uncertainty about the process. Counselors who use silence in initial sessions must ensure clients do not perceive the counselor as bored, hostile, or indifferent. As counseling progresses, clients may gain additional comfort with silence and use it as a way to reflect on content, process information, consider options, and gain self-awareness. Newer counselors may have more difficulty with silence, as they may believe they are not being helpful if they are not talking. Silence is also viewed differently by culture, so cultural awareness is important in understanding and using it as a therapeutic tool.

Summarizing

Counselors may paraphrase and echo clients' verbal statements to acknowledge their feelings. **Summarizing** may involve reflecting back the statements made by the client to clarify what the client has said. Counselors also must summarize communication in order to provide sufficient records of the session. Further, during the end of the session, the counselor may wish to clarify goals and homework assigned for the next week so that the client is clear on the changes that need to take place.

Attending

Attending is the act of the counselor giving clients their full attention. Attending to the client shows respect for their needs, can encourage openness, and can create a sense of comfort and support in the counseling process. There are several ways for counselors to attend actively to clients, including maintaining appropriate eye contact, using reassuring body language and gestures, and monitoring their tone and expressions. Counselors can communicate support and a nonjudgmental attitude through an open posture and eye gaze that shows interest but not intimidation. They should use a caring verbal

tone and facial expressions, which indicate attention to what their clients are saying and can be used in addition to silence to create a positive environment for counseling.

Reflecting

Reflecting is a basic counseling skill designed to build rapport and help clients become aware of underlying emotions. Counselors "reflect back" what a client says, both to indicate they are attending and also to analyze and interpret meanings. Reflecting is more than simply paraphrasing a client's words, as it involves more in-depth understanding and an attempt to elicit further information. An example would be a client stating, "I'm not sure what to do about my current relationship. I can't decide if I should stay or leave." The counselor would reflect by stating, "It sounds like you are conflicted about what to do; this is a difficult decision to make," and follow up with a probing question or allow time for the client to process and react.

The following are additional counseling skills:

- **Restatement**: Clarification through repeating back the client's words, as understood by the counselor

- **Reflection**: Restatement of what the counselor heard from the client, emphasizing any underlying emotional content (can be termed **reflection of feeling**)

- **Paraphrasing**: Repeating back a client's story while providing an empathic response

- **Summarizing**: Reiteration of the major points of the counseling discussion

- **Silence**: Moments during which neither the client nor the counselor speaks; can be used for reflection but may indicate resistance from the client

- **Confrontation**: Technique in which the counselor identifies discrepancies from the client in a supportive manner (counselor may also ask for clarification to determine if content was misheard prior to exposing possible inconsistencies)

- **Structuring**: Used to set goals and agree upon plan for counseling; also used within sessions to make effective use of time and respect boundaries

Errors

Reflecting is one of several active listening and rapport-building skills but should not be overused. It is essential that the counselor be able to offer back meaningful restatements and not simply repeat back what is heard. It is also important that the counselor accurately reflects any feeling and does not project or misinterpret. In some cases, misinterpretation can help the client further clarify and is not detrimental to the relationship. By using reflection and clarification, any errors can be corrected. Even when errors occur, when the counselor clarifies what the client means, it communicates that the counselor is invested in understanding the client. From a cultural awareness standpoint, the counselor should be sensitive to any differences and ensure there is a level of trust prior to engaging in more in-depth reflection.

Methods of Facilitating Communication

Counselors may facilitate communication with the client by verbally encouraging communication or by addressing the client with constructive information concerning the case. Counselors need to recall

information concerning the client from session to session in order to facilitate communication and move forward with the client. Clarifying the client's feelings and statements helps to ensure the counselor understands what is being communicated as well as lets the client know that the counselor is engaged and actively listening. Development of trust with the client may facilitate additional communication, and counselors should be sensitive to the trust-building process because it is the cornerstone of the helping relationship. Counselors may provide clients with homework outside of a session that facilitates communication during the next session.

Mandated clients, including court-ordered clients or clients ordered to counseling from child protective services, may face challenges in communicating with the counselor because they do not choose to be in treatment. Developing trust with these clients to facilitate communication is especially important for progress to be made. It's helpful to acknowledge the client's feelings and possible frustration about the mandated treatment. Clients who require out-of-home placement need clear communication with the counselor to clarify what is happening and make appropriate psychological adjustments to their circumstances.

Furthering and close/open-ended questions are additional communication techniques that are beneficial in counseling:

- **Furthering**: A technique that reinforces the idea that the counselor is listening to the client and encourages further information to be gathered. This technique includes nodding of the head, facial expressions, or encouraging responses such as "yes" or "I understand." It also includes accent responses, whereby counselors repeat or parrot back a few words of a client's last response.

- **Close/Open-Ended Questions**: Depending on the timing or information the counselor is seeking to elicit from the client, one of these types of questions may be used. Close-ended questions, such as "How old are you?" will typically elicit a short answer. Conversely, open-ended questions, such as "What are your feelings about school?", allow for longer, more-involved responses. Open questions are more likely to provide helpful information, as they require the client to express feelings, beliefs, and ideas. Open questions often begin with "why," "how," "when," or "tell me …". Counselors do need to be aware of the limitations of asking questions. Any questions asked should have purpose and provide information that will be meaningful to the counselor and the relationship. Curiosity questions should be avoided, as well as asking too many questions, which may feel interrogating to the client. A counselor can ask follow-up questions for clarification as needed. The counselor should provide the client adequate time to answer questions and elaborate but also allow time for the client to talk freely.

Telemental health is an evolving form of counseling. Since the COVID-19 pandemic, telemental health services have become more prevalent, but the rules and regulations are not firmly established and may differ from state to state. While some insurance companies have started to pay for these services due to no-contact regulations during the pandemic, it is not certain if this will continue to be a covered practice post-pandemic.

Telemental health includes video conferencing, phone calls, chat, text messages, and emails. Individuals, couples, families, and even groups can benefit from these services. Counselors who utilize telemental health must ensure that their devices and software are secure and do not allow recording.

Counselor Characteristics and Behaviors That Impact the Counseling Process

Defense Mechanisms

Sigmund Freud's *psychoanalytic theory* focused on the conflicts, drives, and unacceptable desires in the unconscious mind and how they affect a person. One method of dealing with unconscious conflicts is through *defense mechanisms*, which are the mind's way of protecting a person from unacceptable thoughts. Here are some of the most common defense mechanisms:

- *Repression* is when a person suppresses thoughts or memories that are too difficult to handle. They are pushed out of the conscious mind, and a person may experience memory loss or have psychogenic amnesia related to those memories.

- *Displacement* takes place when someone displaces the feelings they have toward one person, such as anger, and puts it on another person who may be less threatening. For example, someone may express anger toward a spouse, but the person that they are truly angry at is their boss.

- *Sublimation* is when the socially unacceptable thought is transformed into healthy, acceptable creativity in another direction. Pain may become poetry, for example.

- *Rationalization* is when unacceptable feelings or thoughts are rationally and logically explained and defended.

- *Reaction formation* occurs when the negative feeling is covered up by a false or exaggerated version of its opposite. In such a case, a person may display strong feelings of affection toward someone, though internally and unconsciously hate that person.

- *Denial* is refusing to accept painful facts or situations and instead acting as if they are not true or have not happened.

- *Projection* is putting one's own feelings onto someone else and acting as if they are the one who feels that way instead of oneself.

Facilitating Trust and Safety

The nature of the counseling relationship necessitates that clients trust and feel safe with their counselors. Clients reveal personal information to their counselors, and they must be able to trust that the counselor will not spread that information. They should also feel confident that their counselor is reliable, responsible, knowledgeable, and competent to handle their innermost thoughts, feelings, and experiences.

Counselors can facilitate trust with their clients by explaining that they are bound by confidentiality (with some exceptions having to do with harming others or themselves). This allows clients to feel secure when disclosing information that they would not share elsewhere.

Additionally, counselors gain their clients' trust when they respond appropriately to the disclosure of difficult material. When counselors show compassion, care, and concern instead of judgment and condemnation, clients are more likely to develop trust and feel safe.

Building Communication Skills

An individual can communicate verbally and non-verbally through body language or silence. Interviews, two-way casual conversations, and written or verbal standardized assessments can help the counselor determine the individual's communication skills. **Role-playing** a specific situation can help the counselor determine how an individual communicates in certain contexts. Assessing the individual's personal, family, social, or cultural context can also provide valuable insight to communication skills and help validate an assessment.

Counselors use verbal and nonverbal communication techniques to engage clients in completing treatment goals. Verbal communication is vital to the counselor/client relationship, and counselors should be skilled at greetings, summarization, reflection, and the conveyance of new information to the client. The client may misconstrue a counselor's body language if it does not represent openness and trust. Likewise, the counselor needs to be adept at analyzing the client's body language in order to move forward. Clients use both verbal and nonverbal communication to convey their story to the counselor, and communication techniques used by the counselor can be modeled to teach the client improved communication. Clients should be instructed to recognize their own communication techniques in the context of the relationship with the counselor. Clients who are withdrawn or isolated may need especially sensitive communication with the counselor in order to better communicate verbally and nonverbally.

In order to build a strong helping relationship with the client, the counselor must learn to use effective verbal and nonverbal techniques. These skills are necessary throughout the treatment process and especially during assessment and engagement.

Developing and Facilitating Conflict Resolution Strategies

Counselors may engage in conflict resolution with clients by acting as a mediator or advocate. **Mediators** work with clients to intervene in the conflict and develop helpful solutions that reflect all parties involved. For example, the counselor may act as a mediator in family or couples therapy conflicts. Counselors may also work with clients on developing their own conflict resolution skills through methods such as reflection, role-playing, and empty chair techniques. Counselors may also encourage clients to practice the use of *metacommunication*, which is communication about the behaviors and reactions of their regular and possibly dysfunctional method of interactions or communication. Sometimes the client is in conflict with the counselor and transference issues must be resolved before progress can be made. Counselors and clients need to be in collaboration concerning treatment goals and modalities so that conflict is reduced.

In some cases, agencies contract with mediation services outside the agency to assist clients in resolving conflicts. Professional mediators are trained in mediation techniques and are paid by the agency for their services. They can be the final step of resolution when the agency cannot resolve client conflict. Child protective services agencies sometimes use professional mediators to reduce or eliminate conflict in cases involving juveniles.

Developing Safety Plans

Safety plans are problem-solving tools clients can follow when they are unable to think clearly or care for themselves. Counselors can help clients identify tasks to perform when crisis intervention is needed. Safety plans will be dependent on the reason clients require them. Clients with suicidal ideation, victims of domestic violence, and individuals with mood disorders can benefit from establishing a safety plan.

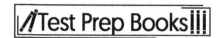

There are a couple of components to a safety plan that should be created in collaboration with the client. Counselors and clients must first be able to recognize the signs of danger.

Clients who verbalize intent to self-harm or harm others are exhibiting signs of a crisis and require intervention. It is also important to be able to identify what the client is able to do on their own to mitigate the negative thoughts and manage stress. Initiation of coping strategies, such as meditation, music, and exercise, that can de-escalate harmful thoughts should be included. Another component to incorporate is the identification of resources. Clients and counselors can work together to create a list of friends, family, or professional resources to be contacted in crisis situations. The goal of a safety plan is to be client-centered, realistic, and achievable.

Reframing or Redirecting

A technique used by counselors to help clients create a different way of looking at a person, situation, or relationship is known as **redirecting** or **cognitive reframing**. This technique helps clients look at situations with a different perspective. For example, reframing thought processes can be effective in counseling teenagers who do not always agree with parental decisions. Anger that results from imposed curfews or punishments for underperforming academically can be redirected by having the client empathize with their parents and analyze the reasons for the restrictions. Effective reframing should acknowledge the client's feelings and help interpret the situation in a different manner. For example, clients who experience fear of failure can use that emotion to reframe their thought process into a positive one. Encouraging them to use fear as a form of awareness as opposed to a paralyzing emotion can help clients look at their situation with a different mindset.

Facilitating Empathic Responses

Empathy is considered an essential counseling skill. It is used not only to initially build trust but also throughout the counseling process. The process of empathy is used to help the counselor understand the client's viewpoint. It is more complex than sympathy, which is somewhat passive and a sense of feeling bad for another person. Empathy focuses on gaining insight into the client's experience to offer effective means to deal with any issues or concerns. Although psychologist Edward Titchener was the first to use the term, it is strongly associated with the client-centered approach of **Carl Rogers**. Rogers believed empathy extended beyond understanding a person's situation; it involved the counselor imagining him or herself in that situation. This level of empathy requires genuineness, acceptance, and a small measure of vulnerability on the part of the counselor.

Self-Disclosure

In rare cases, it may be appropriate for counselors to self-disclose to clients. It is important to remember that the therapeutic process is to help clients, not indirectly benefit counselors. First and foremost, counselors should consider the intent and who will benefit from their self-disclosure. It is not appropriate for clients to be burdened with counselors' emotions, as it could shift the atmosphere and power dynamic of therapy. Counselors can disclose an emotional reaction to content from clients, provided it is for the benefit of the clients. Counselors should be cognizant of their clients' level of functioning and issues prior to any purposeful self-disclosure to ensure professional boundaries are maintained.

Constructive Confrontation

For many clients, there comes a point when goals aren't being reached in counseling. The counselor needs to recognize when progress isn't being made and observe (through active listening) any inconsistencies that are holding the client back. This includes listening for any contradictions the client

makes regarding their behaviors or feelings. These inconsistencies may be the cause of conflict in the client's life. The client may say one thing but do another, or they may say two opposing things. The counselor will need to confront the client about these inconsistencies, but it needs to be done carefully. It is important that a therapeutic and trusting relationship is established before the counselor attempts any confrontation. The client could interpret the counselor's questioning or comments as criticism. The client needs to be approached with empathy to show that the counselor has sincere interest in revealing and understanding their conflicting actions and/or words. When pointing out contradictions, it is best to reflect back what the client has said and delicately inquire about discrepancies. If the client is open to analyzing how this affects their ability to make changes, they may reach a new level of self-awareness and begin to move forward in therapy.

Counselors should be sensitive to the needs of clients they work with. Some clients will respond better than others to confrontation, and the counselor needs to have the skills to identify how and when confrontation should occur. Culture and gender may be a factor in how confrontation will be received. The counselor should also be mindful of the language that is used. Accusatory or harsh language will be met with resistance, while encouraging and positive words are more likely to aid in the therapeutic process. If the confrontation is met with denial, the counselor will need to approach the problem in a different manner at a different time.

Facilitating Awareness of Here-and-Now Interactions

Here-and-now in counseling refers to using the present interactions between the counselor and client or between group members to resolve issues and change behaviors in clients. The idea behind this technique is that interactions or feelings that clients experience during counseling sessions reflect interactions and feelings that occur outside of counseling and that, by addressing them at the present moment, new behaviors and methods of interaction can be learned. In order for here-and-now interactions to be therapeutic and effect change, the counselor has to be aware of these opportunities for working through issues as they arise. After addressing the problem and working through it together, the counselor must summarize what has happened and make the client aware of how this interaction was handled and how this more productive and healthy method can be used to change behaviors and interactions in their daily life.

Counselors who follow the **theory of Gestalt therapy** place an emphasis on the present as opposed to the past or the future. Past experiences are not ignored but are used as milestones for change and growth. For example, clients who are unable to fulfill their interests due to unfinished business can benefit from incorporating the Gestalt method. The counselor can assist the client with redirecting their energy in a positive manner and creating adaptive ways to function despite negative past experiences. Examples of positive energy include optimistic statements, compassionate actions, and self-care. The **Empty Chair Technique** is an exercise that encourages dialogue between the client and an empty chair beside them. The chair should symbolize another person in the client's life, themselves, or a part of themselves in order to engage thoughts, behaviors, and emotions. Role reversal is essential so that the client is able to focus on immediate experiences and work through different aspects of conflicting situations.

Developmentally Relevant Treatment Plans

A client's development level will vary from client to client, and it may even vary for the same client over the full course of an intervention. Therefore, the counselor should make no assumptions about the client's ability to cope, the way the intervention will be accepted and utilized, or any other aspect of the

working relationship. These factors should be assessed upon intake and at regular intervals thereafter, the frequency of which may vary on a case-by-case basis.

Assessments should holistically take into account the client's development, including age, psychological factors, emotional factors, social factors, acute personal conditions (such as an impending divorce or recent refugee status) that may temporarily impact the client's functioning, and any other scope of development that may be appropriate for the client's need. For example, a client who has a history of violent behavior and a history of playing physical sports with extreme contact may find it beneficial to undergo neurological development assessments. By viewing the client through a holistic perspective, counselors can ensure interventions are appropriate across all domains of development; if so, the interventions are more likely to be effective and received positively by the client.

Evidence-Based Counseling Strategies and Techniques for Prevention and Intervention

Licensed professional counselors are obligated to provide their clients with time-limited and effective treatment methods. Time-limited treatments can actualize clients' treatment objectives in the fewest number of sessions possible. Effective methods have been established empirically through scientific research.

Once a counselor determines a diagnosis and understands the clients' treatment goals, they develop a treatment plan. The treatment plan is based on the diagnosis and a particular treatment method. For example, a counselor may choose to use Cognitive Behavior Therapy for a client diagnosed with depression because CBT has demonstrated efficacy in the treatment of depression. The treatment plan would follow CBT protocol, adjusted as necessary to fit the client's needs. The counselor would plan for a limited number of sessions to complete the treatment and would evaluate along the way whether the treatment is effective. If the treatment is not effective, it would be extended and/or altered.

Modeling
Modeling is a technique used in therapy to allow clients to learn healthy and appropriate behaviors. Counselors "model" certain actions and attitudes, which can teach a client to behave in a similar fashion in their own life. Modeling is somewhat indirect. It is not suggested to the client to act in specific ways; rather, the counselor demonstrates desired behaviors, and the client begins imitating them.

Reinforcement
Reinforcement is a tool of behavior modification, used to either encourage or discourage specific thoughts or behaviors. **Positive reinforcement** rewards desired behaviors, thus encouraging the client to continue them. Counselors can provide positive verbal reinforcements, for example, to a client sharing difficult feelings, which in turn will encourage the client to continue sharing. The term **positive** in this case does not refer to a "good" outcome but to the act of applying a reward, such as a positive reaction from the counselor. **Negative reinforcement** works to discourage unwanted thoughts or behaviors by removing a stimulus after a specific action. The negative does not make it "bad"—rather, it is the act of removing a negative stimulus to eliminate a specific thought or behavior.

Extinguishing
Extinguishing is the process of ending, or making extinct, a specific maladaptive thought pattern or behavior. Previously occurring behaviors were reinforced, and when reinforcement (either positive or

negative) ceases, the behavior will eventually be extinguished. It may be a goal in counseling to extinguish unwanted thoughts or behaviors that are harmful or a hindrance to the client.

Cognitive Behavioral Techniques

Cognitive Behavioral Therapy (CBT) is typically a short-term treatment that focuses on transforming behavior by modifying thoughts, perceptions, and beliefs. Conscious thoughts affect behavior. Consequently, to promote consciousness of behavioral patterns in the client, the counselor (in the therapist role) will often assign homework in the form of exercises or journaling. The premise is that by identifying and reframing negative or distorted thoughts, the desired behavioral change can occur. CBT combines techniques and traits of both behavioral (positive and negative reinforcement) and cognitive therapies (cognitive distortion and schemas).

Cognitive restructuring is a concept used in CBT. The goal of cognitive restructuring is to help clients change irrational or unrealistic thoughts so that, ideally, change will lead to development of desired behaviors.

- The steps for cognitive restructuring are as follows:

- Accept that negative thoughts, inner dialogue, and beliefs affect one's feelings and emotional reactions.

- Identify which thoughts and belief patterns or self-statements lead to the target problems. Clients use self-monitoring techniques, including a log to track situations as they occur and the accompanying thoughts or feelings.

- Identify situations that evoke reoccurring themes in dysfunctional thoughts and beliefs.

- Replace distorted thoughts with functional, rational, and realistic statements.

- Reward oneself for using functional coping skills.

In-Life Desensitization

Desensitization is a behavior modification technique designed to replace an anxiety-producing stimulus with a relaxation response. Also known as systematic desensitization, it is a process to help the client manage fear or phobias. The client is taught relaxation techniques, whsich can include breathing, mindfulness, and muscle relaxation. Next, a "fear hierarchy" is created to rank stimulus from least to most fearful. The client is gradually exposed to the object or action that causes anxiety and then moves up the fear hierarchy and practices relaxation techniques. The goal is for the client to reach the most feared object or action and be able to react with calmness and control.

Addiction Issues

Addictions can be in the form of drugs, alcohol, or behaviors that cause financial instability and social impairment. It is important for counselors to distinguish when a behavior or addiction has become problematic for the client. Clients who continue to use substances or participate in behaviors despite legal or social consequences may require a counseling intervention. When assessing for substance abuse addiction, tolerance is an important aspect to consider. **Tolerance** is having to use more of the substance to obtain the same desired effects as before. Additionally, clients who continue taking substances to avoid withdrawal symptoms demonstrate dependence. After establishing a trusting relationship, counselors can encourage addiction recovery by helping their clients locate support groups,

engage in twelve-step programs, secure social connections, and develop a relapse prevention plan. CBT helps clients focus on reducing problematic behavior that is associated with the addiction. The development of coping strategies, such as avoidance and self-control, helps to prevent a relapse. Counselors can assist clients with identifying and modifying cravings, triggers, and risky behaviors that can enable the addictions. Incorporating **motivational enhancement therapy** can encourage clients to address self-destructive behaviors and improve motivation to change.

Cultural Considerations

Culture refers to the way a group of people lives, behaves, thinks, and believes. This can include behaviors, traditions, beliefs, opinions, values, religion, spirituality, communication, language, holidays, food, valued possessions, and family dynamics, among other factors. Geography, social status, economic standing, race, ethnicity, and religion can determine culture. Culture can be found within any organized community, such as in a place of worship or workplace. The following are examples of specific types of culture:

- **Universal**: the broadest category, also known as the human culture, and includes all people

- **Ecological**: groups created by physical location, climate, and geography

- **National**: patterns of culture for a specific country

- **Regional**: patterns for specific areas of a country that can include dialect, manners, customs and food/eating habits

- **Racio-ethnic**: group that shares a common racial and ethnic background

- **Ethnic: group** that shares a common background, including religion and language

Cultural Skills

Counselors should be well versed in **cultural skills**. They must be able to apply interviewing and counseling techniques with clients and should be able to employ specialized skills and interventions that might be effective with specific minority populations. Counselors need to be able to communicate effectively and understand the verbal and nonverbal language of the client. They also should take a systematic perspective in their practice, work collaboratively with community leaders, and advocate for clients when it's in their best interests.

When working with clients from diverse backgrounds, counselors should be able to shift their professional strategies.

Promoting Community-Based Resources

Helping Clients Develop Support Systems

As part of the intake process and initial sessions, counselors need to explore and understand clients' existing support systems. All individuals have varying degrees of social support, which can include friends, family, and community. Counselors can help clients evaluate their level of support and determine how the support system can help during counseling and after it has ended. It may be necessary to help clients find ways to develop additional support, such as through groups or organizations. A support system is necessary to provide help, encouragement, and care.

106

Structured and Unstructured Helping Relationships

Individuals can get help and support from many types of relationships, both structured and unstructured. **Structured relationships** include those with professional helpers, such as counselors, therapists, medical professionals, and counselors. These relationships have clear goals and are time-limited both in session and overall duration. Unstructured relationships also provide support but are more ambiguous and ongoing. These can include community support, groups, friends, family, and activities such as workshops or retreats.

Characteristics of Willingness to Change

Entering into counseling can provoke anxiety, fear, and resistance to change. Clients may have both internal and external reasons to want or need to change but exhibit some unwillingness to do so. Clients with internal or intrinsic motivation understand that they need to change to move forward, grow, and achieve personal goals. External factors, such as mandated counseling, can be motivating, but may create additional resistance. Clients will be more motivated and willing to change when they have a vested interest in the process and believe they will achieve a successful outcome. Commitment to the process is essential, especially considering that counseling may not seem enjoyable or even interesting but may be necessary.

Motivation and resistance impact a client's readiness to change behavior. These are two crucial components to examine when developing an intervention plan. **High motivation** is indicated by self-confidence and self-efficacy, as the client believes they are capable of change. High motivation is also characterized by a client's desire to correct an identified problem, work toward a goal, and reliably show up for sessions. High motivation also shows in the client's belief that implementing a change will improve their overall quality of life.

Resistance can refer to any behavior that indicates the client does not want to work with the counselor or improve their personal situation. Resistance may be indicated by a client's refusal to show up on time, or at all, for sessions. A client involuntarily coming to sessions (such as by a court order) may state that there is no tangible problem to work on, or the client may state they feel no changes are occurring. Counselors should examine resistance holistically to ensure they are not contributing to it. For example, clients may exhibit resistance to counseling sessions if they do not feel comfortable with the counselor, if they do not understand the counselor, or if they are expected to work on issues they do not yet feel ready to address.

Readiness to change occurs in six stages: **pre-contemplation** (where an individual does not believe a need for change exists or is not self-aware), **contemplation** (where an individual recognizes a problem but is not ready to address it), **preparation** (where an individual recognizes a problem and sets the stage for change), **action** (where an individual takes active, involved steps to stop a problem), **maintenance** (where the individual commits to the desired behaviors), and **termination** (where the individual is able to regularly sustain the desired behaviors without relapse).

Motivation and resistance pertain to the individual's readiness to acknowledge and change behaviors. The more the individual feels ready to make a change, the higher the motivation and the lower the resistance. Some indicators of high motivation and low resistance include:

- Awareness and open acknowledgment of the presenting issue
- Willingness to list pros and cons of behavior change

- Willingness to make small steps toward and document outcomes of behavior change
- Acknowledgment that changing behavior is in the individual's best interest

Some indicators of low motivation and high resistance include:

- Lack of recognition of a present problem
- Hostility or apathy towards the counselor (which may be revealed by skipping sessions)
- Discussion of a presenting issue without openness to changing associated behaviors

Counselors can increase the client's motivation by discussing changes positively in terms that demonstrate benefit to the client's life, allowing the client to set his or her own goals and providing assistance only for those specific goals, highlighting the tools the client possesses to make changes, and acknowledging and respecting the client's fears about change.

Reassurance

Reassurance is an affirming therapeutic technique used to encourage and support clients. Reassurance can help alleviate doubts and increase confidence. Counselors use reassurance when a client experiences setbacks or an inability to recognize progress. Clients can be reminded of past successes to help bolster their ability to solve current problems. It is important that reassurance is genuine and not overused by counselors to pacify clients, but rather as a tool to validate and inspire continued growth.

Improving Interactional Patterns

Improving relationships for the client requires minimizing maladaptive interaction patterns. Interaction patterns that can harm a relationship include negative interpretations, shutting down, defending, complaining, and disapproving. A **validating style of interaction** is characterized by partners respecting each other's opinions and emotions, compromising, and resolving problems mutually. Volatile patterns lead to arguments and conflict, followed by reconciliation. The **avoiding style** is characterized by not dealing with problems at all. An example of a therapy method that attempts to improve interactional patterns is the Gottman Method. The **Gottman Method** includes assessment of the relationship and the development of a therapeutic framework with primary interventions. The areas addressed include conflict management, creation of a shared meaning, and development of friendship. The interventions assist with replacing negative conflict patterns with positive interactions to strengthen a relationship. The overall goal of this method is to achieve a sense of understanding, awareness, empathy, and interpersonal growth.

Availability of Community Resources

There is a wide range of community resources available, making it confusing for some clients to navigate the system and identify what would be most helpful for them. Therefore, a case manager plays a critical role in helping the client to find and utilize the community resources that would be most beneficial. When seeking resources, it is useful to look at the different domains of life—physical, psychological,

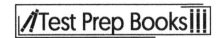
emotional, spiritual, and educational—and then compile a collection of resources that may be useful for the client in each of these domains.

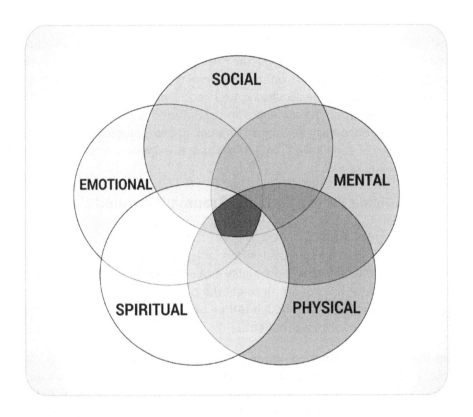

Physical needs can include food, shelter, clothing, or medical care, and there are many government programs available for these needs, such as free health care, affordable housing, and food stamps. For the elderly or disabled, their greatest need may be related to the accessibility of physical resources. In that case, the delivery of meals through Meals on Wheels or transportation services may be the most appropriate recommendation. Another help would be prescription assistance programs offered by some pharmaceutical companies to those with low income, which provide medications for free or at reduced cost. Other resources for the elderly can be accessed through the Administration on Aging and other local departments for elder care.

Ensuring the provision of adequate emotional and psychological services would first involve making sure the client is receiving emotional support from family and friends, or getting involved in support groups with others who have similar struggles. For the elderly, there may be community centers with programs to help seniors connect with each other and stay active. When it comes to finding the right psychological resources, both therapeutic and psychiatric, there are many options, so the client must be involved in the process of deciding what type and format of therapy would be best.

An often overlooked area of whole-person care is the spiritual needs of the client. In addition to providing spiritual support, religious organizations are often nonprofits that can assist the client in physical or emotional ways as well. Fraternal organizations may provide similar benefits to a person, offering emotional, social, and spiritual components.

Educational resources should not be disregarded, especially in the case of someone who has mental or physical health needs. Whether formal training or informal learning through the library or online, there

are many resources for gaining knowledge in almost any area. As discussed, education related to the individual's specific health needs is a crucial element of self-management care, client activation, and empowerment.

Calling United Way's helpline at 211, checking the U.S. government website, or conducting an internet search are easy and effective means of identifying the relevant community resources in the client's locality. Collaborating with other service providers can also make use of those who already know the client and can also prevent overlap in the provision of services. Finally, and perhaps most important, help the client to find resources through the people and organizations with whom they are already connected. Not only does this encourage self-determination and empowerment by helping the client see how many resources they already have in their life, but many clients will be most comfortable with places and people they already know.

Crisis Intervention, Suicide Prevention, and Trauma-Informed Care

Crisis Intervention and Treatment Approaches

A **crisis** can occur whenever a client is in physical danger or has an extreme emotional need that goes unmet. For example, suicidal threats or ideation qualify as a crisis situation. When a crisis arises, the very first concern is always safety. It is important to get the client into a safe situation, protected from themselves or others. After safety is established, it is then possible to assess the level of need and what should happen next in order to best assist the client.

Another important strategy is **de-escalation**. When there is a crisis, extreme emotions are usually involved. If possible, a client should be guided through relaxation techniques to help calm them down. Oftentimes, a calm and neutral party who can facilitate a conversation or listen to the client empathetically, but without feeding the emotion, will automatically de-escalate the situation. **Confrontation** or matching the client's emotions will escalate the situation. Allowing the client to communicate the situation fully may help them to become less emotional and more focused on the facts. At this point the client may be able to focus on the next steps and specific tasks that need to be done. If possible, help the client to regain emotional control so that extreme options such as restraints are unnecessary.

In cases where a client is suicidal, it is important to establish if there is a suicide plan or means of committing suicide in place. These two things will determine the severity of suicidal ideation and how at-risk the client is. If it is determined that a client is at imminent risk of suicide, they should be admitted to the hospital or a mental health facility for their own protection.

Creating crisis plans ahead of time, in collaboration with clients, may assist them in preventing crisis situations or more quickly regaining control when the crisis arises. If clients have been part of the planning process, they may feel empowered, even when their emotions are overwhelming them. Part of the plan should be to identify the potential triggers or warning signs, and have immediate steps that can be taken to avoid a crisis. This could be engaging in relaxation strategies, or calling a supportive friend, family member, or clinician.

Critical Incident Stress Debriefing

Designed to support individuals after a traumatic event, **Critical Incident Stress Debriefing (CISD)** is a structured form of crisis management. Specifically, it is short-term work done in small groups but is not considered psychotherapy. Techniques used include processing, defusing, ventilating, and validating thoughts, experiences, feeling, and emotions. CISD is best for secondary trauma victims, not primary

110

trauma victims. For example, in cases of workplace violence, any employees who witnessed an event or who were indirectly impacted could benefit from CISD. Employees who were first-degree victims would need more individualized, specialized care and therapeutic intervention. It is important that CISD is offered as quickly as possible after an event; research has indicated it is most effective within a 24- to 72-hour time frame and becomes less effective the more time lapses after the event. CISD can be managed by specially trained personnel and could include mental health workers, medical staff, human resources, or other professionals. Trained Crisis Response Teams can be ready or quickly available to provide support directly following a traumatic situation.

Trauma-Informed Care

Trauma-informed care systems ensure that trauma and its effects are understood by health services providers and that signs and symptoms of trauma are recognized even when not explicitly stated by the client. Trauma-informed care means that trauma-informed practices are integrated into all procedures of the care system. Incorporating these aspects into care involves ensuring a sense of safety and security for the client and the client's family. Trauma-informed care also ensures that the client feels they can trust the social worker and that all procedures are communicated and transparent. It provides a network of support, empowers the client to collaborate with their health care providers to develop a suitable intervention, and encourages the client to ask questions and voice concerns at any time. Trauma-informed care also accounts for each client's specific personal history, cultural and social norms, and other unique factors. Interventions encourage respect, self-efficacy, hope for future outcomes, and identify that various behaviors correlate as coping mechanisms to specific instances of trauma. Trauma-informed care is a model that is encouraged with any social services client, but it is especially beneficial for survivors of abuse, those experiencing eating disorders or addiction, or those who grew up in poverty or violence.

Developing a Personal Model of Counseling

Assessing Competency to Work with Specific Clients

Licensed professional counselors are required to work within the scope of their competence. This means that all counselors must have specialized academic training and receive clinical supervision during their practicum and internship. Counselors can also receive additional training through **Continuing Education Units (CEUs)** or other certifications that qualify them to use certain techniques and methods. For example, a counselor is working with a military veteran suffering from PTSD. The client experiences angry, emotional outbursts with his family, uses substances to cope with the intrusive images he witnessed while in the military, and he has not been able to maintain employment since his discharge. The counselor believes that **Eye Movement Desensitization and Reprocessing (EMDR)** would be the best treatment approach. However, prior to treating a client with EMDR, the counselor must have received specialized training and supervised clinical experience. If the counselor does not have such training, they need to refer the client to a clinician who specializes in EMDR. Otherwise, they could use an alternative treatment method for which they are properly trained.

Skills or Strategies for Dealing with Problems

An important aspect of counseling is helping people work through challenging events in their life. The counselor's role is to facilitate awareness and help clients resolve their internal conflicts. There are various strategies a counselor can use to guide clients to develop their own strategies for problem resolution. The first step is to ask the client what they are trying to accomplish with counseling and how committed they are to creating change. Understanding the presenting concern is a crucial aspect in developing a treatment plan and setting goals. A model of assessment known as the **DO A CLIENT MAP**

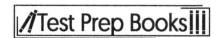

takes a broad range of variables into consideration before establishing a treatment plan. The client map focuses on areas such as objectives, treatment models, resources, and timing. For example, a client dealing with anger issues will require certain steps in counseling to uncover the underlying cause of the rage, such as unprocessed trauma, sadness, or fear. One key component of anger therapy is **emotional regulation**, which includes relaxation techniques to maintain control of uncertain situations. Other skills for anger management include skill development for crisis prevention and cognitive restructuring for balanced thinking patterns. Other examples include increasing self-awareness for clients with control issues, building trust in clients with paranoia, and cognitive restructuring for clients with social anxiety.

Counseling strategies will be dependent on the client's overall goals, motivation, and readiness for change. For example, a client wanting to overcome codependency issues may seek treatment when feelings of resentment and emptiness overpower their daily activities. Counselors may initiate interventions, such as placing the client in a support group that follows a twelve-step model. **Co-Dependents Anonymous (CoDA)** helps clients learn self-compassion and set personal boundaries. Once clients learn to develop self-care and communicate needs clearly, counselors can progress to evaluating therapy goals.

Cognitive and/or Behavioral Interventions
Cognitive Approaches
Cognitive approaches to the counseling process involve changing the way the client thinks in order to facilitate progress and problem-solving skills. Cognitive approaches tend to be evidence based and favored by insurance carriers, as they are efficacious for a variety of client issues, including substance use and personality disorders. Cognitive approaches focus on changing maladaptive thinking and cognitive distortions, and thus may help clients engage in behavior change. Cognitive distortions involve fallacious thinking patterns engaged in by the client, such as black-and-white thinking. Types of cognitive approaches may include cognitive behavior therapy, rational emotive behavior therapy, and solution focused brief therapy. There are many modalities of cognitive therapies and counselors should implement them when necessary.

Behavioral Approaches
Behavioral approaches, which originated with **Skinner and Pavlov**, include methods of changing and motivating client behaviors toward reaching constructive goals. The underlying concept is that if clients can change behavior, they may also alter the way they think. Skinner and Pavlov believed that all behavior is learned, and they believed in conditioning. Tokens may be awarded for positive behavioral changes in the client; this occurs in what is called a token economy. Cognitive behavioral therapies, which focus on both the cognition and the behavior of the client, are considered evidence based and are favored by managed care insurers.

Problem-Solving Approaches
The **problem-solving therapeutic model** serves to teach clients how to manage stressors that come in life. Often clients do not possess skills that allow them to effectively navigate negative events or emotions without increasing personal harm. The goal of the problem-solving model is to teach clients the skills necessary to deal with negative life events, negative emotions, and stressful situations. In particular, goals of this model should be to assist clients in identifying which particular situations may trigger unpleasant emotions, understanding the range of emotions one might feel, planning how to effectively deal with situations when they arise, and even recognizing and accepting that some situations are not able to be solved.

The counselor, however, may be an instructional guide to facilitate problem solving for the client. Because problem-solving skills are one of the primary methods of resolving issues, and often are skills that clients lack, the counselor may need to model them for the client so that the client can then develop their own skills. Counselors need to maintain empathy and congruence with the client during the problem-solving process, and even though they may have verbally instructed or modeled problem-solving methods, they need to maintain rapport in the relationship.

Components of the Problem-Solving Process

When working with clients to develop problem-solving skills, counselors must first engage and prepare clients by discussing the benefits of improving such skills and encouraging clients to commit to the problem-solving process during the goal setting/contracting phase.

Steps in the problem-solving process:

- Step 1: Assess, define, and clarify the problem. As with goal setting, counselors should assist clients in clearly determining and defining the specific problem. Counselors should focus on the current problem and ensure clients do not become distracted by other past or current difficulties. Examine specific aspects of the problem, including behaviors and the needs of those involved.

- Step 2: Determine possible solutions. Counselors should lead discussion among participants to determine possible solutions and encourage client(s) to refrain from limiting options at this point. The purpose is for clients to gain practice in solution development. In the case of family work, all capable members should be allowed to offer solutions and should feel safe to do so without fear or criticism from other members.

- Step 3: Examine options and select/implement a solution. Counselors should assist clients in examining the benefits and drawbacks of each possible solution and choose an option that best meets the needs of those involved.

- Step 4: Evaluate and adjust. Counselors should help clients to determine the success of the solution. Client(s) can use a practical form of tracking solution effectiveness (charts, logs, etc.). If it is determined the solution is not working, the client can return to the solution-generating stage.

Rational Problem-Solving Process

Rational problem solving is based on facts and clear consequences. It is an analytical approach that relies on predictability and understood outcomes. The rational decision-making process has distinct steps to define a problem and then weigh and rank the decision-making criteria. Next, the client must develop, evaluate, and select the best alternative. It is also important to explore consequences as well as what might happen if no decision is made and no action is taken.

Intuitive Problem Solving

Intuitive problem solving is based on feelings and instinct. It is an approach based on emotions and a "gut feeling" about what might be the right decision. Although in some cases it may be the right way and result in the correct decision, it is important for the counselor and client to work together on understanding any problem and possible solutions. It is also important to know when to utilize rational decision making versus intuitive or when to employ both strategies.

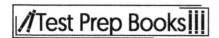

Counseling and Helping Relationships

Strengths-Based and Empowerment Practice

Empowerment is a strengths-based modality, and the goal is that all clients should feel empowered based on their personal identities. Clients need to feel in control of most of their lives and circumstances, and this is what empowerment permits. Working from a strengths-based perspective empowers clients to facilitate change in their own lives. Counselors may seek to empower clients by focusing on strengths and bolstering clients' social constructs. Clients may need to be empowered from a racial, ethnic, religious, gender, or age perspective because they have suffered discrimination in these areas. Counselors may act as political advocates in these realms to combat social oppression affecting clients. The counselor should take into account the differences each client possesses due to their race, religion, or circumstance, and use these differences as strengths.

Teaching Coping Strategies to Clients

Teaching coping skills is an important role of the counselor in the therapeutic relationship. **Coping skills** enable individuals to manage stressful situations, solve problems, handle uncertainty, and develop resilience. Coping skills can include solution-focused problem solving, removing negative self-talk, learning mindfulness or other stress management techniques, and gaining support through friends, family, and community. Individuals may learn how to identify specific patterns to their feelings and behaviors, and thus, learn new and healthier responses. As there are many ways for individuals to develop and practice coping skills, counselors can provide options and unique plans for clients to best meet their needs.

Counselors may act in the role of teacher to instruct clients about coping and other skills. Coping skills may include relaxation techniques, deep breathing, time out, and improved communication skills. Common diagnoses that often require the instruction of coping skills include stress reduction, anxiety, and major depression. Clients may be able to utilize coping and acceptance skills for these diagnoses because they are frequently chronic, and clients will need to cope with them on an almost daily basis. Clients often need to learn a plethora of new skills to manage their issues and complex problems, and they and the counselor should collaborate on coping and other skills to manage these circumstances. Counselors can partialize and brainstorm with clients concerning coping and other treatment skills. Clients sometimes need detailed instructions in order to succeed with treatment goals. Clients need to be engaged in therapy outside of sessions and learn how to cope when the counselor is not present, so assigning clients' homework between sessions is a method of skills building. While the counselor may offer suggestions to the client for coping and other skills, the client is ultimately the most effective arbiter of their own treatment.

Finding Happiness

Happiness can be defined in many ways, and individuals may have challenges in arriving at a state where they feel entirely happy. Research on happiness shows that it is small things, like activities, and not hypothetical future events or material possessions that create the most happiness. Counseling can assist in helping individuals explore times when they felt happy and work on ways to increase and maintain their happiness. By asking clients about past happy times and what about those times made them feel happy, the counselor will be able to help clients explore how to feel happier in the present. It is important to recognize that future achievements may not produce desired happiness, such as "I will be happy when …". Rather, counselors should focus on helping clients appreciate what makes them happy in the present moment and how to use that happiness to feel more fulfilled each day.

114

This material is provided for exam preparation purposes only and does not indicate an endorsement of any specific scientific, political, or religious point of view. © TPB Publishing. You have been licensed one copy of this document for personal use only. Any other reproduction or redistribution is strictly prohibited. All rights reserved.

Steps in Skill Development

Clients frequently need to develop better coping strategies or improved social, communication, or life skills. Examples of skills that counselors may help clients develop include anger management, parenting, and substance abuse management. Skill training can take place in individual, family, group, or classroom formats. Steps in skill development include:

- Step 1: Skill identification. Identify and describe the skill(s) to be developed and how the client will benefit by acquiring the new skill(s). Engage clients and garner motivation to build skill development.

- Step 2: Demonstrate use of the skill. Give the client a visual example of what the skill looks like by modeling and performing role-play of the desired skill. This can be completed by a counselor and the client or in a family or group situation with another client.

- Step 3: Use of the skill outside of session and evaluation. The client should use the skill in everyday situations. The counselor can use sessions to discuss and evaluate a client's mastery of the skill and whether further skill development is needed.

Models of a Helper

Gerard Egan developed a model for helping outlined in his book, *The Skilled Helper*. Egan drew from several theorists, including **Rogers**, **Carkhuff**, and **Albert Bandura**, to create a **three-stage model for helping**. The phases of the model are identifying the present situation or scenario, defining the desired scenario, and developing a strategy to achieve it. The model provides a framework and map that clients can internalize for use when faced with a problem. It was designed to empower individuals to develop skills and confidence to solve problems outside of a helping relationship.

Imagery

Guided imagery can be a powerful tool in the counseling process. **Guided imagery**, which draws upon the mind-body connection, can be used to help the client alleviate anxiety, relax, and control or change negative thoughts or feelings. A counselor, who helps the client envision a place of relaxation and calm, guides the process. The counselor encourages the client to visualize and relax into the details of the image. Clients can also envision the successful outcome of a situation or imagine themselves handling a stressful situation. Once learned, clients can practice imagery on their own to help reduce stress and anxiety.

Role-Play

Role-play is a type of modeling and is also called behavior reversal. This technique enables clients to view the different ways a person may handle a challenging situation. It also allows a client to view a non-tangible behavior in a more tangible way. When clients practice skills and develop new and more productive methods of coping, they are able to take an active role in treatment, increasing their sense of empowerment and self-determination.

Assertiveness Training

Assertiveness training is an intervention that can be used in multiple settings with an assortment of interpersonal difficulties. This type of training helps individuals learn to express their emotions, thoughts, and desires, even when difficult, while not infringing on the rights of others. There are ways in which individuals can assert themselves, including saying no to a request, having a difference of opinion with another person, asking others to change their behavior, and starting conversations. Counselors

must respect cultural differences when working with clients to develop assertiveness skills. For example, some cultures feel it is inappropriate for women or children to assert themselves. Role-play is an effective technique to help clients develop assertiveness skills.

Role Modeling

Role modeling, which offers the client a real-life view of desired target behaviors, can be an important tool to learn new skills. The counselor can request that clients demonstrate the behavior before modeling it, thereby allowing the counselor to assess a client's current skills and abilities. Counselors can demonstrate a coping model showing the skill or desired behaviors, including difficulties, anxieties, or challenges. The counselor can also demonstrate a mastery model, which shows confidence and competence with the desired behaviors. Each method has benefits and drawbacks. In coping mode, the client and counselor can process the interaction and identify improvements or changes that can be made to the desired behaviors or actions. There are several types of modeling:

- **Symbolic Modeling**: Client watches a visual representation of the modeled behavior (i.e., video, TV, images)

- **Live Modeling**: Client watches while a person performs the behavior

- **Participant Modeling or Guided Participation**: Client observes model performing behavior and then performs the behavior and/or interacts with the model

- **Covert Modeling**: Client visualizes the desired behavior

Promoting Relaxation

As part of the counseling process, clients may need to learn basic relaxation techniques, which can be simple to learn and practice. Stress can cause increased anxiety and tension; thus, relaxation techniques help reduce both mental and physical stress. Clients may present with racing thoughts, fatigue, or headaches; techniques such as awareness, breath work, and progressive relaxation can be of great benefit. Clients who have a reduction in their stress level may be more engaged in the counseling process and better able to manage difficulties outside of sessions. **Meditation** is a powerful relaxation tool to help build awareness and the ability to calm oneself. Relaxation can help diminish the activity of stress hormones in the body, reduce feelings of anger and frustration, lower heart rate, and improve confidence.

Guidelines for Giving Advice

There are two main types of advice: substantive and process. **Substantive advice** can be considered directive and may involve the counselor imposing their opinions onto clients. Process advice is more empowering and helps clients navigate options for solving their own issues. An example would be a client who is struggling with anxiety. Substantive advice would be the counselor telling the client he or she should practice deep breathing. **Process advice**, in the same example, would be teaching the client how relaxation techniques can lessen anxiety and providing examples. Counselors can offer process advice to help clients better understand their problems and possible solutions. Clients may ask for advice, and in some situations, it may be appropriate for the counselor to offer process advice; it is less likely that substantive advice should be given. Providing counseling is more complex than simply giving advice; thus, counselors should explore when, why, and how to give advice, if needed. As the goal of counseling is to help individuals gain a better self-awareness and competence, giving advice may

116

undermine the process by not allowing clients an opportunity to learn ways to solve their own issues both within and after counseling.

Practice Quiz

1. What is one of the most important tasks a counselor must accomplish within the first couple of sessions?
   a. Payment method
   b. Therapeutic alliance
   c. Diagnosis
   d. Treatment Plan

2. Clients who distance themselves from others to prevent feeling dependent and getting hurt have an anxious-avoidant attachment style. What kind of practice will help prevent loneliness in these clients?
   a. Focusing on the future
   b. Personalizing situations
   c. Initiating a relationship with a partner who also has an avoidant attachment style
   d. Practicing empathy

3. A client tells the counselor she has developed healthy coping mechanisms for her anger issues and is ready to terminate therapy. What strategy will the counselor perform next?
   a. Obtain client feedback prior to ending the therapy session
   b. Reflect on the client's progress and how they plan to continue growth
   c. Encourage the client to continue therapy to ensure progress
   d. Offer the client an opportunity to visit the office as desired

4. During couples counseling, one of the clients expresses that she rarely voices her opinions to her partner for fear of starting a conflict. What kind of communication style is characterized by this behavior?
   a. Aggressive
   b. Assertive
   c. Passive
   d. Obstructing

5. Which of the following Gestalt therapy techniques focuses on role reversal and engaging the client's thoughts and behaviors?
   a. The Hunger Illusion
   b. The Empty Chair
   c. The Miracle Question
   d. Virtual reality

See answers on next page

Answer Explanations

1. B: The therapeutic alliance is critical to the client's decision to stay in treatment. Choice *A*, payment method, is not one of the most important tasks in the first session; it should be agreed upon prior to the beginning of treatment. Choice *C*, diagnosis, might not be possible to formulate in the first couple of sessions. Choice *D*, treatment plan, may or may not be established in the first couple of sessions.

2. D: Clients with an anxious-avoidant attachment style who practice empathy and increase their closeness with others can experience decreased feelings of depression and loneliness. Choice *A* can cause more anxiety in the client; anxious-avoidant attachment styles are encouraged to practice mindfulness and focus on the present. Choice *B* will worsen the negative attachment style; taking everything personally will damage social relationships. Choice *C* will result in a toxic relationship; communication is important for healthy interactions.

3. B: Reflecting on the client's growth and plan for progress can help ease the transition. Choice *A* is important for the counselor but not a priority in transitioning the client out of therapy. Choice *C* is incorrect; the client's choice to terminate therapy due to progress should be respected. Choice *D* crosses the professional boundary; clients should only return when they need therapy again.

4. C: Passive communicators do not openly express their opinions and can be taken advantage of by others. Choice *A* is a communication style characterized by an inappropriate expression of feelings that violates the rights of others. Choice *B* is a communication style that is clear, direct, and honest. Choice *D* is not a type of communication style.

5. B: The Empty Chair Technique allows a client to use the chair as a symbol of a person in their life or a part of themselves; the dialogue encourages conflict resolution. Choice *A* is used for clients who want to overcome habitual behavior; the technique is a simple process that involves noticing automatic motivations, stopping the action, and keeping track of the resulting emotion. Choice *C* is a solution-focused technique that helps clients envision the future and focus on achievable goals. Counselors ask the client a question that describes what the perfect situation for them would be like. It assists the counselor with determining what the client wants out of therapy. Choice *D* is used in clients requiring exposure therapy for anxiety or fear disorders; clients are introduced to a virtual world that increases exposure to negative stimuli in a controlled setting.

119

Group Counseling and Group Work

Theoretical Foundations of Group Counseling

Group counseling is a method of therapy in which clients with similar needs are grouped together to help share experiences and work toward an individual goal. The counselor's decision to place a client in group therapy is based on several factors, including the client's readiness to change, needs, preferences, and the services required. The decision to place a client in group therapy should be a joint decision between the client and the counselor. Clients should never be forced to participate in group counseling. Before the client can participate in group therapy, rules and expectations should be discussed with the counselor. Counselors will benefit from having a client sign an agreement delineating rules and expectations. Some of the rules group members may be expected to adhere to are confidentiality, privacy, maintaining dignity, abstaining from violence, and regular attendance to the sessions.

Clients should clearly understand that anything said in group counseling should not be shared and no group member is required to answer questions or engage in all activities. A clear expectation of attendance should be explained to the client. Clients are encouraged to remain in group counseling until the group members jointly decide it is time for a member to terminate their group therapy. Counselors acting as group leaders can guide members in determining when a group member is ready to leave. Some of the reasons clients may terminate group counseling include progress toward achieving their goals, a reduction or elimination of their primary symptoms, and the ability to independently cope with their issue. Alternatively, if a client no longer wants to participate in group therapy, their decision to leave should be respected.

Dynamics Associated with Group Process and Development

Several theories outline the developmental stages of a group. One of the most well-known is **Bruce Tuckman's four-stage model**: forming, storming, norming, and performing. **Forming** is the stage where the group members are just beginning to get acquainted and may be anxious and less vocal. **Storming** involves conflict, discord, and struggles to agree upon a leader. **Norming** is the agreement stage, during which a leader is chosen and conflicts begin to resolve. **Performing** is the point at which the group becomes effective at achieving defined tasks. A fifth stage, **Adjourning**, was added, which defines the point at which the group terminates. Other group development theories include that of **Irvin D. Yalom**, whose three-stage model included orientation, conflict/dominance, and development of cohesiveness.

Gerald Corey's stages included initial, transition, working, and termination. All three theories share similar progressions of the group process.

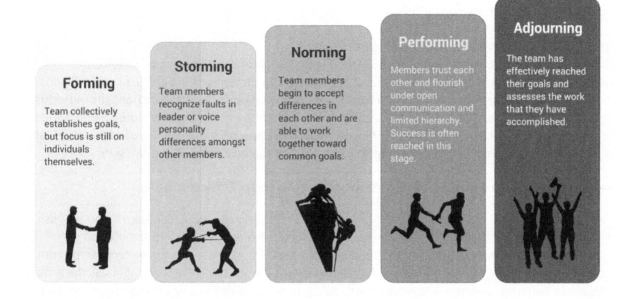

Other group development theories include that of Irvin D. Yalom, whose three-stage model included orientation, conflict/dominance, and development of cohesiveness. Gerald Corey's stages included initial, transition, working, and termination. All three theories share similar progressions of the group process. A general method of categorizing the group process is the beginning, middle, and end stages. Each stage is classified by different activities, processes, and tasks:

Beginning Stage

Counselors determine the group's purpose, members, objectives, and other logistical tasks (time, location, etc.). Group formation occurs at this stage as new members come together. The counselor fosters a safe and trusting environment by establishing acceptable group norms. As group members become more comfortable, conflicts arise as power and control behaviors emerge. Group roles and alliances begin to form. The counselor's role is to help guide the group through these challenges and process any conflicts that arise within the group.

Middle Stage

This stage is where most group work is done. Members share information, openly address issues, and work through conflicts. Some groups do not make it to this stage for several reasons, including member dynamics and a lack of investment of the group members. Group cohesion or the connectedness of the members is extremely important at this stage. The role of the counselor is to help members focus on methods and the meaning of communication, working through group differences and confronting members when necessary. Counselors should also help develop more intensive levels of cohesiveness while building on member individuality.

End Stage

Group members come to resolutions on the issues addressed during the group process. Members may have strong reactions to termination, especially if there was a high level of cohesion developed during

the group process. The counselor should lead the group in discussing feelings about termination and be aware of negative reactions that may surface. When these types of emotions occur, counselors should address any challenges that arise with members. The counselor should also help group members identify and reflect on the skills learned in the group process and how those skills can benefit the members with future challenges.

Working with Individuals in the Group Context

It is the role of the counselor to encourage all members to participate in the group process. The counselor can solicit feedback from each member of the group throughout the group process. Clients typically take on various roles during group treatment. **Roles** can be defined as functions the individual members of the group are fulfilling or performing that facilitate the group process. Some roles include that of a clown, scapegoat, mediator, etc. The counselor must be aware of the roles of each individual and how those roles are affecting the group so interventions can be made when necessary.

Therapeutic Factors and Their Contribution to Group Effectiveness

Counselors can foster the emergence of therapeutic factors to help the group successfully accomplish its goals. One of the most important initial therapeutic factors in group therapy is the promotion of cohesion, and counselors can accomplish this in several ways. For example, group leaders can promote cohesion by responding well when someone challenges their authority. The leader might ask the group if they agree with the challenge and what they think could be done differently to help the group. This, in turn, can help members bond with each other. Group leaders can also encourage empathy among members by calling upon individuals to check in with those who become emotionally dysregulated during sessions.

Counselors can promote therapeutic factors by helping members deal with conflicts appropriately. Instead of fearing conflict, the group can learn how to disagree without violating relationships within the group. The leader is often an important figure during conflicts because they monitor and provide space for safe discussions.

Counselors can also facilitate the emergence of therapeutic factors by showing care for all group members. When the leader demonstrates equal care for everyone in the group, members will likely feel safe to disclose more personal information. Not only does this encourage deeper disclosure, but it also provides the group members with an example of how they should act towards one another.

Additionally, counselors can provide insight to members about their behaviors and interchanges with each other. Counselors can use the group setting as a microcosm of the members' real-life situations by bringing about changes within the group that will result in outside transformations.

Characteristics and Functions of Effective Group Leaders

Counselors should encourage their clients who are in group therapy to interact with the group leader. The leader is there to not only facilitate the group, but also to help the group members get as much out of the group as possible. Groups may have multiple leaders. Co-leadership is widely used in group therapy sessions and is found to have many beneficial aspects. **Co-leadership** may be used as a way to train therapists to lead groups and is found to have positive impacts, especially in larger groups. Having two leaders can help ensure that all members get attention, can actively participate, and assist the group in accomplishing more. Co-leadership can be detrimental if leaders do not get along or cannot form a cooperative and united management team for the group.

Linking and Blocking

Blocking is the act of the group leader stopping unwanted behaviors from members that may be harmful or hurtful or violate confidentiality. This helps to set appropriate standards for how the group should behave. With linking, the group leader relates members' stories or situations to enhance interaction and cohesion of the group.

Management of Leader–Member Dynamics

Broadly speaking, anything that impacts the group can be considered dynamic. The word *dynamic* means change, activity, or progress. Thus, a group is constantly adapting and evolving. **Dynamics** are the interrelationships between the members, which include the leadership style, decision-making, and cohesiveness. **Cohesiveness** is the degree to which the group sticks together. There are two types of cohesion: task and social. Task is the level at which the group works to achieve a common objective. **Social cohesiveness** refers to the interpersonal relationships within the group.

There are three main styles of leading groups:

- **Autocratic**: This leader is authoritarian and sets clear rules, boundaries, and goals for the group. This type can be beneficial in situations where there are time or resource limitations, constant changes to membership, or the need to coordinate with other groups. This type of leadership can create resentment and dissatisfaction, as it is unilateral and strict.

- **Democratic**: This leader is considered the fairest by taking into consideration ideas and choices of the group. Not to be confused with the political usage, these leaders do not wield specific power or prestige; rather, they work to maintain a participatory style and harmonious atmosphere.

- **Laissez-Faire**: This is the most relaxed style of leadership; group members are responsible for all aspects of decision-making. Laissez-faire is an absence of leadership, which works best with motivated, self-directed members.

Group Formation and Members Roles

Members serve different roles in the group and can change their roles as the group progresses. There are both functional and nonfunctional roles. Functional roles assist the group and include the energizer, harmonizer, tension reliever, and gatekeeper. Nonfunctional roles can disrupt and hinder the group and include the interrogator, dominator, monopolizer, aggressor, and recognition seeker. Other roles include victim, scapegoat, and follower, who are not overtly negative but do not assist in positive group functioning. Counselors should encourage positive interactions between group members and guide and encourage members to assume positive roles that benefit themselves as individuals and the group as a whole.

Promoting and Encouraging Interactions Among Group Members

It is the role of the counselor to encourage all members to participate in the group process. Members serve different roles in the group and can change their roles as the group progresses. Roles can be defined as functions the individual members of the group are fulfilling or performing that facilitate the group process. Clients typically take on various roles during group treatment. There are both functional and nonfunctional roles. **Functional roles** assist the group and include the energizer, harmonizer, tension reliever, and gatekeeper. **Nonfunctional roles** can disrupt and hinder the group and include the

interrogator, dominator, monopolizer, aggressor, and recognition seeker. Other roles include victim, scapegoat, and follower, who are not overtly negative but do not assist in positive group functioning.

The counselor must be aware of the roles of each individual and how those roles are affecting the group, so interventions can be made when necessary. The counselor can solicit feedback from each member of the group throughout the group process. The counselor can use blocking to stop unwanted behaviors from members that may be harmful or hurtful or violate confidentiality. Counselors should encourage positive interactions between group members and guide and encourage members to assume positive roles that benefit themselves as individuals and the group as a whole. To enhance interaction and cohesion of the group, the counselor can use the technique of linking by relating members' stories or situations. Members who have similar issues can assist one another in therapy.

Groups can take on characteristics that are often seen in families. As group members become comfortable with one another, their true personalities emerge and behavioral patterns from their families of origin tend to surface. Counselors can take note of these dynamics and use them within the group setting in a way that helps members see their familial patterns and make changes in line with their treatment goals. For example, if there is one person in a group who is viewed as everyone's favorite and who can do no wrong, then this person likely played the role of favorite child at home or as teacher's pet in school. Another example is a person who wants to be the leader's favorite; these individuals vie for the counselor's attention and attempt to curry favor by the way they respond to the leader. The counselor must be sensitive to all types of themes appearing in the group and be sure not to succumb to the subtle pressure to keep members in the roles they have played all their lives. Instead, the counselor's job is to identify these patterns and use them as therapeutic tools for transformation.

Types of Groups

Groups are designed to fulfill different tasks. **Supportive groups** (those used for severe mental illness or medical conditions) sometimes encourage interaction outside of the group. Forming genuine friendships outside of the group could be beneficial for members. **Psychodynamic groups** (those designed to affect personality changes while focusing on relationship issues and interpersonal dynamics) often prohibit outside group involvement. This is done to prevent interference with therapy goals. **Cognitive behavioral groups** (designed for treating symptoms of psychiatric conditions or for acquiring new coping skills) also discourage members from interacting outside the group. **Self-help groups** (designed around themed life issues such as AA or grief support groups) often encourage members to interact outside of the group. The therapeutic purpose of the group determines whether members are allowed to have contact outside of the group.

For a therapy group to be successful, leaders must fill crucial roles that change depending on the stage of the group's development. One important duty of the leader is ensuring that group members are safe from harmful group interactions. Sometimes a group member will behave in a destructive manner or say hateful things to other members. The **therapeutic group** is one in which the potential for conflicts exists, and leaders know that some conflict is productive and necessary when diverse people share intimate details about their lives. However, when a group member becomes aggressive or hostile to another member in a damaging way, the leader must confront the member. This must be done in a way that is straightforward, caring, and professional. The leader must stop the aggressive behavior and also attend to the offended member.

Transitions in Group Membership

There are two kinds of groups in counseling: open and closed. A **closed group** has a specific starting date, and only the clients who begin on that date are admitted to the group. Once the group starts, no other clients are permitted to join. In an **open group**, clients can begin and end treatment at any time during the life of the group. Prior to the beginning of either type of group, counselors should interview all potential members individually to determine their suitability for the group. Once new members are admitted, the counselor should go over the group's rules and describe the limits of confidentiality. When a group is coming to end, counselors should prepare their clients in advance.

This can be done by addressing issues such as the sadness some members may experience because they have come to rely upon the group for support or they have formed bonds within the group. Counselors can facilitate this process by having open conversations and encouraging clients to express their feelings. In preparation for termination, counselors should also talk about the progress made by the group members. Additionally, counselors can provide referrals to individual counselors if clients need or desire further treatment. Helping clients transition out of group therapy is an important stage of the process.

Practice Quiz

1. Dynamics deal with the interrelationships between the members, which include the leadership style, decision-making, and cohesiveness. Which of the following defines the dynamics of a group?
   a. Positive leadership
   b. Anything that impacts the group
   c. Lack of cohesiveness
   d. Norming

2. The empty chair technique is used by what type of group therapy and for what reason?
   a. Person-centered, to put oneself in another's situation and build empathy
   b. Gestalt, to resolve emotional issues with another person
   c. Psychoanalytic, to resolve issues with parents or authority figures
   d. Transactional analysis, to understand and edit life scripts

3. Conflict resolution requires a mutual agreement by both parties. Which of the following is required for successful conflict resolution?
   a. Assertive opinions
   b. Defining the solution
   c. Good communication
   d. Giving advice

4. When a group counselor sees that members' conflict with each other is escalating to an unhealthy level, what is the most beneficial tactic for the counselor to use?
   a. Address the conflict between the group members, but let it run its course
   b. Address the conflict and help resolve it because it may cause damage to the group
   c. Stay out of the conflict entirely
   d. End the group

5. A psychodynamic therapy group has been meeting for six months. Some group members have formed friendships and want to have dinner together. Is this possible in a psychodynamic group and, if so, under what conditions?
   a. Yes, if the group leader goes with them.
   b. Yes, with or without the group leader.
   c. No, psychodynamic groups cannot have outside contact.
   d. Yes, if all the group members go out together.

See answers on next page

Answer Explanations

1. B: The word *dynamic* means activity, change, or progress; thus, dynamics are anything that affect (or change) the group. Group dynamics refers to any interactions and processes of the group. Choice *A*, positive leadership, can be part of a leadership style of a group, but it does not define group dynamics. Choice *C*, lack of cohesiveness, is the inability to form a united whole, and is incorrect. Choice *D*, norming, is one of the stages of group development and involves the time where the group becomes a cohesive unit.

2. B: The empty chair technique is used in Gestalt to help resolve feelings toward another person. The other choices are merely the goals of those types of therapies. In person-centered therapy, Choice A, the goal of the counselor is to put himself or herself in another's situation and have empathy toward that person. One goal of psychoanalytic therapy, Choice C, is to resolve issues with parents or authority figures. Finally, in transactional analysis, Choice D, therapists work with clients to understand their life scripts and how they may be edited to have a more functional life.

3. C: Conflict resolution is dependent on good communication; both parties should respect each other's opinions and eliminate negative verbal obstacles. Choices A and D are considered obstacles for effective communication and conflict resolution; forceful statements and unsolicited advice can disrupt rapport. Choice B is incorrect; conflict resolution involves defining the problem before reaching a solution.

4. B: When a conflict reaches an unhealthy level, it is important for the counselor step in and help the members successfully resolve it; otherwise, the members may lose trust in the effectiveness of the group and may even leave the group. Choice A is not a good option because the conflict has already reached an unhealthy state. Choice C would not help the group navigate to a healthy resolution. Choice D is not warranted and could cause psychological harm to the members.

5. C: Under no circumstances do members participating in psychodynamic therapy meet outside of group time. Therefore, Choice C is correct, and the remaining choices are incorrect.

Assessment and Testing

Initial Assessment

Diagnostic Interview

The **problem system** refers to factors that are relevant to the client's presenting problem, which may include other people or environmental elements the client deems relevant to the situation. It is important that questions be asked to determine what the client's perception of the presenting problem is. Additionally, the counselor should determine if there are other legal, medical, or physical issues related to the problem. For a **comprehensive assessment**, the client should also be asked how long the problem has been present and if there are any triggers they believe contribute to the problem. Identification of external supports and access to resources is also key when examining and discussing the problem system.

The presenting problem is generally revealed in the client's statement about why they have come in for treatment. If collateral sources are used, information can also be gathered from one or more of the collateral sources who have insight as to why the client is in need of assistance. Disclosure of the presenting problem allows the counselor to determine the prevailing concerns deemed important by the client. Counselors can gain a sense of how distressed the client is about the problem or situation and what client expectations are for treatment. The manner in which the client describes the presenting problem can also provide insight as to how emotionally tied the client is to the problem and whether or not the client came in under their own volition.

It is important to determine the true root causes of the presenting problem. Although a client may come in and voice a concern, it may not be the root cause of the issue. Rather, this concern may simply be an item the client feels comfortable discussing. For example, a client who is experiencing sexual issues may initially speak about anxiety before disclosing the actual problem. This may require an investment of time to allow the client to become comfortable trusting the counselor. The history of the problem is important to address because it clarifies any factors contributing to the presenting problem, as well as any deeper underlying issues. Gathering background information on the problem history is also helpful for developing interventions. There are three key areas to address when reviewing the problem history: onset, progression, and severity.

- **Onset**: Problem onset addresses when the problem started. It usually includes triggers or events that led up to the start of the problem; these events may also be contributing factors.

- **Progression**: Assessment of the progression of the problem requires determining the frequency of the problem. The counselor should ask questions to determine if the problem is intermittent (how often and for how long), if it is acute or chronic, and if there are multiple problems that may or may not appear in a pattern or recurring cluster.

128

- **Severity**: Counselors should determine how severe the client feels the problem is, what factors contribute to making the problem more severe, and how the situation impacts the client's adaptive functioning. This may be determined by addressing the following questions:

  o Does the problem affect the client at work?

  o Is there difficulty performing personal care because of the problem?

    ▪ The counselor should ascertain whether or not the client has access to resources that can provide adequate care (running water, shelter, and clothing).

    ▪ The client's living situation should be explored if there are difficulties with personal care activities.

    ▪ The counselor should also ask if there are others for whom the client is responsible, like children or elderly parents/relatives.

  o Has the problem caused the client to withdraw from preferred activities?

  o Has the client used alcohol or other controlled substances to alleviate or escape the problem? If so, for how long and to what degree?

In order for an assessment to be comprehensive, the counselor must gather information and assess the individual holistically, which includes examining systems related to the biological, psychological, and social or sociocultural factors of functioning. In some cases, a spiritual component may be included. This process is based off of the **biopsychosocial framework**, which describes the interaction between biological, psychological, and social factors. The key components of the biopsychosocial assessment can be broken down into five parts: identification, chief complaint, social/environmental issues, history, and mental status exam.

Identification
Identification consists of the details or demographic information about the client that can be seen with the eye and documented accordingly. Some examples of identification information are age, gender, height, weight, and clothing.

Chief Complaint
This is the client's version of what the over-arching problem is, in their own words. The client's description of the **chief complaint** may include factors from the past that the client views as an obstacle to optimal functioning. It could also be an issue that was previously resolved but reoccurs, thus requiring the client to develop additional coping skills.

Social/Environmental Issues
This involves the evaluation of social development and physical settings. **Social development** is critical to understanding the types of support systems the client has and includes information about the client's primary family group, including parents, siblings, and extended family members.

The client's peers and social networks should also be examined. There should be a clear distinction between peers available online (such as through online social networks) and peers the client interacts with face-to-face, as online systems may provide different forms of support than in-person systems.

The client's work environment and school or vocational settings should also be noted in this portion of the assessment. The client's current housing situation and view of financial status is also included to determine the type of resources the client has. Legal issues may also be included.

History

This includes events in the client's past. Clients may need to be interviewed several times in order to get a thorough picture of their **history**. Some information in a client's history, such as events that occurred during the stages of infancy and early childhood, may need to be gathered from collateral sources. Obtaining the client's historical information is usually a multi-stage process and can involve the following methods of data collection:

Presenting Problem

Clients should be asked to describe what brings them in for treatment. Although a client may attempt to delve into information that is well in the past, the counselor should redirect the client to emphasize the past week or two. Emphasis is placed on the client's current situation when assessing the presenting problem.

Past Personal

When reviewing a client's history, noting biological development may determine whether or not the client hit milestones and the ensuing impact it had on their health. In reviewing biological development, other physical factors should also be assessed for impact on current emotional well-being, including those that may no longer persist, like a childhood illness. As much information regarding the client's entire lifespan (birth to present) should be gathered, with attention paid to sexual development.

Medical

During the medical component of the assessment process, information should be obtained on the client's previous or current physiological diagnoses. These diagnoses can contribute to the client's current situation.

For example, a client with frequent headaches and back pain may be unable to sleep well and therefore may be experiencing the physical and psychosocial effects of sleep deprivation. Additional information on other conditions, such as pregnancy, surgeries, or disabilities, should also be explored during this time.

Mental Health

Previous mental health diagnoses, symptoms, and/or evaluations should be discussed. If a client discloses prior diagnoses or evaluations, the counselor should determine the following:

- Whether or not the client has been hospitalized (inpatient)

- If the client has received supervised treatment in an outpatient setting (to include psychotherapeutic intervention)

- Whether the client has been prescribed medications

- If the client has undertaken other treatments related to mental health diagnoses

The client's psychological development should also be reviewed. It is important to gather details on how clients view their emotional development, including their general affect.

130

The client's cognitive development, in relation to information previously obtained regarding the biological development, should also be reviewed.

Substance Use

Without demonstrating judgment, counselors should encourage clients to disclose whether or not they have used controlled substances. It is important that thorough information is gathered and symptoms related to substance abuse are assessed BEFORE rendering a primary mental health disorder diagnosis.

Should a client disclose that they have engaged in the use of substances, information as to the type of substance, frequency of use, and duration of exposure to the lifestyle should be gathered. Additionally, information on what the client perceives as the positive and negative aspects of substance use should be gathered, noting whether or not the client perceives any consequences of substance abuse, such as job loss, decreased contact with family and friends, and physical appearance.

Mental Status Exam

A mental status exam is a concise, complete evaluation of the client's current mental functioning level in regard to **cognitive and behavioral aspects** (rapport-building, mood, thought content, hygiene). There are mini-mental status examinations available that allow counselors to provide a snapshot of the client's overall level of functioning with limited resources and time available. Mental status examinations are usually conducted regularly and discreetly through questioning and noting non-verbal indicators (such as appearance) in order for the counselor to best guide the session.

DSM-5-TR Cultural Formulation Interview

How individuals think about their symptoms or mental illness is greatly influenced by their cultural context. The **Cultural Formulation Interview (CFI)** is designed to evaluate these perspectives in order to gain a comprehensive understanding of the individual's specific experience. It consists of a set of sixteen questions that are typically asked when first meeting a new client during an initial interview. The CFI covers four domains of cultural assessment: cultural definition of the problem; cultural perceptions of cause, context, and support; cultural factors affecting self-coping; and past help seeking.

When obtaining cultural information about the client, counselors should do so in an inviting and welcoming manner. The CFI emulates a person-centered process, meaning that counselors encourage clients to explore their thought processes and experience. By using this approach, the diagnostic assessment becomes more valid and the individual becomes more engaged in the process. Stereotypic thinking is also controlled for as much as possible by this interview because counselors have the ability to understand how the client's particular culture affects their clinical presentation. Other variations of the CFI have been developed in order to assess certain populations such as children and adolescents, the elderly, immigrants, and refugees.

The CFI is such a vital part of diagnostic assessment as it provides extraordinary emphasis on the way mental illness is perceived through a cultural lens. Level of distress, one of the main indicators of psychological illness, can vary in the way it is expressed from culture to culture in how it is communicated (if at all), understood, or felt. A specific psychological experience that is shared among individuals in certain cultural groups, known as a cultural syndrome, may be presented through the CFI. Additionally, cultural idioms of distress and cultural explanations are able to be highlighted and understood through the process of the CFI. Culture will always affect the way in which mental illness presents. By extracting information about the client's experience in this context, counselors can avoid

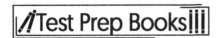

misdiagnosis, obtain useful clinical information, improve rapport and client engagement, guide clinical research, and possibly clarify cultural epidemiology.

Using Assessment Results to Determine Diagnoses

Diagnostic and Statistical Manual of the American Psychiatric Association

The current American Psychiatric Association manual for the classification of mental disorders is the *Diagnostic and Statistical Manual of Mental Disorders, Fifth Edition, Text Revision*, or the **DSM-5-TR**. It is an updated and revised version of the APA's previous classification and diagnostic tool from 2013, the **DSM-5**. The **DSM-5-TR** serves as an authority for mental health diagnosis and functions as a tool for counselors to make treatment recommendations. The *DSM-5-TR* is organized in accordance with the developmental lifespan. In addition to guiding diagnosis, the updated framework of the *DSM-5-TR* is designed to help researchers and clinicians better understand how disorders relate to one another and ultimately improve treatment outcomes for patients.

There are several notable changes to the *DSM-5-TR* as of 2022:
the addition of scientific knowledge accumulated since the 2013 update

- the recognition of the role of culture in psychiatric diagnosis

- the revision of language used regarding race, gender, and gender identity

- the description of a Cultural Formulation Interview for use in the counseling intake process

- the correction of ICD codes for mental health disorders

- the addition of more precise criteria for childhood conditions

- the addition of a new mental disorder, Prolonged Grief Disorder, to the category of Trauma- and Stressor-Related Disorders

- the addition of new conditions of clinical attention

- the updated names of two disorders, Functional Neurological Symptom Disorder and Intellectual Development Disorder

- the addition and removal of diagnosis specifiers, including those for Bipolar I, Bipolar II, Obsessive-Compulsive Related Disorder, Persistent Depressive Disorder, and Gender Dysphoria

Complete Listing of *DSM-5-TR* Diagnostic Criteria Chapters

- Neurodevelopmental Disorders
- Schizophrenia Spectrum and other Psychotic Disorders
- Bipolar and Related Disorders
- Depressive Disorders
- Anxiety Disorders
- Elimination Disorders
- Other Mental Disorders and Additional Codes
- Obsessive-Compulsive and Related Disorders
- Trauma- and Stressor-Related Disorders
- Dissociative Disorders
- Somatic Symptom and Related Disorders

132

- Feeding and Eating Disorders
- Sleep-Wake Disorders
- Sexual Dysfunctions
- Gender Dysphoria
- Disruptive, Impulse-Control and Conduct Disorders
- Substance-Related and Addictive Disorders
- Neurocognitive Disorders
- Personality Disorders
- Paraphilic Disorders
- Medication-Induced Movement Disorders and Other Adverse Effects of Medication
- Other Conditions That May Be a Focus of Clinical Attention

Assessing Risk of Aggression, Danger to Others, Self-Inflicted Harm, or Suicide

Ongoing Assessment for At-Risk Behaviors

The counselor conducts **risk assessments** to determine any influence that could result in harm or increased risk of harm to the individual. Assessing risk can be an ongoing process, as it's important to always have updated, accurate information. Risk-assessment methods will also vary depending on the circumstance (e.g., criminal justice, child abuse or neglect, community care). Some common methodology themes in risk assessment include the following:

Universal Risk Screening

This is a general screening for certain risky behaviors (e.g., violent behavior, substance abuse problems, self-harm) that may result in additional screenings, referral for treatment, or stronger outcomes such as institutionalization (in the instance of high suicide risk, for example). This screening often takes place in initial consultations or as part of the individual's intake forms and may be administered on an ongoing basis (e.g., at every session) to remain current.

Unstructured Methods

These typically include clinical assessments without any specific, prepared structure. While high-level professionals often make judgments during this process, outcomes can sometimes be considered biased and unreliable.

Actuarial Methods

These include highly logical, regimented tests and scales used to predict the likelihood of certain behavior patterns in a specified time frame. While scientific and evaluative in nature, some argue that these methods may place undue blame on individuals or be too inflexible to allow for the likely interplay of many influencing factors in an individual's presenting issue.

Structured Professional Judgment

This combination of the previous two methods is generally the most accepted. It uses structured tools appropriate for the scope of the case but allows for the judgment and flexibility of the counselor to decide what information is useful and to note any external information that may not be caught by standardized assessments.

Client's Danger to Self and Others

Counselors should always be alert to indicators that individuals may pose a threat to themselves or others. These indicators may be obvious or discreet and may include:

- Substance use and abuse
- Sudden apathy towards others or society
- Sudden lack of personal care or grooming
- Isolation
- Apparent personality change
- Drastic mood shifts
- Marked change in mood. Both depressed mood and a positive change in mood can be associated with suicidal thoughts or plans. A sudden positive change may indicate that the individual has made a decision and is no longer experiencing personal turmoil.
- Verbalization of feelings such as extreme self-loathing, desire to be dead, being a burden to others, or volatility toward others.

Risk Factors for Danger to Self and Others

A client who presents as a danger to self or others should be assessed through a biopsychosocial lens. In addition, tailoring crisis management techniques to the immediate problem can help de-escalate the situation. Open-ended questions should be used to gather as much information from the client as possible. It is also important to consult collateral information from any nearby family members to document other pertinent information about the client.

- The client should be asked if there are plans to harm anyone. If the client states yes, the counselor should determine what the plan entails.

- Any and all threats made should be taken seriously and reported to the proper authorities. Colleagues may be consulted to determine the validity of a threat, if the counselor is unclear on the client's intent.

- Identifying the critical event and antecedent that preceded it is important. The client should be asked to provide as much information on this as they are willing, in order for the counselor to gain a better perspective of the client's point of view.

- Determining whether or not the client has engaged in self-injurious behaviors (SIB) is also important. Here are a few examples of SIB:

  - Excessive use of alcohol or other substances

  - Cutting

  - Banging one's head against a hard object

  - Ignoring necessary medical advice (not taking prescribed pills, leaving a hospital against medical advice)

- The counselor should also evaluate the social and cultural factors that contribute to how the client reacts to stressful situations, including the following:

  o   History of violence

  o   Stability of relationships (school, work, and home)

  o   Social isolation or withdrawal from others

  o   Limited access to social resources

- Any recent life stressors that would lead to the client carrying through with a plan to harm self or others

- Assessing the client's current thought process is important. Do they present with confusion, clarity of the situation, or irrational thinking?

- If the client has a clear, concrete plan of action, then the risk for harm to self or others should be considered high.

Risk Factors Related to Suicide

The following are risk factors related to suicide:

- Previous attempts at committing suicide
- History of cutting
- Multiple hospitalizations related to self-injurious or reckless behavior, such as those noted below:
- Drug overdose
- Alcohol poisoning
- Inhalation of carbon monoxide
- Statement of a plan to commit suicide/suicidal ideations and access to the means to complete it
- Ownership or access to a lethal firearm
- Stated plan to cut one's wrists "the right way"
- Warnings or statements that suicide is planned
- Other factors related to suicide risk
- Age—middle-aged adults present highest suicide risk over other age groups
- Gender—males are more likely to commit suicide than females
- Adolescents—high suicide risk, especially those heavily-entrenched in social media groups as a means of support and socialization
- Presence of a mental health disorder
- Life stressors from work or school
- Family history of suicide
- Family discord or other relationship trauma (divorce, break-up, widowed)
- Excessive drug or alcohol use
- Chronic illness
- Job loss

135

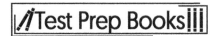

Identifying Trauma and Abuse

In normal circumstances, an individual is typically able to return to a calm state after a stressor passes. Traumatic stress and violence, however, cause long-term effects, and the patient may not be able to recover to a normal state. Indicators of traumatic stress and violence include:

- Unexplained anger or outbursts
- Substance use and abuse
- Uncontrolled behaviors such as binge eating, compulsive shopping, gambling, hoarding, or sex addiction
- Attachment issues
- Chronic and intense feelings of shame, regret, guilt, and/or fear
- Obsessive thoughts or behaviors related to the traumatic event
- Eating disorders
- Self-harm, self-injury, or other self-destructive behaviors
- Sleep problems such as insomnia or sleeping too much
- Intense anxiety, especially in social or crowded situations
- Fear, clinginess, aggression, withdrawal, or regression in developmental behavior in children

Trauma occurs when a client experiences a deeply disturbing experience that yields an intense emotional response. Traumatic events may interfere with a client's baseline level of functioning. It is important for the counselor to have an understanding of the detrimental effects, both visible and invisible, that traumatization can have on a client.

The counselor should have an understanding of the client's baseline level of functioning. This information may be gathered first-hand from the client or through collateral sources if the client is unable or unwilling to provide that information.

The counselor should have an understanding of how to guide the client gently through describing the traumatic experience and the emotions related to it. In doing so, the counselor should have an understanding of the widespread, lasting effects that trauma can have, as well as the multiple recovery and treatment options. This knowledge also helps prevent re-traumatizing the client.

An adult client may present with traumatic stressors due to one or more events that occurred during childhood. Symptoms of anxiety, depression, or other mood disorders that are actually related to the traumatic event(s) may present in session and daily functioning. A counselor should be aware that symptoms of trauma could manifest in places and interactions outside of the client, such as within the family system, with peers, and at work.

Assessing Substance Use

During the intake stage of the counseling process, a counselor may screen clients for substance abuse. The depth of screening will be determined by several factors. Many clients will confess to using substances recreationally or medicinally. The frequency of use, simultaneous use of other substances, and associated medical comorbidities should all be assessed. Counselors should also be aware of the differences between substance abuse and substance dependence. A client who is dependent on a substance is unable to function normally without it. The presence of polydrug use and dependency of substances for social survival should direct the counselor to do an in-depth assessment. Counselors should expect variations in the willingness of clients to respond to substance use questions.

136

Teenagers will be hesitant to respond honestly for fear of parental involvement. Examples of alcohol and drug screening tools include the Alcohol Use Disorder Identification Test (AUDIT) and the CAGE (cut-annoyed-guilty-eye) questionnaire. The **CAGE questionnaire** is a screening tool that determines the likelihood of alcohol problems. The risk is determined by the number of "yes" responses recorded. The **CAGE-Adapted to Include Drugs (AID)** questionnaire is similar to the CAGE tool but includes drug use in its questions. Substance abuse may cause clients to become suicidal or homicidal. Alternatively, chemical dependency may be the result of a suicidal state of mind. It is important to perform a suicide risk assessment concurrently when treating clients with substance abuse. The ultimate goal will be to assist clients in identifying and utilizing alternative coping mechanisms.

Obtaining Client Self-Reports

One of the ways to obtain data from clients is through self-reporting. **Self-reports** allow clients to disclose their own symptoms, beliefs, attitudes, and behaviors and can be done using a paper survey or electronic test. The **Minnesota Multiphasic Personality Inventory (MMPI)** is a common tool used to measure personality traits and can help diagnose mental health disorders. **Interest inventories** are a type of affective test that can help clients identify their areas of interest and match these preferences to work contexts. **Symptom checklists** can evaluate the presence and intensity of symptoms that appear with certain disorders and are useful in monitoring symptom reduction after treatment has been established. Examples of symptom checklists include the Beck Depression Inventory, the Connors 3 Rating Scales, and the Child Behavior Checklist. Counselors should be aware of client bias when they report their symptoms. Other factors to consider are the validity and reliability of the chosen test.

Forms of Testing

Some tools used to screen clients for appropriate services include questionnaires, checklists, rating scales, and standardized tests. **Standardized testing** is a formal process that produces a score and can be interpreted using a set of guidelines. Examples include personality and aptitude tests, such as the Minnesota Multiphasic Personality Inventory-2 or the SAT. Frequently used projective personality tests include the Thematic Apperception Test (TAT) and the Rorschach Inkblot Test (Rorschach). Objective personality tests rely on the client's personal responses and are considered a form of self-reporting. Examples include the Sixteen Personality Factors Questionnaire (16PF) and the Edwards Personal Preference Schedule (EPPS). Counselors should choose the screening tool that can best examine the client's presenting problem further.

Selection, Use, and Interpret of Appropriate Assessment Instruments

Psychological and educational tests play a critical role in understanding client backgrounds, belief systems, and perspectives as part of the overall assessment. They also indicate any current or potential psychological, social, or physical needs that the client may have. These pieces of information shape the way counselors develop and tailor interventions for a specific client; they also allow counselors to maintain the highest level of safety for the patient as well as themselves. Psychological testing usually includes an interview component in which the counselor may conduct the initial intake assessment, ask the client personal and family-related questions, and notice body language and other physical behaviors.

Answers to interview questions and body language observations are incorporated into assessments by indicating potential risk or protective factors, individual capacity to accept and receive services, and strengths and challenges that the counselor can incorporate into the client's treatment plan. Clients are also often tested for their communication, comprehension, reasoning, and logic skills in order to determine which methods of intervention will be best received. For example, a client who is unable to

communicate verbally may not benefit from simply listening to the counselor providing counseling; a non-verbal, interactive approach will need to be developed for such a client. Clients may also take personality and behavior tests, which allow the counselor to incorporate aspects of the client's beliefs, attitudes, perspectives, and reactions into the assessment.

Many psychometric instruments exist to assess and diagnose psychological functioning. Some of the most common tests include:

Beck Depression Inventory-II (BDI-II)
BDI-II is a twenty-one-question inventory used to measure presence and severity of depression symptoms in individuals aged thirteen years and older.

Bricklin Perceptual Scales (BPS)
BPS is a thirty-two-question inventory designed for children who are at least six years old. It examines the perception the child has of each parent or caregiver and is often used in custody cases.

Millon Instruments
Millon Clinical Multiaxial Inventory III (MCMI-III): This 175-question inventory is used to determine indicators of specific psychiatric disorders in adults aged eighteen years and older.

Millon Adolescent Clinical Inventory (MACI): This 160-question inventory is used to determine indicators of specific psychiatric disorders in adolescents aged thirteen to nineteen years.

Millon Adolescent Personality Inventory (MAPI): This 150-question inventory is used to determine specific personality indicators in adolescents aged thirteen to eighteen years.

Millon Behavioral Health Inventory (MBHI): This 165-question inventory is used to determine psychosocial factors that may help or hinder medical intervention in adults aged eighteen years and older.

Minnesota Multiphasic Personality Inventory (MMPI-2)
MMPI-2 is a 567-item inventory. It is one of the most widely administered objective personality tests. It is used to determine indicators of psychopathology in adults aged eighteen years and older.

Myers-Briggs Type Indicator
Myers-Briggs is a 93-question inventory widely used to help people aged fourteen years or older determine what personality traits influence their perception of the world and decision-making processes. A preference is identified within each of four different dimensions: extraverted (E) or introverted (I); sensing (S) or intuitive (I); thinking (T) or feeling (F); and judging (J) or perceiving (P).

Quality of Life Inventory (QOLI)
QOLI is a 32-question inventory that determines the perception of personal happiness and satisfaction in individuals aged seventeen years and older.

Thematic Apperception Test (TAT)
TAT is a narrative and visual test that typically requires the individual to create a story and allows the counselor insight into the individual's underlying emotional state, desires, behavioral motives, and needs. It's used for individuals aged five years and older.

Rorschach Test
Rorschach test is a visual test that records an individual's perception and description of various inkblots. It's used to determine underlying personality or thought disorders in individuals aged five years and older.

Wechsler Adult Intelligence Scale – Fourth Edition (WAIS-IV)
WAIS-IV is a series of subtests that assesses cognitive ability in individuals aged sixteen years and older.

Pre-Test and Post-Test Measures for Assessing Outcomes
Counselors can employ **pre-tests** before an intervention to serve as a baseline data set, and they can employ a **post-test** to measure changes from the baseline. Counselors can also administer surveys, Likert scale questionnaires, or specific intervention evaluation assessments to the client or client system. These tools can measure quantitative results as well as provide an option for anecdotal or testimonial information. Entrance and exit interviews with the client or the client system can also provide a wealth of evaluation information. When evaluating clients face-to-face or through a survey, it's important to create an environment that fosters comfort, open dialogue, and honesty. Clients may feel pressured to provide positive evaluations if they are answering directly to the counselor or if they feel as though a satisfaction survey that they are completing can be traced back to them. This can bias the evaluation process and produce skewed results.

Formal and Informal Observations
Qualitative data can be collected through interviews, observations, anecdotes, and surveys, and by reviewing literature and other relevant documents. Qualitative data collection methods are often subjective and cannot be generalized to larger samples or populations. **Quantitative data** can be collected from experiments, recordings of certain events and timed intervals, surveys in which an answer choice must be selected for each question, data management systems, and numerical reports. Quantitative data methods are often objective and abstract, and they can be generalized to explain relationships between variables in large populations.

Evaluating Interactional Dynamics
Interpersonal relationships refer to interactions (often of a close, friendly, romantic, or intimate nature) between people. They can form due to shared personal, professional, social, charitable, or political interests. Strong interpersonal relationships are built over time as participants are willing to honestly communicate on a regular basis, support one another's well-being, and develop a shared history. Psychological, evolutionary, and anthropological contexts suggest that humans are an inherently altruistic, community-oriented species that relies on interpersonal relationships to survive and thrive. These types of relationships (when healthy) provide security, a sense of belonging, an exchange of benefits and rewards, and a sense of self-esteem. **Healthy interpersonal relationships** are characterized by mutual respect, care, and consideration between members. Almost all groups assemble into a power structure of some kind, with natural leaders taking over decision-making, resource sharing, and other tasks that affect the group as a whole. **Dysfunctional interpersonal relationships** may be characterized by an extreme power imbalance and dominance by one or more involved members, often leading to submissiveness, learned helplessness, and feelings of low self-esteem in the relationship's less powerful members. Submissive members of a group may find themselves without material resources or respect from the rest of the group.

In some cases, information about interactional relationships, as well as the client's current functioning and past history, can be obtained from collateral sources. **Collateral sources** are persons other than the

139

client, such as family members, police officers, friends, or other medical providers, who can provide information related to the client's levels of functioning, life events, and other potential areas of significance in the client's treatment.

Prior to obtaining collateral information from any source, a signed **release of information (ROI)** form should be obtained from the client (or from a parent/ guardian if the client is a minor). The necessity for an ROI may be waived if there is explicit legal consent granting access to collateral sources. This is most commonly seen during forensic interviews. It is important to explain the purpose behind collecting an ROI to the client. Relatedly, it is also important to make the collateral source aware of the reason behind the request for information on the client.

Information from collateral sources is useful in cases when the client is unable to provide reliable information. The inability to provide reliable information could be due to a number of factors, such as substance abuse issues, severe cognitive impairment, or severe mental illness/disorder. Based on the client's background, there could be a number of collateral sources from which to solicit information. Thus, it is important to filter these sources based on those who have had regular or recent contact with the client.

It is important to select collateral sources that can provide information about significant experiences and events relating to the client's presenting problem. Collateral sources can provide a level of objectivity when discussing the client's situation. Additional examples of collateral sources include physician's reports, police reports, reports from other medical professionals or mental health agencies, school reports, and employment records.

Use of Assessments for Various Counseling Areas

Determining Level of Care Needed

A client's need for care can fall on a wide spectrum. Some clients may comfortably live in their own residence but attend regularly scheduled meetings with a counselor to receive care. Other clients, after being appropriately assessed, may require institutional care where they can receive medical and therapeutic support as often as is needed. Institutional care may be a long-term or short-term solution for a client. The level of care required for a client is assessed by examining a number of self-sufficiency factors, such as the presence of any formally diagnosed developmental disabilities, physical disabilities, or mental disorders.

Additionally, the client's ability to communicate needs, IQ level, ability to complete self-care tasks (such as dressing, toileting, grooming, etc.) alone or with assistance, and risk of voluntary or involuntary harm to self or others will also be taken into consideration. Based on the client's health and caretaking needs, they may receive outpatient services (such as regular therapeutic appointments), inpatient services (such as a behavioral program that lasts for a predetermined period of time), assisted living in a facility such as a nursing home, or in-home support (such as a home health nurse). Regardless of where a client falls on the care spectrum, services for mental wellness and adjusting to this new context of life will likely be beneficial to care.

Determining Appropriate Modality of Treatment

When utilizing a holistic approach for client assessment and treatment planning, counselors should utilize evidence-based research to support the selected interventions and treatment modalities. The interventions and treatment modalities selected will be based on a number of things, including the client's current level of functioning (based on the biopsychosocial assessment), level of care needed,

140

presenting symptoms, and the counselor's background. Here are some things a counselor will want to consider when constructing interventions or treatment modalities:

- Are the selected interventions evidence-based?

- Do the selected interventions arise from a strengths-based perspective specifically tailored around the client's strengths, interests, and needs?

- Do the associated risks with the selected interventions outweigh the possible positive outcomes?

- Is the selected intervention culturally-sensitive and culturally-appropriate?

- Did the client participate in the construction of the intervention selection and/or consent to it?

- Does the counselor feel comfortable and well-versed in the selected intervention to increase the levels of intensity as needed and provide a continuity of care for the selected modalities?

- Does the selected intervention coincide with the client's financial ability to pay?

Assessing the Presenting Problem and Level of Distress

While formulating the treatment plan, the counselor should assess the level of care needed for a client with the whole person in mind and a desire for continuity of care. As the counselor starts where the client is, the treatment plan process should reflect levels of care that are in line with the client's needs, adjusting the intensity up or down based on the level of need as reflected in ongoing assessments and review processes.

For example, geriatric care is similar to behavioral health care as the client may present with a need for the most basic level of care, conducted through routine visits with a counselor, either at the counselor's office or at the client's residence. The intensity may move up to increased sessions with the counselor.

The highest level of intensity would be a multidisciplinary team approach in a residential or inpatient setting. For geriatric care, the highest level of need would be represented in a skilled nursing facility. For child welfare or special needs, an inpatient medical facility would also represent the highest level of need.

Indicators of Client's Strengths and Challenges

Noticing a client's different characteristics can indicate particular strengths. Strengths are biological, physical, mental, social, spiritual, or emotional abilities that help them to solve problems and keep the mind, body, and spirit in a stable state. The counselor might also notice areas requiring intervention or treatment plans for the individual's overall growth. Focus is on the following indicators:

- Intelligence quotient (IQ) and cognitive ability
- Willingness to learn
- Willingness to understand oneself without judgment
- Ability to accept both positive feedback and constructive criticism
- Desire for personal growth
- Willingness to change
- Ability and desire to learn new concepts

- Temperament
- Optimistic or pessimistic thought patterns
- Reaction patterns to stressors (both initially and over time)
- Self-esteem
- Self-efficacy
- Self-worth
- Accountability for one's actions
- Emotional quotient (EQ), also called emotional intelligence (EI)
- Status and complexity of close relationships and friendships
- Ability to trust and depend on others
- Ability to be trustworthy and dependable
- Ability to empathize and sympathize
- Perspective on society at large
- Self-awareness
- Moods and what external events or internal thought processes affect them
- Involvement in social institutions (e.g., religious groups, social clubs)
- State of physical health
- State of finances
- Socioeconomic status

Evaluating an Individual's Level of Mental Health Functioning

Ideas about what is normal versus what is abnormal with regard to behavior are society-dependent. People tend to equate *normal* with "good" and *abnormal* with "bad," which means that any behavior labeled as abnormal can potentially be stigmatizing. Use of person-centered language is one way to reduce stigma attached to abnormal behavior or behavior health issues (e.g., saying "a person with schizophrenia," rather than "a schizophrenic.")

The **"Four Ds" of Abnormality** assist health counselors when trying to identify a psychiatric condition in their clients. Deviance marks a withdrawal from society's concept of appropriate behavior. **Deviant behavior** is a departure from the "norm." The *DSM-5* contains some criteria for diagnosing deviance. The second "D" is dysfunction. **Dysfunction** is behavior that interferes with daily living. Dysfunction is a type a problem that may be serious enough to be considered a disorder. The third "D" is distress. **Distress** is related to a client's dysfunction. That is, to what degree does the dysfunction cause the client distress? A client can experience minor dysfunction and major distress, or major dysfunction and minor distress. The fourth "D" is danger. **Danger** is characterized by danger to self or to others. There are different degrees of danger specific to various types of disorders. **Duration** is sometimes considered a fifth "D," as it may be important to note whether the symptoms of a disorder are fleeting or permanent.

Screening Clients for Appropriate Services

The **treatment plan** is dependent on the goals set by the client and counselor. Part of the intake process is obtaining a general overview of why the client is seeking counseling services. Data collection can be performed using various methods. The primary tool used to gather information about the client is an unstructured client interview. Counselors can also observe nonverbal behavior and build rapport during an unstructured interview. Structured interviews are used to ask clients questions that will improve reliability and ensure collection of specific information.

Practice Quiz

1. Which of the following is NOT a personality test?
a.   Minnesota Multiphasic Personality Inventory (MMPI-2)
   b. Beck Depression Inventory
   c. Stanford-Binet Intelligence Scale
   d. Myers-Briggs Type Inventory (MBTI)

2. What concurrent assessment is important to perform with substance abuse clients?
   a. A cognitive assessment
   b. A suicide risk assessment
   c. A fall risk assessment
   d. An environmental assessment

3. Which of the following clients would benefit from substance abuse treatment?
   a. A 21-year-old male who drinks three days a week and is an A student at school
   b. A 50-year-old accountant who drinks a glass of wine daily after work
   c. A 35-year-old female artist with a history of back pain who takes narcotics for pain relief
   d. A 46-year-old male who reports marijuana use and works two jobs to manage increasing debt

4. Which of the following is an index that measures someone's cognitive, critical, and abstract thinking abilities?
   a. Intelligence
   b. Intellectual Achievement
   c. Intelligence Quotient
   d. Emotional Quotient

5. What kind of test is used to explore the client's unconscious attitudes or motivations?
   a. Objective test
   b. Projective test
   c. Free choice test
   d. Vertical test

See answers on next page

143

Answer Explanations

1. C: The Stanford-Binet Intelligence Scale is an intelligence test. The other three answers, Minnesota Multiphasic Personality Inventory (MMPI-2), Beck Depression Inventory, and Myers-Briggs Inventory (MBTI), are types of personality tests.

2. B: Clients with substance abuse problems may be prone to suicide or homicide and should be screened appropriately. Choice *A* is appropriate for clients who display memory impairment. Choice *C* is not an appropriate assessment for a client with a primary problem of substance abuse. Choice *D* is a holistic evaluation of how the environment affects the client, family, or group.

3. D: One of the signs of substance abuse is financial struggles; clients will prioritize purchasing substances over essentials. Choice *A* is still able to perform well academically. Choice *B* does not depict binge behavior. Choice *C* is socially functional, and the substance is used for medical purposes.

4. C: Intelligence Quotient. More commonly known as IQ, this index measures someone's intellectual ability. The average person's IQ falls between 90 and 110. Over 125 is considered exceptional and under 70 is considered intellectually deficient. Choices *A* and *B* are too broad to be considered actual terms in psychology. Choice *D* is an index used to measure someone's ability to show empathy and connect with others, so this is incorrect.

5. B: A projective test would be given to explore the client's unconscious attitudes or motivations. An objective test, Choice *A*, gives questions with clear correct or incorrect answers and is not open to interpretation. A free choice test, Choice *C*, allows for an open-ended response, but this is a much more general answer choice than Choice *B*, making it incorrect. A vertical test, Choice *D*, is a same-subject test given to different levels or ages, which is incorrect.

Research and Program Evaluation

Identification of Evidence-Based Counseling Practices

Treatment evaluation is a necessary part of direct practice. Counselors should strive to exercise best practice techniques by using evidence-based practice evaluation. It is beneficial for clients to see the progress they have made, while simultaneously providing information to funders and insurance companies that typically require documentation and outcome measures for reimbursement of services. Other benefits include providing indicators that interventions should be modified or that treatment is complete and termination is warranted. Several factors are important in the evaluation of a client's progress, including identifying specific issues to be addressed; creating appropriate goals, objectives, and tasks; using effective and relevant techniques and tools to measure success; and routinely documenting progress.

Collaborating with Client to Establish Treatment Goals and Objectives

Goal setting should occur in collaboration with a client's treatment plan. Intervention strategies, tasks, and timeframes should correspond with the desired goal and objectives. The primary goal should be to assist clients in returning to pre-crisis functioning. However, there will likely be additional and related goals and tasks as the plan of action is implemented.

Whenever possible, counselors should invite their clients to take a collaborative perspective in designing interventions, establishing objectives, and developing program goals. This allows the client to feel empowered and engaged as an active member of the problem-solving process. These factors are associated with higher incidences of positive outcomes, as they encourage clients to feel accountable for their behaviors, actions, and personal changes.

Collaboration should begin at the intake process. This is a period in which the counselor can make assessments, but they can also get information directly from clients about why they are in the session and what they hope to achieve. The counselor can also ask clients the steps they believe they need to take to reach their desired outcomes. While clients may or may not provide useful or feasible answers, this process still sets the tone that allows clients to feel acknowledged and involved in their own care.

In the intake session or in the sessions that immediately follow, the counselor can invite the client to develop SMART objectives to reach their goals. This may also include establishing accountability tools, documenting plans of action to address potential barriers and how to overcome them, and any other support protocols that clients may need for their individual situations. Depending on the client's specific case, this process may take one session or may take much longer. Counselors should continuously show patience, compassion, and a welcoming desire to engage the client in the process.

Establishing Short- and Long-Term Counseling Goals Consistent with Diagnoses

Setting goals is an important aspect of the therapeutic process. Talk therapy may seem unstructured or capable of lasting for long periods of time; however, both the client and the counselor are responsible for setting and working toward measurable change. Goals of counseling can include the desire for physical change, such as getting into shape or losing weight, and career aspirations and/or social goals, such as gaining increased support or modifying relationships. Other types of goals can be emotional, spiritual, and intellectual. Goals can be immediate, short term, or long term, and clients may want to achieve several goals at different paces.

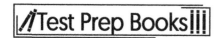

Identifying Barriers to Client Goal Attainment

Goal setting must be specific to each client and should be mutually agreed upon. Setting clear time frames that are supported by the counselor is essential to success. Goal setting may cause issues if goals are too ambitious or vague or have no identifiable benefit. It is also important to explore what motivation exists for a client to work toward a goal. If adequate motivation is present, the counselor also needs to consider what will happen if the goal is not met. In some cases, failure to meet goals can cause a client to become highly discouraged and unwilling to stick with the process of reformulating goals. During the process of working toward goals, a client may realize another goal is better suited. It's important to reevaluate goals during the process to help the client grow and embrace personal change.

Referring Clients to Different Levels of Treatment

When planning a client's treatment, the counselor will need to decide which type of therapeutic environment will coincide best with the client's needs. The most extreme level of treatment is inpatient. **Inpatient treatment** provides professional supervision and monitoring along with daily counseling sessions. Clients who require inpatient treatment will be diagnosed with more problematic and complicated mental health issues or issues that are chronic or unusual. Inpatient treatment will provide an orderly routine, allowing focus to be on therapy, and it will eliminate environmental factors that aggravate the client's issue. This level of treatment is best for clients who can commit to weeks or months in a treatment facility. Inpatient treatment should be chosen for clients who are in danger of harming themselves or others and/or if their condition is interfering with day-to-day functioning. In cases of substance use, if the client has attempted treatment in the past and relapsed, inpatient treatment is a viable option.

The next level under inpatient treatment is residential. This type of treatment environment is more like a home. Clients are monitored but not to the same degree as they would be in inpatient treatment. Inpatient treatment is preferable for problems such as eating disorders or substance abuse. The daily focus will be on treatment. Counselors should refer clients to **residential treatment** if they don't need constant supervision but still need to get out of an environment that encourages or provokes the problem. In residential treatment, clients benefit from the group environment where others who are going through the same problems support and push each other to reach their goals.

The most flexible option for treatment is outpatient as it allows clients to continue working or going to school while going through therapy. Clients who only need to meet for sessions once a week or once a month should receive **outpatient treatment**. Outpatient treatment allows clients to retain privacy regarding treatment while learning how to cope in their usual environment. The options for outpatient treatment include short- and long-term counseling and individual, group, or family therapy. Typically, clients who are referred to outpatient treatment show more motivation to change and will show signs of being able to commit to this level of treatment. Outpatient treatment is acceptable for clients who suffer from disorders such as depression or anxiety. Occasionally, after inpatient treatment, patients will need to maintain treatment in an outpatient setting.

Referring Clients to Others for Concurrent Treatment

Counselors sometimes work concurrently with other providers of mental health services. One of the most common examples is when counselors work with psychiatrists. If a counselor believes that their client is not making sufficient improvement or their symptoms are worsening, they can refer the client to a psychiatrist for medication evaluation while continuing to counsel the client.

Counselors can also refer their clients to another counselor if the client desires another type of therapy (e.g., marriage counseling). In such cases, individual counselors may maintain communication with the other counselor, but they are not required to do so. The level of collaboration with other mental health providers should always be done with the client's best interests in mind.

Termination Process and Issues
An important part of treatment planning is discharge planning. There are numerous reasons that services for a client may end. Clients may feel that they no longer need the services, that they are not compatible with the counselor providing the services, that an increased level of care is needed that is beyond the scope of the counselor, or they may have successfully met goals for treatment.

Discharge planning should begin with the onset of the initial assessment for the client. The counselor should not delay discharge planning, as discharge may occur at any time. Making the client aware of the choices for discharge and the discharge planning process empowers the client during treatment. It also provides continuity of care for the client.

The main purpose of **discharge planning** is to develop a plan of care that goes beyond the current treatment sessions to promote success once services have concluded. In the event the client is going to a higher level of care or to a different professional, effective discharge planning is useful in disseminating pertinent information about the client to assist in continuity of care and effective treatment. In this sense, the current counselor should prepare to become a collateral source linked to the client's level of care for the next professional.

In addition to benefitting the other counselors the client may meet with, effective discharge planning is a benefit to the client as well. If services have been completed successfully and the client has met the stated goals, then discharge planning ensures the client has a plan to sustain a stable level of function and maintain the successes achieved. This is particularly useful with clients who suffer from substance use or other addictive behaviors, as effective discharge planning can prevent relapse.

Upon the conclusion of the client discharging from services, a discharge summary should be created and placed in the client's file. The *discharge summary* should include the following information:

- Reason for discharge
- Description of treatment goals and the degree to which they were met
- Client's response to the interventions
- Description of the client's levels of functioning
- Baseline
- Progress during treatment
- Functioning at discharge
- Recommendations for follow-up care
- Links to community resources
- Appointment dates for other providers (if available)
- Provision of additional contacts, client supports
- Description of potential risks post-discharge
- Contact information for post-discharge support and crisis intervention

Needs Assessments

Often the urgency of immediate client services takes precedence over program evaluation, but evaluation is a necessary step in ensuring that an organization provides effective and affordable services for clients. Program evaluation can be conducted during the formative stage of a program, in order to establish the best objectives and methods, but it can also be summative, evaluating outcomes of the program at a later stage. Summative evaluations can be used to determine what changes should be made or even if the program should continue.

Needs assessments, which explore the needs of constituents or clients, play a pivotal role in developing programs. Needs assessments provide evidence for the necessity of a program trying to obtain funding and measure program usefulness. **Cost-effectiveness** looks at whether programs are being conducted in a way that makes the best use of the available money. **Cost-benefit analysis** is a process of comparing the beneficial outcomes of a program to the amount of money spent on them to see if the benefits are worth the cost. Both of these cost-related aspects of program evaluation are important, especially for grant proposals. Ultimately, program evaluation seeks to do outcomes assessments, something frequently requested by funding agencies. **Outcomes assessments** look at the program's effectiveness at meeting its objectives and in making the expected changes.

Outcome Measures for Counseling Programs

Client progress may be measured using a quantitative or qualitative approach used in research. Quantitative measures relate to the rate of occurrence or severity of a behavior or problem. When performing quantitative evaluation, first establish a baseline, which is a measurement of the target problem, prior to intervention. Qualitative measures are more subjective and reflective of the client's experience (information is gathered largely from observation and different forms of interviewing) and provide a view of whether progress is being made.

Evaluation of Counseling Interventions and Programs

There are several techniques to evaluate client progress, including self-reporting by the client, quantitative measures that are collaboratively discussed by the social worker and the client, and narrative approaches that utilize a textual basis for describing progress. Social workers may ask client scaling questions to measure client mood and/or progress. Client progress should be measured at regular intervals in order to assist with treatment planning and intervention efficacy. Clients should be informed of progress, and social workers should develop progress notes to reflect client progress. Social workers need to be aware of client progress and compliance in order to accurately measure the steps the client is taking to move forward.

Using Assessment Instrument Results to Facilitate Client Decision-Making

Psychometric assessment tools can provide valuable pieces of information. Many assessment tools are available for free, while others must be purchased. **Assessment tools** often come with rating scales that indicate the level of training needed to interpret the results. Assessment instruments can be used at the beginning of treatment to help counselors make diagnostic decisions. Counselors can also have clients take personality assessments, which can provide them with information about the best ways to work with their clients. Some counselors use a battery of tests that provide them with multifaceted views of their clients' disorders and personality structures. Assessment tools can also be used throughout counseling to give counselors feedback on the effectiveness of their treatment methods. If the testing

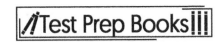

devices indicate that a client's symptoms are remaining the same or worsening, then counselors might consider changing their treatment plans.

Qualitative, Quantitative, and Mixed Research Methods

Non-Experimental Quantitative Research

Quantitative research utilizes logical, empirical methods of collecting information. This information is called data and is often analyzed using statistics. **Non-experimental quantitative research** includes forms of data collection where the researcher collects data that's already available in some form. They then analyze this dataset to describe the relationship between pre-determined variables. The researcher does not set up a novel system of trials to produce new data, and they can't randomize any data collected. The researcher has no part in manipulating any variables or establishing a separate control group to which they can compare collected data. The lack of a control group, lack of variable manipulation by the researcher, and lack of randomization are often seen as weaknesses in non-experimental quantitative research studies. Some examples of non-experimental quantitative research designs are depicted below:

- **Survey Designs**: These can be conducted through telephone or face-to-face interviews. They can also be conducted through paper or electronic questionnaires (either at an external facility or at the study participant's home). Survey designs are generally used when research about a particular topic is limited so that more information can be gathered to better shape the research question or topic. Surveys are easy (and usually cost-efficient) to administer, but they can also result in low or biased participant response rates.

Correlational Designs: These analyze the strength of the relationship between two variables in one group. One unique type of correlational design is found in ex post facto studies. The researcher examines two existing groups and analyzes the correlation between the variables of interest. Another unique type of correlational design is found in prediction studies, where the researcher determines a correlation between variables and then uses it to predict other correlations, related events, or future events. The strength and description of the correlation is indicated by the correlation coefficient (r), which falls between -1 and 1. If $r = 0$, it indicates there's no relationship between the two variables, while $r = 1$ indicates a direct, perfect correlation. If r equals a negative value, it indicates an inverse relationship between the two variables. If r equals a positive value, it indicates a direct relationship between the two variables. Regardless of how strong the correlation is between two variables, it doesn't indicate that one causes the other. It simply indicates that these two variables tend to occur (or not occur) together to some degree.

- **Comparative Designs**: These examine data trends to determine a relationship in two groups or datasets that have already been established.

Qualitative Research

Qualitative research is commonly employed in social sciences, including the field of counseling. It typically focuses on the analysis of a group of people (which is sometimes biased) to understand different aspects of human behavior, relationships, and social interactions. The researcher does not manipulate variables when conducting qualitative research. Qualitative research is primarily conducted without rigid structures in place. Data is collected through the following:

- **Case Studies**: These are detailed and documented examples of the topic of interest. They can be real or hypothetical situations. Case studies often record data over a period of time to examine

149

a specific variable of interest. They can examine a situation involving one individual, a family, a larger community of people, or an organization. Case studies frequently look at how people relate to one another and/or to their physical or emotional environment.

- **Focus Groups**: These bring together a relatively small group of individuals. The group can be diverse in nature or have many similar interests. A facilitator guides a discussion within the group to discern information about individual or collective viewpoints about a specific issue.

- **Interviews**: These are typically more personal in nature. Interviews can be conducted in person, over the telephone, or via e-mail or regular mail. The interviewer asks the individual or group a series of meaningful questions related to the research topic. The interview can be structured with the interviewer having pre-set questions to ask, or it can be unstructured with the interviewer asking questions based on the flow of conversation and the answers given by the interviewee(s).

- **Observation**: In an observation, the researcher simply watches the individual or group of interest. However, a number of additional factors usually shapes the development of the observation study. The researcher can observe the participant(s) in a specific situation or highly controlled context, or the researcher can observe the participant(s) in their day-to-day routine. The participant(s) may or may not know that they are being observed for specific behaviors. The researcher can involve themselves in the context and become part of the observation study. The researcher can also freely write down data from the observations or use a pre-made scale or data sheet to document specific behaviors.

Experimental and Quasi-Experimental Quantitative Research

Experimental quantitative research employs highly controlled processes with the hope of determining a causal relationship between one or more input (independent) variables and one or more outcome (dependent) variables. It uses random sampling and assignment methods to make inferences for larger populations. Typically, it compares a control group (serving as a baseline) to a test group. Ideally, experimental studies or experiments should be able to be replicated numerous times with the same results. The ultimate goal of a well-designed experiment is to declare that a particular variable is responsible for a particular outcome and that, without that variable, the associated outcome wouldn't occur.

Quasi-experimental quantitative research employs many of these same qualities, but it often doesn't use random sampling or assignment in its studies or experiments. Consequently, quasi-experimental research produces results that often don't apply to the population at large. They do, however, often provide meaningful results for certain subgroups of the population.

Designs Used in Research and Program Evaluation

Identifying Strengths That Improve Likelihood of Goal Attainment

Goals can take the form of **SMART goals**, which are specific, measurable, achievable, relevant, and time-bound. **Specific** means detailing why you want to accomplish the goal, what specifically there is to accomplish, who is involved, the setting for the goal, and what kind of resources are involved. **Measurable** means designating a system of tracking your goals in order to stay motivated. **Achievable** is making sure that the goal is realistic, such as looking at financial factors or other limitations. **Relevant** means making sure it's the right time for the goal, if it matches your needs, or if the goal seems worthwhile to pursue. Finally, **time-bound** is developing a target date so that there is a clear deadline to

focus on. A client's strengths should also be identified and recognized when the goal is set, as this will help the client feel empowered in the attainment of the goal.

Creating SMART objectives allows for data-driven and measurable intervention plans. When creating objectives, counselors should be able to measure the desired behavior that is exhibited, the number of times the desired behavior is exhibited over a period of time, the conditions in which the desired behavior must be exhibited, and progress from the undesired behavior to the desired behavior through baseline evaluation and evaluation at pre-determined intervals.

Statistical Methods Used in Conducting Research and Program Evaluation

Simply defined, **research** means to systematically investigate an experience either to understand what causes it or to develop a theory about how that experience can cause a future event. Systematic investigation can occur through a number of different scientific methods. **Deductive research** focuses on a specific theory and then establishes hypotheses to methodically test the theory in order to support or discredit it. Deductive research often involves setting up experiments, trials, or data collection surveys to collect information related to the theory. **Inductive research** examines information that's already available (such as established datasets like the U.S. Census Report) to highlight data trends and make inferences and/or projections from those patterns. **Research designs** determine how to structure a study based on factors such as variables being tested, the level to which the researcher is manipulating a variable in the study, the types of subjects in the study, what the study is testing or looking for, the frequency and duration of data collection, and whether the data collected is qualitative or quantitative in nature.

Analysis and Use of Data in Counseling

External Validity
External validity illustrates how well inferences from a sample set can predict similar inferences in a larger population (i.e., can results in a controlled lab setting hold true when replicated in the real world). A sample set with strong external validity allows the researcher to generalize or, in other words, to make strongly supported assumptions about a larger group. For a sample to have strong external validity, it needs to have similar characteristics and context to the larger population about which the researcher is hoping to make inferences. A researcher typically wants to generalize three areas:

- Population: Can inferences from the sample set hold true to a larger group of people beyond the specific people in the sample?

- Environment: Can inferences from the sample set hold true in settings beyond the specific one used in the study?

- Time: Can inferences from the sample set hold true in any season or temporal period?

If results from the sample set can't hold true across these three areas, the external validity of the study is considered threatened or weak. External validity is strengthened by the number of study replications the researcher is able to successfully complete for multiple settings, groups, and contexts. External validity can also be strengthened by ensuring the sample set is as randomized as possible.

Research and Program Evaluation

Internal Validity
Internal validity illustrates the integrity of the results obtained from a sample set and indicates how reliably a specific study or intervention was conducted. Strong internal validity allows the researcher to confidently link a specific variable or process of the study to the results or outcomes. The strength of a study's internal validity can be threatened by the presence of many independent variables. This can result in confounding, where it's difficult to pinpoint exactly what is causing the changes in the dependent variables. The internal validity can also be threatened by biases (sampling bias, researcher bias, or participant bias) as well as historical, personal, and/or contextual influences outside the researcher's control (natural disasters, political unrest, participant death, or relocation). Internal validity can be strengthened by designing highly controlled study or experiment settings that limit these threats.

Sampling
Sampling is the method of collecting participants for a study. It's a crucial component of the research design and study process. There are a number of different ways to select samples, and each method has pros, cons, and situations where it's the most appropriate one to use.

Simple Random Sampling
For this type of probability sampling, the participants are taken directly from a larger population with the characteristics of interest. Each individual in the larger population has the same chance of being selected for the sample.

- Pros: closely represents the target population, thus allowing for results that are the highest in validity

- Cons: obtaining the sample can be time consuming

- Use When: a highly controlled experiment setting is necessary

Stratified Random Sampling
For this type of probability sampling, the researchers first examine the traits of the larger population, which are often demographic or social traits like age, education status, marital status, and household income. They then divide the population into groups (or strata) based on these traits. Members of the population are only included in one stratum. Researchers then randomly sample across each stratum to create the final sample set for the study.

- Pros: closely represents the target population, which allows for results that are highest in validity. Since the sampling method is so specific, researchers are able to use smaller samples.

- Cons: obtaining the sample can be tedious. Researchers may first need to compile and become acutely knowledgeable about the demographic characteristics of the target population before selecting a representative sample.

- Use When: a highly controlled experiment setting is necessary; demographic, social, and/or economic characteristics of the target population are of special interest in the study; or researchers are studying relationships or interactions between two subsets within the larger population

This material is provided for exam preparation purposes only and does not indicate an endorsement of any specific scientific, political, or religious point of view. © TPB Publishing. You have been licensed one copy of this document for personal use only. Any other reproduction or redistribution is strictly prohibited. All rights reserved.

Systematic Random Sampling

For this type of probability sampling, researchers pick a random integer (n), and then select every *n*th person from the target population for the research sample.

- Pros: a simple, cost-effective sampling technique that generally provides a random sample for the researchers. It ensures that sampling occurs evenly throughout an entire target population.

- Cons: researchers need to ensure that their original target population (from which the sample is selected) is randomized and that every individual has an equal probability of being selected. Researchers need to be familiar with the demographics of the target population to ensure that certain trends don't appear across the selected participants and skew the results.

- Use When: a highly controlled experiment setting is necessary; researchers are short on time or funding and need a quick, cost-efficient method to create a random sample

Convenience Sampling

This is a type of non-probability sampling where researchers select participants who are easily accessible due to factors like location, expense, or volunteer recruitment.

- Pros: saves time and is cost-effective since researchers can create their sample based on what permits the easiest and fastest recruiting of participants

- Cons: highly prone to bias. It's difficult to generalize the results for the population at large since the sample selection is not random.

- Use When: conducting initial trials of a new study, when researchers are simply looking for basic information about the larger population (i.e., to create a more detailed hypothesis for future research)

Ad Hoc Sample

For this type of non-probability sampling, researchers must meet a set quota for a certain characteristic and can recruit any participant as long as they have the desired characteristics.

- Pros: allows for greater inclusion of a population that might not otherwise be represented

- Cons: results won't be indicative of the actual population in an area

- Use When: it's necessary that a group within the larger population needs a set level of representation within the study

Purposive Sampling

Another non-probability sampling method used when researchers have a precise purpose or target population in mind.

- Pros: helps increase recruitment numbers in otherwise hard-to-access populations

- Cons: usually unable to generalize the results to larger populations beyond the sample's specific subset

- Use When: researchers have a precise purpose for the study, or a specific group of participants is required that isn't easy to select through probability sampling methods

Levels of Measurement

Levels of measurement describe the type of data collected during a study or experiment.

- **Nominal**: This measurement describes variables that are categories (e.g., gender, dominant hand, height).

Ordinal: This measurement describes variables that can be ranked (e.g., Likert scales, 1 to 10 rating scales).

- **Interval**: This measurement describes variables that use equally spaced intervals (e.g., number of minutes, temperature).

- **Ratio**: This measurement describes anything that has a true "zero" point available (e.g., angles, dollars, cents).

Independent and Dependent Variables and Type I and Type II Errors

A **variable** is one factor in a study or experiment. An **independent variable** is controlled by the researcher and usually influences the **dependent variable** (the factor that's typically measured and recorded by the researcher).

In experiments, the researcher declares a hypothesis that a relationship doesn't exist between two variables, groups, or tangible instances. This hypothesis is referred to as the **null hypothesis**. Errors can be made in accepting or rejecting the null hypothesis based on the outcomes of the experiment. If the researcher rejects the null hypothesis when it's actually true, this is known as a type I error. A **type I error** indicates that a relationship between two variable exists when, in reality, it doesn't. If the researcher fails to reject the null hypothesis when it's actually false, this is known as a type II error. A **type II error** indicates that a relationship between two variables doesn't exist when, in reality, it does. These errors typically result when the experiment or study has weak internal validity.

T-Test

A **t-test** is a statistical testing method used to determine the probability that, when comparing two separate sample sets with different means, the difference in the means is statistically significant. In other words, researchers can infer that the same difference will be found between the same two groups in the target population as opposed to only being found between the two specific sample sets. Usually the t-test is only used when the data sets have normal distributions and low standard deviations. The calculated t-test statistic corresponds to a table of probability values. These values indicate the likelihood that the difference between groups is simply due to chance. Traditionally, if the t-test statistic corresponds with less than a 5 percent probability that the differences between the two data sets are by

chance, then researchers can assume that there's a statistically significant difference between the two sample sets.

Forms of Hypothesis
A hypothesis typically takes one of two forms:

- **Null Hypothesis**: declares there is no relationship between two variables
- **Alternative Hypothesis**: declares a specific relationship between two variables, or simply states that the null hypothesis is rejected

Analyses of Variance
Variance tests examine the means of two or more sample sets to detect statistically significant differences in the samples. **Analyses of variance tests** (commonly referred to as **ANOVA** tests) are more efficient and accurate than t-tests when there are more than two sample sets. There are multiple types of ANOVA tests. One-way ANOVA tests are used when there's only one factor of influence across the sample sets. Consequently, two- and three-way ANOVA tests exist and are used in the case of additional factors. ANOVA tests can also analyze differences in sample sets where there are multiple dependent and independent variables.

ANOVA tests work by creating ratios of variances between and within the sample sets to determine whether the differences are statistically significant. Calculating these ratios is fairly tedious, and researchers generally use statistical software packages such as SPSS, SAS, or Minitab to input the data sets and run the calculations. SPSS stands for Statistical Package for the Social Science and is one of the most popular packages that performs complex data manipulation with easy instructions. SAS stands for **Statistical Analysis System** and is a software developed for advanced analytics, data management, business intelligence, multivariate analyses, and predictive analytics. **Minitab** is an all-purpose statistical software created for simple interactive use.

Analyses of Covariance
This analysis is a type of ANOVA. This analysis is used to control for potential confounding variables and is commonly referred to as **ANCOVA**. Say a researcher is testing the effect of classical music on elementary students' ability to solve math problems. If the students being tested are in varying grades, then their grade level must be taken into account. This is because math ability generally increases with grade level. ANCOVA provides a way to measure and remove the skewing effects of grade level in order to better understand the correlation that's being tested.

Chi-Square and Bivariate Tabular Analysis
Similar to statistical testing methods like t-tests and ANOVA tests, a **chi-square test** analyzes data between independent groups. However, chi-square tests focus on variables that have categorical data rather than numerical data. They can only be run on data with whole integer tallies or counts, and they're typically used when a researcher has large, normally distributed, and unpaired sample sets.

Bivariate tabular analysis is a basic form of analysis used when the value of an independent variable is known to predict an exact value for the dependent variable. This is most commonly illustrated by a traditional XY plot graph that marks independent variable (X) values across the horizontal axis, and marks dependent variable (Y) values along the vertical axis. Once all of the values are plotted, a relationship (or lack thereof) can be seen between the independent and dependent variables.

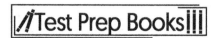

Post Hoc and Nonparametric Tests

Post hoc tests are usually performed after running other tests (e.g., t-tests or ANOVA tests) where it's been determined that statistically significant differences exist between two or more sample sets. At this point, researchers can pick and choose specific groups between which to analyze similarities or differences. Some common post hoc tests are the Least Significant Difference test, Tukey's test, and confidence interval tests, which are often similar to running multiple t-tests. Post hoc tests can be complex and time-consuming to calculate by hand or with simple software, so they often must be completed using sophisticated statistical software packages.

Nonparametric tests are typically used when datasets don't have pre-set parameters, are skewed in distribution, include outliers, or are unconventional in some other way. As a result, nonparametric tests are less likely to be valid in showing strong relationships, similarities, or when differences between groups exist. It's also easier to make a type I error when running nonparametric tests. Some common nonparametric tests include the Mood's Median test, the Kruskal-Wallis test, and the Mann-Whitney test.

Research Ethics

Research performed on living creatures, especially humans, is always scrutinized for ethical concerns. Such research often uses experiments for which the outcomes are unknown. Therefore, it is possible that any research performed on a person may have unintended, unwanted, or otherwise harmful psychological, physiological, emotional, or social effects. Research ethics are intended to protect participants, ensure that research is being conducted for some public benefits, and ensure that participants who are involved have been provided with informed consent. Informed consent involves explaining to an individual, in as much detail as possible, the processes of the experiment or study, all potential side effects or outcomes, and the opportunity to make an educated decision independently about participation in such a study. Informed consent also documents the fact that the participant may leave the study at any time. Informed consent paperwork is usually signed by the participants, the researcher, and an independent third party. Some controversy still exists over research that affects vulnerable populations, such as those with psychological disorders, the elderly, children, the poor, and others who cannot easily make objective decisions or could be persuaded by experiment incentives (such as gift cards or the like).

An **Institutional Review Board (IRB)** is any independent group that reviews research and clinical trial designs that have human participants to ensure there are no potential ethical violations. IRBs are accredited by the US Food and Drug Administration. These groups can request changes, additions, and eliminations to any study proposal; they can also completely deny a proposal for approval. Without IRB approval, research designs cannot come to the experiment phase. While research is in session, IRB committees conduct regular audits to ensure compliance is still intact. Noncompliance can result in heavy fines, penalties, criminal investigation, and termination of a study.

Practice Quiz

1. Which of the following is a popular statistical software program?
   a. SPSS
   b. SAS
   c. Minitab
   d. All of the above

2. Fluid Intelligence refers to what type of abilities?
   a. Thinking and acting quickly, solving new problems
   b. Utilizing learned skills
   c. Adapting to new situations
   d. Developing opportunity from adversity

3. Tina is conducting a research study about underage drinking habits on college campuses on football game days. As she's scoring her collected data, she notices the test group is primarily made up of freshman students and the control group is primarily made up of sophomore students. What does Tina realize about this distinction?
   a. It's to be expected.
   b. It may confound her results.
   c. It won't make a difference if she runs enough ANOVA tests.
   d. It should be tabulated in a chi-square cross section.

4. A study is considered to have strong external validity if the researcher can replicate and generalize its findings across multiple instances of what three factors?
   a. Population, time, and environment
   b. Gender, age, and height
   c. Animal studies, human studies, and non-living object studies
   d. Infant years, adolescent years, and adult years

5. A researcher is grouping participants into sample sets by gender. In this instance, gender is an example of what type of measure?
   a. Interval
   b. Nominal
   c. Ordinal
   d. Ratio

See answers on next page

157

Answer Explanations

1. D: All of the above. SPSS, SAS, and Minitab are all popular statistical software programs. These programs make it easier to analyze and run tests on large datasets. Choice *A*, SPSS, stands for Statistical Package for the Social Science and is one of the most popular packages that performs complex data manipulation with easy instructions. Choice *B*, SAS, stands for Statistical Analysis System, and is a software developed for advanced analytics, data management, business intelligence, multivariate analyses, and predictive analytics. Choice *C*, Minitab, is an all-purpose statistical software created for simple interactive use.

2. A: Fluid intelligence refers to the ability to think and act quickly and solve new problems. It is independent of education and culture, making the other choices incorrect.

3. B: Tina realizes that this distinction may confound her results. Confounding occurs when any results found correlate with multiple variables, therefore preventing a clear correlation between a particular independent variable and a particular dependent variable. In this instance, the fact that a majority of the test group and control group are each made up of a particular year of students may influence the presence of any habits that Tina is trying to study.

4. A: Population, time and environment. If a research design can produce the same outcomes across multiple types of people, multiple seasons or temporal periods, and across a variety of settings and situational contexts, it is considered to have high external validity. Any results are likely generalizable to the target population.

5. B: In this case, gender is an example of a nominal measure. A nominal measure describes variables that are categorical in nature. An interval measure, Choice *A*, describes variables that use equally spaced intervals (e.g., number of minutes, temperature). An ordinal measure, Choice *C*, describes variables that can be ranked (e.g., Likert scales, 1 to 10 rating scales). A ratio measure, Choice *D*, describes anything that has a true "zero" point available (e.g., angles, dollars, cents).

Practice Test #1

1. When working with a client who has a phobia, a counselor should NOT encourage the client to do which of the following?
    a. Talk about why they fear the object or situation
    b. Progressively face the feared object or situation
    c. Avoid the feared object or situation
    d. Practice deep breathing

2. Which of the following refers to the perspective someone holds about society on a domestic and global scale?
    a. Worldview
    b. Cultural Encapsulation
    c. Ethnicity
    d. Ethnocentrism

3. What entity was responsible for supporting and expanding professional counseling services?
    a. The first mental health clinic in the United States
    b. The United States Department of Veterans Affairs
    c. The United States Army
    d. Carl Rogers' first privately funded organization

4. A counselor is teaching her client about gender differences that are evident in young preschool children's language skills. This is an example of which of the following?
    a. Racism
    b. Gender bias
    c. Psychoeducation
    d. Shaping

5. A counselor is working with a married couple. Often, the husband speaks to his wife in a demeaning tone, moves his body aggressively toward her, looks down at her, and speaks loudly. The counselor demonstrates for the husband a different way to speak to his wife. This is an example of which of the following?
    a. Negative feedback loop
    b. Overstepping the husband's boundaries
    c. Confrontation
    d. Building communication skills

6. Some issues that adults over sixty face and may want to discuss in counseling include what?
    a. Bereavement, ageism in the workforce, and unemployment
    b. The Millennial generation, religion, and politics
    c. Sagging skin, hair loss, and cancer
    d. None of the above

159

7. A counselor has spent several months working with a woman who was initially diagnosed with anxiety. Her symptoms have greatly improved, and the counselor can see that the end of treatment is approaching. What would be the least appropriate action for the counselor to take?
   a. Have a discussion with the client about her progress and inform her that treatment is about to end
   b. Ask the client if she has any other issues that she would like to address
   c. Avoid talking about the end of treatment to prevent the client's anxiety from returning
   d. Discuss how ending the counseling relationship may cause feelings of sadness or fear

8. When determining whether to give a diagnosis of enuresis or encopresis, the counselor should consider which of the following?
   a. Chronological age
   b. Whether the symptoms are voluntary or involuntary
   c. Developmental age
   d. Whether the symptoms occur during the day or night

9. Harry Harlow noticed that monkeys who did not receive consistent warmth or affection from a maternal figure were more likely to be which of the following?
   a. Less warm or affectionate to their own offspring
   b. Aloof and/or angry
   c. Socially impaired
   d. All of the above

10. Which of the following is a reason clients may terminate group counseling?
   a. A reduction in primary symptoms
   b. Regression of goal achievement
   c. Dependent coping
   d. An independent decision by a group leader

11. A 65-year-old male counselor is working with a 25-year-old male client. When the client comes to sessions, he is often short-tempered. Which of the following would be the most beneficial to the client?
   a. The counselor talks with the client about his short temper.
   b. The counselor overlooks the client's tone in an effort not to break the therapeutic bond.
   c. The counselor angrily replies to the client to demonstrate what it feels like to be treated in that manner.
   d. The counselor refers the client to another counselor.

12. A counselor has been working with a client for the past nine months. The counselor first diagnosed the client with major depressive disorder after administering the Beck Depression Inventory (BDI) that resulted in a high score for depression. Three months into treatment, the BDI was administered again, and the client's symptoms were unchanged. In the ninth month of treatment, the BDI was administered again, and at that time showed slight improvement in the client's symptoms. What would the counselor most likely conclude from these test results?
   a. The client was faking symptoms at the initial assessment.
   b. The BDI is an untrustworthy assessment tool because of its inconsistent results.
   c. The client should be referred to another counselor because he is not making adequate improvement and the counselor is concerned about suicide risk.
   d. The treatment may be working, but alterations to the treatment plan may be needed.

13. The cycle of violence follows which of the following sequences?
   a. Honeymoon, explanation, tension building
   b. Tension building, honeymoon, explanation
   c. Explosion, honeymoon, reunification
   d. Tension building, explosion, honeymoon

14. A counselor who has been working with an anorexic client arranges a session to discuss treatment progress. Which of the following would be the least beneficial in helping the client move toward her treatment goals?
   a. Asking the client to show the counselor her personal journal
   b. Showing the client her pre-treatment, mid-treatment, and current psychometric assessment scores
   c. Asking the client to bring her recent medical tests for discussion
   d. Asking the client if her family relationships are improving or declining

15. What is the main concern of a counselor when their client shows signs of hopelessness?
   a. The client may be suicidal.
   b. The treatment has been ineffective.
   c. The client needs a referral for medication.
   d. The client is depressed.

16. A counselor is working with a family and observes that whenever the father belittles the mother, the adolescent son corrects the father. This is an example of which of the following?
   a. Electra Complex
   b. Parentification
   c. Paradoxical Intervention
   d. Motivational Interviewing

17. During an initial interview, counselors should ask questions pertaining to which of the following realms?
   a. Work, rest, play
   b. Scholastic, interpersonal, medical
   c. Biological, social, psychological
   d. Psychological, occupational, social

18. What occurs during the pre-group preparation phase of group therapy?
   a. Informed consent is obtained, previous group experiences are discussed, and group members learn about each other's diagnoses.
   b. Alliance with the leader is established, informed consent is obtained, and client goals and limits of confidentiality are discussed.
   c. Informed consent is obtained, limits of confidentiality are discussed, and group members learn about each other's diagnoses.
   d. A waiver of confidentiality is signed and the leader's role and client goals are discussed.

19. Which of the following indicates that a client is at high risk for suicide?
   a. The client has attempted suicide previously.
   b. The client is thinking about suicide but has no definite plan.
   c. The client has been diagnosed with depression.
   d. The client does not have a healthy support system.

20. A type II error _____ a _____ null hypothesis.
    a. Rejects; true
    b. Rejects; false
    c. Fails to reject; true
    d. Fails to reject; false

21. In what year did the ACA launch the National Board for Certified Counselors?
    a. 1963
    b. 1973
    c. 1983
    d. 1993

22. What is the approximate rate of divorce for second marriages in the United States?
    a. 65 percent
    b. 35 percent
    c. 50 percent
    d. 85 percent

23. Counselors can help clients learn how to handle their negative emotions in a healthy way by having them acknowledge the emotions for what they are and then teaching them how to gain personal distance from the emotions so that they are not controlled by them. This technique is known as which of the following?
    a. Cognitive defusion
    b. Psychogenic fugue
    c. Enmeshment
    d. Differentiation

24. According to Erikson's psychosocial model of development, what is the main task during the Generativity vs. Stagnation stage?
    a. Learning to trust others
    b. Finding oneself
    c. Contributing to the next generation
    d. Developing self-sufficiency

25. Which of the following is a holistic model that helps clients focus on the present and work toward personal growth and balance?
    a. Gestalt
    b. Person-centered
    c. Rational Emotive
    d. Jungian

26. If a client reports that she has been eating soap for the past two months, the counselor should consider which of the following?
    a. Admitting the client to a hospital
    b. Diagnosing the client with pica
    c. Sending the client for a brain scan
    d. Diagnosing the client with anorexia nervosa

27. What are groups called that provide guidance, problem prevention, and skills building?
    a. Psychoeducational
    b. Structured
    c. Gestalt
    d. Psychodynamic

28. When does negative transference occur?
    a. When counselors project feelings onto clients
    b. When clients project feelings toward another person in the past onto the counselor
    c. When multiple roles exist between a therapist and a client
    d. When clients become angry or hostile toward counselors

29. Which of the following is a symptom of schizophrenia?
    a. Multiple personalities present in one individual
    b. Hallucinations
    c. Sleep walking
    d. Night terrors

30. A student receives daily threats from a classmate via text messages. Which of the following defines this kind of bullying?
    a. Cyberbullying
    b. Physical bullying
    c. Relational bullying
    d. Group bullying

31. A 30-year-old client calls his counselor at 8:00 p.m. indicating that she is "at her wit's end." Upon further probing, the counselor learns that the client has a gun in her home, has thoughts of killing herself, and is feeling hopeless. The client lives alone. Which of the following would NOT be an acceptable step for the counselor to take?
    a. Call the police and give them the client's name, address, and phone number
    b. Call the client's neighbor and ask him to check on the client
    c. Ask the client to drive to the nearest hospital for an evaluation
    d. Call the client's fiancé who has come to counseling on several occasions

32. One fundamental difference between probability sampling and non-probability sampling is that probability sampling uses _____ while non-probability sampling does not.
    a. Convenience
    b. Randomization
    c. Volunteerism
    d. Referral

33. Which of the following statements regarding sexual dysfunction is true?
    a. Sexual dysfunction only occurs during the orgasm phase.
    b. Sexual dysfunction is a medical problem, and the client should be referred to a physician.
    c. Sexual dysfunction only occurs in 10 percent of the population.
    d. Sexual dysfunction can occur during any of the four phases of the sexual response cycle.

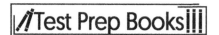

34. Social workers strive to consider cultural impact on individual values. How should cultural differences and values be addressed?
   a. Cultural values and differences should be pointed out so that the client knows the social worker is aware of them.
   b. Cultural values and differences should be learned by the social worker and worked around when issues arise.
   c. Cultural values and differences should be learned by the social worker and used as strengths and to empower change.
   d. Cultural values and differences should be compared to the greater society to find similarities.

35. Blocking refers to what type of act in group counseling?
   a. Leader putting a stop to negative behavior
   b. Members being disruptive to process
   c. Leader locking the door to prevent members from exiting
   d. Existing members not welcoming new members to group

36. Joe's parents divorced when he was six years old, and his father moved out of the house. He is now receiving therapy and has become very angry with his male therapist, fearing the therapist will abandon him. Joe's reaction is an example of what?
   a. Remorse
   b. Fixation
   c. Negative reinforcement
   d. Transference

37. A client starts to consume an addictive substance more frequently after seeing a counselor for several months. The counselor should consider referring the client to a residential treatment facility if:
   a. the client is unable to perform their daily responsibilities.
   b. the client's family members keep contacting the counselor about the excessive consumption.
   c. the client receives a DWI.
   d. the client does not want to attend Alcoholics or Narcotics Anonymous.

38. What is the main difference between Persistent Depressive Disorder and Major Depressive Disorder?
   a. Over/under eating
   b. Hallucinations
   c. Feelings of hopelessness
   d. The length of time that symptoms are present

39. Maslow's hierarchy of needs is composed of five levels. Which needs are included in Level 4?
   a. Cognitive and aesthetic
   b. Food and shelter
   c. Safety and order
   d. Love and belonging

40. When a person with schizophrenia believes that the world is going to come to an end by a tsunami, that belief would be considered which of the following?
    a. Persecutory delusion
    b. Nihilistic delusion
    c. Grandiose delusion
    d. Referential delusion

41. A counselor has been using Adlerian therapy with a client for several months to help her overcome shyness but has not made significant progress. At this time, what should the counselor do?
    a. Refer the client to a psychiatrist for medication evaluation
    b. Refer the client to another counselor
    c. Use the empty chair technique
    d. Consider using another treatment method

42. Which of the following is NOT a factor of a mental status exam?
    a. Orientation to time
    b. Whether the client is guarded or unguarded
    c. Appropriate displays of emotion
    d. Authenticity

43. Which of the following is an index that measures someone's ability to connect with others, develop relationships, and show empathy?
    a. Intelligence Quotient
    b. Emotional Quotient
    c. Emotional Achievement
    d. Emotional Handling

44. A counselor is working with a client who has difficulty making and keeping friends. The counselor gives the client feedback about his inappropriate statements at various times to teach him social skills. Which of the following would NOT be an appropriate tool/technique for the counselor to use?
    a. EMDR
    b. Modeling socially appropriate statements
    c. Role playing with the client
    d. Having the client watch a movie that demonstrates both appropriate and inappropriate social skills

45. The phrase "neurons that fire together, wire together" describes which of the following?
    a. The process of repetition by which neural pathways in the brain are formed
    b. The process by which memories are formed in the brain
    c. The process by which neurotransmitters send chemical messages from one to another
    d. The process by which nuclei of brain cells send chemical messages within the cell body

46. Which of the following is NOT a physical symptom of anxiety?
    a. Feeling the need to urinate
    b. Having trouble sleeping
    c. Feeling weak or tired
    d. Sweating

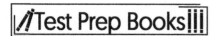

47. Claudia is coming to counseling for the first time. She meets her counselor, Susan, and Susan tells her what she can expect from treatment. Claudia says that she understands the process of counseling, as well as the risks, and that she is excited to begin. Susan makes a note of their discussion and begins her assessment. Has Susan satisfied the informed consent requirement, and why or why not?
   a. Yes. Susan discussed the process and risks of counseling, and the client agreed.
   b. No. Susan didn't ask Claudia if she understood everything fully.
   c. No. Susan did not have Claudia sign a consent form.
   d. Yes. Susan made a note that Claudia agreed as part of her documentation.

48. A small country like Denmark—where most people hold the same cultural beliefs, education status, dress, and traditions—is considered a/an _____; a larger country like the United States—where people come from many diverse backgrounds and many have emigrated from other countries—is considered a/an_____.
   a. Narrow country; broad country
   b. Ethnography; demography
   c. Homogenous society; heterogeneous society
   d. Heterogeneous society; homogenous society

49. Risky shift phenomenon refers to what aspects of group dynamics?
   a. Groups becoming increasingly risk-averse
   b. Groups become less risk-averse
   c. Leaders encouraging individual members to take risks
   d. Closed groups considering taking on new members

50. A young client who was adopted at age 12 has been skipping school, is verbally aggressive toward his adoptive parents, and does not follow house rules. The counselor should recognize that this may be occurring for which of the following reasons?
   a. The adoptive parents are setting house rules that are too strict.
   b. The client is going through a normal stage of development.
   c. Behavior issues are significantly more common in adopted children.
   d. The client is experiencing bullying at school.

51. A client tells her counselor, "I'm afraid that I'm going to die every time I have a panic attack. It feels like I'm having a heart attack." The counselor responds, "When you have a panic attack, you feel physical sensations in your heart that can make you feel like something is physically." This is an example of which of the following?
   a. Modeling
   b. Reflection
   c. Congruence
   d. Unconditional positive regard

52. What is one of the most important elements of an intake interview?
   a. Making an accurate diagnosis
   b. Obtaining a recent medical report from the client's doctor to rule out medical conditions that may masquerade as psychological conditions
   c. Asking open-ended questions
   d. Obtaining permission to break confidentiality if the client becomes suicidal

53. What are the main components of the Cognitive Information Processing (CIP) career development theory?
    a. Communication and Analysis
    b. Synthesis and Valuing
    c. Valuing and Executing
    d. Content and Process

54. Which of the following is another term for horizontal interventions in group counseling?
    a. Interpersonal
    b. Intrapersonal
    c. Individual
    d. Organizational

55. Positive interactions help develop the therapeutic relationship and encourage clients to meet their goals. What are the four stages of a positive interaction in counseling?
    a. Exploration, consolidation, planning, and termination
    b. Initiation, clarification, structure, and relationship
    c. Initiation, consolidation, planning, and termination
    d. Exploration, clarification, planning, and relationship

56. Client information is protected by confidentiality. However, in the instance where a client makes a threat against another individual during treatment, the social worker is required to warn the individual, thus breaking confidentiality. What court case established the duty to warn?
    a. *Tarasoff vs. Regents of University of California*
    b. *Regents of University of California vs. Bakke*
    c. *Blonder-Tongue vs. University of Illinois*
    d. *Fisher vs. University of Texas*

57. An individual leaves early for their commute to work to avoid traffic. This is an example of what?
    a. Modeling
    b. Negative reinforcement
    c. Positive reinforcement
    d. Classical conditioning

58. When parents disagree over a parenting issue, a counselor should instruct them to do all of the following EXCEPT:
    a. Disagree calmly in front of the child to display conflict resolution.
    b. Disagree in private where the child cannot hear what they are saying.
    c. Concede to each other at times.
    d. Set the issue aside until they can talk about it with the counselor at the next session.

59. During which stage of the transtheoretical model is the client most motivated to create change?
    a. Precontemplation stage
    b. Contemplation stage
    c. Preparation stage
    d. Maintenance stage

60. When performing a mental status examination, a counselor asks their client what she would do if she found a wallet with money inside. The counselor is assessing which of the following domains?
    a. Short-term memory
    b. Abstract reasoning
    c. Spatial orientation
    d. Judgment

61. Sixteen-year-old Jake is at his great-grandfather's 95th birthday party. Jake is talking with his great-grandparents, grandparents, parents, and siblings. Jake's great-grandparents, who have been married for over seventy years, believe couples should stick it out no matter what. Jake and his siblings believe most people will divorce once in their lifetimes. The grandparents believe divorce can usually be avoided, and the parents believe divorce is sometimes necessary. This is an example of which concept of the Murray Bowen's family systems theory?
    a. Differentiation of Self
    b. Family Projection Process
    c. Multigenerational Transmission Process
    d. Emotional Cutoff

62. A counselor believes that a client's relationship with her fiancé is worsening her depression because he is emotionally abusive. Which of the following would NOT be an appropriate action for the counselor to take?
    a. Tell the client to stop seeing her fiancé
    b. Help the client identify her fiancé's abusive treatment
    c. Have the client bring her fiancé to counseling
    d. Recommend a book about emotional abuse

63. Which of the following is a focus area when counseling adult clients with attention-deficit hyperactivity disorder (ADHD)?
    a. Depression
    b. Conflict resolution
    c. Group therapy
    d. Dependency

64. A male counselor is working with a group. One of the male group members has berated several of the other members at various times. On one occasion, the therapist yells at the belligerent group member to give feedback. Which of the following is true?
    a. If the group member and the counselor were both females, this would be appropriate.
    b. If the counselor was a female and the member was a male, this would be appropriate.
    c. This would be appropriate if it demonstrated protection of the group.
    d. This would never be appropriate.

65. The REACH model offers five steps to achieving forgiveness. Which of the following are components of that model?
    a. Remember, Expect, Acquiesce, Consider, Harbor
    b. Reflect, Examine, Acknowledge, Consider, Hold
    c. Recall, Excel, Accept, Count, Happiness
    d. Recall, Empathize, Altruistic Gift, Commit, Hold

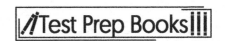

66. Under what conditions is it appropriate to discuss spiritual issues with clients?
    a. The client and the counselor are of the same faith.
    b. The client and the counselor do not attend the same church.
    c. The client and the counselor are of different faiths.
    d. The client has agreed to discuss spiritual issues in counseling.

67. In a group counseling session, the therapist asks, "Why didn't anyone say something about Samuel missing the last two meetings?" This is an example of which of the following?
    a. Giving interpersonal feedback
    b. Uncovering psychodynamic transference reactions
    c. Therapist transparency
    d. A therapist would not make this kind of remark.

68. At every level of professional development, it is important to continually participate in education opportunities. Why is this important to the values of counseling?
    a. Continuing education is necessary to maintain a level of competence in expertise areas that the counselor practices.
    b. Continuing education is required to maintain licensure, and licensure ensures that the counselor is regarded as a capable professional.
    c. Conferences and learning situations provide networking opportunities that can aid in interdisciplinary collaboration.
    d. Education is an ongoing personal journey.

69. A counselor is meeting with a client for the first time. After hearing the client describe multiple issues, what is the best course of action for the counselor to take?
    a. The counselor should ask the client what he would like the focus of treatment to be.
    b. The counselor should tell the client what the focus of treatment should be.
    c. The counselor should send the client to a psychiatrist for a medication evaluation.
    d. The counselor should send the client to a psychologist to run a battery of psychological assessments.

70. Which of the following is a reason client confidentiality may be breached without consent?
    a. A client expresses he wants to physically harm his partner.
    b. A client expresses feelings of sadness throughout the day.
    c. A client's friend calls the counselor to ask about the client's progress.
    d. The client states he wants to terminate treatment.

71. According to Murray Bowen's family systems theory, a strong sense of self is associated with _____, while a weak sense of self is associated with _____.
    a. Confidence and pragmatism; seeking approval from others
    b. Only children; many siblings
    c. Authoritative parenting styles; laissez-faire parenting styles
    d. Physical strength; physical weakness

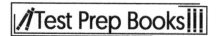
72. A counselor is working with a combat veteran who was recently discharged. Which of the following is NOT likely to be a symptom that the veteran would display?
    a. Nightmares
    b. Avoidance of people he/she cares about
    c. Angry outbursts
    d. Psychosis

73. What are the stages for Kubler-Ross' five-stage model for grief?
    a. Anger, denial, bargaining, resolution, sadness
    b. Denial, anger, bargaining, depression, acceptance
    c. Denial, panic, sadness, anger, frustration
    d. Sadness, anger, bargaining, denial, acceptance

74. If a counselor were to shame a client for disclosing hidden aspects of their life, the counselor would NOT be demonstrating which of the following?
    a. Congruence
    b. Unconditional positive regard
    c. Modeling
    d. Genuineness

75. Desensitization is a behavior modification technique designed to replace an anxiety-producing stimulus with a relaxation response. Which is NOT one of the stages of desensitization?
    a. Exposure to the object or action of fear
    b. Avoidance of the object or action of fear
    c. Creation of a fear hierarchy
    d. Learning relaxation techniques

76. Critical Incident Stress Debriefing (CISD) is short-term work done in small groups and is not considered psychotherapy. Techniques used include processing, defusing, ventilating, and validating thoughts, experiences, feeling and emotions. CISD is designed for which of the following?
    a. Primary trauma victims
    b. Human resources professionals
    c. First responders
    d. Secondary trauma victims

77. According to the Substance Abuse and Mental Health Services Administration (SAMHSA), all of the following are considered protective factors against suicide EXCEPT:
    a. Membership in a place of worship
    b. Intact marriage
    c. Attendance in a twelve-step group
    d. One year of sobriety

78. A counselor has been working with a female client who has bipolar disorder for several months. Upon seeing no improvement in her symptoms, the counselor reminds her that completing the homework assignments is akin to taking medication; if she does not comply, she will likely not get better. Under what condition would this be appropriate?
    a. The psychiatrist agrees with the counselor.
    b. The counselor believes that the client is not complying with the treatment directives.
    c. A counselor should not make a comparison between medication compliance and homework assignments.
    d. The treatment has been occurring for more than 6 months.

79. When conducting an initial interview, counselors should rely most heavily on which of the following when formulating a diagnosis?
    a. Socioeconomic status
    b. Cultural background
    c. Client's self-report of symptoms
    d. Psychometric assessments

80. One of the three main styles of leadership for managing a group is an autocratic leadership. What are autocratic leaders most likely to lead with?
    a. Consensus and belonging
    b. Little to no structure
    c. Empathy and goal setting
    d. Control and power

81. According to Erikson's stages of psychosocial development, in what stage is a five-year-old child?
    a. Initiative vs. Guilt
    b. Trust vs. Mistrust
    c. Autonomy vs. Shame and Doubt
    d. Identity vs. Confusion

82. Family units need guidance just as individuals do in dealing with problems and learning how to function more effectively. Which is NOT a goal of family therapy?
    a. Resolving intrapsychic conflicts
    b. Increasing effective communication
    c. Creating more effective patterns
    d. Improving overall functioning and stability

83. Counselors require feedback to gauge the effectiveness of therapy. Which of the following questionnaires is given to clients at the beginning of a counseling session?
    a. The Counselor Competencies Scale (CCS)
    b. The Session Rating Scale (SRS)
    c. The Outcome Rating Scale (ORS)
    d. The Group Session Rating Scale (GSRS)

171

84. Susan has been seeing a client, Christine, for about six months. Christine has three young children and a previous drug addiction. Susan suspects that Christine may be using again and decides to confront her at their session. When Christine arrives, she appears to be under the influence, and she has her two-year-old with her. Susan also notices that the two-year-old is covered in bruises. When she comments on the bruises, Christine becomes defensive. Christine has disclosed in the past that she sometimes gets so angry at her small children that she feels like she could beat them, but that she never would. What is the ethical concern?
    a.   Christine has disclosed past drug abuse and violent thoughts toward her children. Susan now suspects both are occurring, but she would have to break confidentiality to report her suspicions.
    b.   Christine may be on drugs again, but she's already been defensive with Susan, so it will be difficult for Susan to bring it up without damaging their relationship.
    c.   Christine has made disclosures in the past regarding drug use and also seems to need childcare so she can go to therapy. Susan knows a good babysitter who can help, but also knows that would be establishing a dual relationship.
    d.   Christine seems to be neglecting her children. Christine could possibly use education about parenting issues. Susan isn't sure if Christine would be open to a referral for parenting classes.

85. Under what conditions would it be inappropriate for a counselor to contact a client who was discharged from treatment six months ago?
    a.   The counselor cares about the client and wants to make sure they are still doing well.
    b.   The counselor remembers that the client had other issues that should be addressed.
    c.   It is the client's birthday.
    d.   It is the client's anniversary.

86. Which of the following is a method used in therapy to address sleep disorders?
    a.   Tell the client how many hours of sleep he or she should be getting.
    b.   Encourage the client to take a sleeping aid nightly.
    c.   Have the client keep a sleep diary.
    d.   Suggest the client change the sleep-wake schedule as needed.

87. Which of the following often leads to preconceived notions, stereotyping, and unsupported assumptions of others who come from different backgrounds?
    a.   Acculturation
    b.   Assimilation
    c.   Cultural encapsulation
    d.   Worldview

88. Symptoms of professional burnout consist of fatigue, headache, insomnia, depression, anxiety, or boredom, among others. When does burnout in counselors and helping professionals occur?
    a.   When countertransference is not managed
    b.   When counselors become desensitized to client issues
    c.   When counselors are overworked
    d.   When clients regularly cancel or don't show

89. A client has disclosed to his counselor that he has been secretly viewing pornography for years. The counselor can do all of the following EXCEPT:
   a. Encourage the client to speak with his wife about it.
   b. Call the client's wife and ask her to come with her husband to his next session, without revealing anything about the pornography in the phone call.
   c. Allow the client to withhold the information from everyone in his life.
   d. Demonstrate a non-judgmental attitude toward the client.

90. During the Strange Situation test, a counselor observes that the child becomes upset when the caregiver leaves the room and also avoids eye contact with strangers. What kind of attachment style does this behavior represent?
   a. Anxious-resistant insecure
   b. Depressed
   c. Secure
   d. Anxious-avoidant insecure

91. What do Yalom's stages of group development include?
   a. Forming, norming, storming, and performing
   b. Orientation, storming, working, and adjourning
   c. Orientation, conflict/dominance, and development of cohesiveness
   d. Initial, transition, working, and termination

92. A teenager receiving counseling for anger management discloses to the counselor that she is upset with her parents because they took away her car keys after she continually disobeyed curfew hours. What kind of technique can the counselor use to help the teenager understand the reasoning behind these actions?
   a. Cognitive reframing
   b. Reminiscence therapy
   c. Cognitive processing
   d. Ego state therapy

93. A counselor is working with a client who is talking to other people who are not present during the session. The client is likely having what experience?
   a. Auditory hallucinations
   b. Delusions of grandeur
   c. Dissociative fugue
   d. Depersonalization

94. Which of the following symptoms is NOT part of the diagnostic criteria for attention-deficit/hyperactivity disorder (ADHD)?
   a. Inability to pay attention to teachers
   b. Inability to focus on video games
   c. Inability to follow instructions from parents
   d. Inability to stay organized

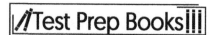

95. A practitioner is reviewing her appointment schedule and notices that her next client has a traditional Chinese name. The practitioner should assume _____.
   a. that the office translator will need to be present for the session and should be summoned immediately in order to ensure the client's comfort.
   b. that the client is an only child.
   c. that the client is male.
   d. nothing.

96. A marriage counselor is working with a couple experiencing a lot of conflict. The counselor encourages the couple to have arguments and yell at each other during the session so that he can analyze their conflict. This is an example of which of the following?
   a. Cognitive Behavioral Therapy for Marriage
   b. Gottman's Marriage Therapy
   c. Reality Therapy for Married Couples
   d. This is not part of any specific marriage therapy.

97. What is the most difficult part of forgiveness called?
   a. Emotional
   b. Decisional
   c. Situational
   d. Conditional

98. Which of the following needs to be considered when determining the usefulness of an evaluation tool?
   a. The cost of the test
   b. The technology used to administer the test
   c. The validity of the test
   d. The time it takes the client to take the test

99. In which of the following stages of the family life cycle might parents experience "Empty Nest Syndrome"?
   a. Independence
   b. Parenting
   c. Launching adult children
   d. Retirement

100. When a person who has been diagnosed with cyclothymia experiences a major depressive episode with no manic or hypomanic episodes, what change should be made to the diagnosis?
   a. The cyclothymia diagnosis is dropped, and the diagnosis is changed to major depressive disorder.
   b. The cyclothymia diagnosis is kept, and the secondary diagnosis of major depressive episode is added.
   c. The cyclothymia diagnosis is kept, and the primary diagnosis of major depressive episode is added.
   d. The cyclothymia diagnosis is kept, and the primary diagnosis of bipolar I is added.

101. Vertical interventions occur when the group leader focuses on which of the following?
    a. Individuals rather than the group
    b. The group rather than individuals
    c. Both the individuals and the larger group
    d. Group dynamics

102. Which of the following is unethical?
    a. Referring a client to another counselor because the counselor does not have the proper training to treat the client's issues
    b. Referring a client to another counselor because the counselor does not like the client's religious preference
    c. Accepting a referral from another counselor because the other counselor does not like the client's religious preference
    d. Accepting a referral from another counselor because the other counselor has not been trained to treat the client's issues

103. A client is experiencing obsessive thoughts about a recent relationship breakup. The counselor could do all of the following EXCEPT:
    a. Use CBT to help the client adjust his perspective on the relationship.
    b. Use EMDR to help the client overcome his sadness.
    c. Have the client journal his thoughts and feelings about the breakup.
    d. Encourage the client to get together with friends.

104. A counselor shares with her client that she was hospitalized for depression years ago. Which of the following is true?
    a. The counselor should not share personal information because it would derail the client's trust in her.
    b. This is appropriate if it would benefit the client.
    c. This is appropriate if the client had been previously hospitalized for a mental illness.
    d. This is appropriate if the counselor was about to hospitalize the client for depression.

105. Who is associated with the concept of birth order and the influence that sibling position has on personality?
    a. Abraham Maslow
    b. Alfred Adler
    c. Albert Bandura
    d. Anna Freud

106. Which of the following must the counselor determine to distinguish between bipolar I and bipolar II disorders?
    a. If the client has experienced a decreased need for sleep
    b. If the client has engaged in excessive shopping, gambling, or sexual activity during a depressive episode
    c. If the client has ever had a full manic episode
    d. If the client has ever had a full major depressive episode

107. Which of the psychologists below was a pioneer in humanistic theories?
    a. Wilhelm Wundt
    b. Sigmund Freud
    c. Carl Rogers
    d. Raymond Cattell

108. Which of the following clients would benefit from a safety plan?
    a. A 7-year-old boy who is being bullied at school
    b. A 39-year-old man with anger issues who uses meditation as a coping skill
    c. A 25-year-old female who occasionally binge-drinks with her friends
    d. A 36-year-old female in a physically abusive relationship

109. All of the following could help the development of a healthy support system EXCEPT:
    a. Encouraging church attendance
    b. Encouraging participation in a self-help group like AA
    c. Helping the client heal broken family relationships
    d. Encouraging the client to engage in regular exercise

110. A counselor asks a client what methods they have previously used to overcome problems in their life. What type of treatment strategy is the counselor using?
    a. Identification of cognitive distortions
    b. A gestalt approach
    c. Strengths-based counseling
    d. Regression

111. According to Dr. John Gottman's theory of marital distress, what are the four communication styles that can predict the end of a relationship?
    a. Contempt, controlling, belittling, stonewalling
    b. Contempt, stonewalling, confronting, scapegoating
    c. Contempt, criticism, stonewalling, defensiveness
    d. Criticism, confronting, belittling, controlling

112. What are the five stages of change in Motivational Interviewing?
    a. Motivation, contemplation, preparation, action, change
    b. Considering, contemplation, preparing, action, behavioral change
    c. Precontemplation, contemplation, preparation, action, and maintenance
    d. Motivation, preparation, reconsideration, action, change

113. How does group therapy help clients develop outside social interactions?
    a. Members act on the instincts of others within the group.
    b. Group therapy requires members to participate in free-form dialogue.
    c. Clients no longer have issues with conflict resolution after group therapy.
    d. It allows members to practice open expression of thoughts and feelings within a group.

114. A large, multi-story building that serves as the primary office for a business corporation in the United States only has stairs available to access each floor and the main front door. There are no elevators within in the building, and there is no ramp anywhere outside of any of the external doors. Additionally, all of the doors that lead into the building are revolving doors, which the corporation cites as being more energy-efficient. This organization is in direct violation of _____.
 a. Individuals with Disabilities Education Act (IDEA)
 b. Americans with Disabilities Act of 1990 (ADA)
 c. Workforce Innovation and Opportunity Act
 d. The Hidden Job Market

115. A client tells her counselor that she thinks her life is over because of her recent breakup. The counselor says, "You feel like this breakup has many negative ramifications for you." This is an example of which of the following?
 a. Confronting
 b. Reframing
 c. Mirroring
 d. Underestimating

116. Trainee counselors who come from highly conflictual families of origin should consider all of the following EXCEPT:
 a. Getting personal counseling
 b. Taking courses in conflict resolution
 c. Not allowing families to argue during sessions
 d. Talking with a supervisor about highly conflictual families they are counseling

117. Sometimes in group counseling, group members may think of the leader as an authority figure in their lives, such as their father or mother. This is an example of which of the following?
 a. Resistance
 b. Countertransference
 c. Transference
 d. Role Reversal

118. A school-aged child is constantly being bullied and has presented with signs of depression and anxiety. The counselor realizes that the child is displaying which stage of development?
 a. Mistrust
 b. Shame and doubt
 c. Guilt
 d. Inferiority

119. A counselor is working with an adult female client who suffered continuous sexual abuse from ages six to fourteen by a male relative. To establish safety and trust, the counselor should do all of the following EXCEPT:
 a. Allow her to express feelings of rage about the abuse.
 b. Hug her when she is crying.
 c. Allow her to sit near the door.
 d. Express empathy when she describes the abuse.

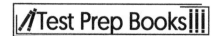

120. Which of the following is NOT reason a counselor would administer a test or assessment to a client?
    a. Aid the counselor in sharing pertinent information with the client's loved ones
    b. Ensure a client's needs are within the counselor's scope of practice
    c. Help the client gain a better understanding of themselves
    d. Evaluate the effectiveness of counseling interventions

121. Which of the following guidelines is endorsed by the American Counseling Association Competencies for Counseling with Transgender Clients?
    a. Refer to the client by whatever gender the counselor perceives it to be.
    b. Use nonsexist language when communicating with the client.
    c. Encourage the client to accept their biological gender.
    d. Avoid talking about gender-role stereotyping.

122. When working with counseling clients online, one way to maintain the privacy section of the ACA Code of Ethics is to do which of the following?
    a. Encrypt all client intake information, communications, evaluations, and other related records
    b. Use personal servers to store client information
    c. Print all of the client's records and store them in a filing cabinet
    d. Let the client know before you begin treatment that you cannot guarantee any privacy when working virtually

123. What are some specific issues cited as commonly discussed by women in counseling?
    a. Infertility, marital conflict, and eating disorders
    b. Balancing a career and family, self-esteem, and mitigating societal expectations/pressures
    c. Exhaustion, joint pain, and postpartum depression
    d. Anxiety, work-life balance, and finances

124. When does modeling occur in the counseling process?
    a. When counselors model clients' feelings back to them
    b. When clients provide counselors with an ideal image of themselves to achieve
    c. When clients are told how to behave by counselors
    d. When counselors demonstrate appropriate reactions and behaviors for clients to follow

125. A group member starts crying because of something another member just shared. The counselor encourages the person sitting next to her to explore these elicited emotions. This is an example of which of the following?
    a. The leader is being too controlling in the group.
    b. The leader is trying to develop empathy between group members.
    c. The leader is trying to help the member to stop crying so he can attend to what the other member said.
    d. The leader is trying to form an artificial bond between members.

126. Which of the following is NOT a central component of Carl Roger's Client-Centered Therapy?
    a. The counselor demonstrates unconditional positive regard.
    b. The therapist is congruent with the client.
    c. The counselor empathizes with the client.
    d. The counselor is a good listener.

127. A client is using marijuana to the point where it interferes with his ability to get up and go to work every day. What should the counselor do?
    a. Encourage the client to begin an addictions program like Narcotics Anonymous
    b. Not consider this a problem since marijuana is legal in the state where the client lives
    c. Call the police since marijuana use is illegal in the state where the client lives
    d. Refer the client to a psychiatrist who can prescribe medication to treat the addiction

128. Which of the following is part of good sleep hygiene?
    a. Exercising for thirty minutes before bedtime
    b. Staying away from screens at least twenty minutes before bedtime
    c. A regular sleep routine
    d. Eating chocolate left on one's pillow

129. When a client is sleeping less than three hours per night, the counselor should consider all of the following EXCEPT:
    a. Refer the client to a sleep testing clinic
    b. Refer the client to a psychiatrist for medication
    c. Offer the client a bottle of Melatonin since it is all natural
    d. Teach the client progressive relaxation techniques

130. A counselor is providing telemental health services to her clients via email. Under what condition(s) would this be ethical?
    a. The email server is secure and no one in the counselor's home has access to it.
    b. The counselor is in the same state as the client.
    c. The counselor tells her clients that the email service is insecure.
    d. Email communications are not allowed in telemental health counseling.

131. A counselor is working with an adult who has anger management issues and minor cognitive impairment due to methamphetamine abuse. Which of the following would be the most appropriate method of treatment?
    a. Psychoanalysis
    b. Cognitive behavioral therapy
    c. Group therapy
    d. Gestalt therapy

132. When is Critical Incident Stress Debriefing (CISD) most effective?
    a. When it is provided to individuals
    b. When it is provided by trained mental health professionals
    c. When it is provided within seven days of the incident
    d. When it is provided within 24 to 72 hours

133. During a session, the counselor is silent and notices the client speaking to himself. When prompted, the client tells the counselor he is responding to the questions he heard from a voice in his head. What follow-up question is important for the counselor to ask?
    a. "Are the voices telling you to harm yourself?"
    b. "When did you start hearing the voices?"
    c. "Is there an activity you would like to perform to distract you from the voices?"
    d. "Are you experiencing emotional distress at the moment?"

134. The statistically most common and normative behaviors of a society are referred to as what?
    a. Culture
    b. Modal behavior
    c. Tripartite
    d. Ethnology

135. Genograms are useful tools that help clients understand which of the following?
    a. The influence of generational patterns on present familial functioning
    b. The impact of past trauma on current behavioral patterns
    c. Psychodynamic influences on present relationships
    d. Intrapsychic influences on present behaviors

136. Albert Roberts designed a seven-stage model to deal with a crisis and provide effective intervention and support. What are the initial three tasks of Roberts's seven-stage model of crisis intervention?
    a. Assessments, identifying problems, and referring out
    b. Establishing contact, providing counseling, and referring out
    c. Assessments, establishing rapport, and identifying cause of crisis
    d. Intervention, assessments, and treatment

137. Research studies have indicated which of the following?
    a. Males develop language earlier than females.
    b. Males and females develop language at the same rate.
    c. Females develop language earlier than males.
    d. No determination for rate of language development has been made.

138. During an initial interview with a client, counselors should consider all of the following when formulating a diagnosis EXCEPT:
    a. Mental health history
    b. Length of time that symptoms have been present
    c. Cultural background
    d. Occupation

139. A client indicates that she recently suffered from a blackout when drinking alcohol. What would be the most appropriate next step for the counselor to take?
    a. Have the client admitted to an inpatient alcohol treatment program
    b. Ask additional questions about the client's alcohol consumption
    c. Begin treating the client for alcoholism
    d. Refer the client to an outpatient alcohol program such as AA

140. Which of the following activities can help increase the mental and emotional stability of a client who just retired?
    a. Call the client's children and suggest the client be placed in a nursing home.
    b. Have the client wake up at the same time every day to establish a routine.
    c. Encourage the client to continue working a high-stress job to avoid mental instability.
    d. Tell the client to perform the same activities every day.

141. A counselor sees signs of abuse in a child with whom she is working. Which of the following would be unethical for her to do?
    a. Report the abuse to the local authorities without the parents' knowledge.
    b. Let the parents know she is going to report the abuse while she is reporting the abuse.
    c. Talk to the child's teacher to confirm that she is seeing the same signs.
    d. Ask the child questions about the suspected abuse.

142. A 25-year-old, unemployed male who has recently returned from combat claims to experience reoccurring nightmares, angry outbursts, and feelings of depression. A counselor who wants to use a theory-based treatment method for this client would likely decide which of the following?
    a. The client has PTSD and should have Psychoanalysis.
    b. The client has major depressive disorder and should have CBT.
    c. The client has PTSD and should have EMDR.
    d. The client is faking symptoms so that he will not have to find a job.

143. Which of the following is a major concern when providing counseling services electronically?
    a. Technology limitations cannot be discussed with the client.
    b. Rapport with the client cannot be established.
    c. There are limitations to client confidentiality.
    d. Counselors will need to establish a social media account.

144. Why is depression a greater concern in older adults?
    a. Older adults do not have coping mechanisms to deal with depression.
    b. Depression does not happen in the older adult population.
    c. Older adults are incapable of asking for help.
    d. Symptoms of depression are often overlooked in older adults.

145. How does instrumental grieving differ from intuitive grieving?
    a. Instrumental is thinking; intuitive is feeling.
    b. Instrumental is action-oriented; intuitive is passive.
    c. Instrumental is more feminine; intuitive is more masculine.
    d. Instrumental is anger; intuitive is acceptance.

146. All end-of-life concerns are suitable for a counselor to work with a client about EXCEPT:
    a. Medication management
    b. Religious issues
    c. Financial matters
    d. With the client's written consent, communication with their family

147. Which of the following affective tests can measure personality traits?
    a. Myers-Briggs Type Indicator (MBTI)
    b. Beck Depression Inventory (BDI)
    c. Connors 3 Rating Scales
    d. Child Behavior Checklist

148. A counselor is working with a client who is bothered by ruminating thoughts about losing his job two months ago. The counselor should consider all of the following EXCEPT:
    a. Working with the client using a five-column CBT chart
    b. Teaching the client progressive relaxation
    c. Referring the client to a psychiatrist for medication
    d. Using the empty-chair technique

149. What are the differences between substantive advice and process advice?
    a. Substantive is nondirective; process is directive.
    b. Substantive is directive; process is encouraging.
    c. Substantive is directive; process is empowering.
    d. Substantive is fact-based; process is feeling-based.

150. What are the main components of a safety plan?
    a. Initiation of coping strategies and identification of resources during crisis
    b. Mitigation of negative thoughts and group-centered interventions
    c. Recognition of danger signs
    d. Goals that are community-centered, realistic, and achievable

151. When working with individuals in the LGBT community, it's important for a counselor to do what?
    a. Be an active member of the LGBT community
    b. Assist the client in locating gender-neutral jobs
    c. Consult with other professionals and refer out when necessary
    d. Reach out to employers to provide education about discriminatory hiring practices

152. Which of the following signs indicate that a client needs to be hospitalized?
    a. The client is homeless.
    b. The client is hallucinating.
    c. The client scored high for depression on a psychometric test.
    d. The client has recently beaten his wife.

153. Studies on gratitude have found that it is correlated with all of the following EXCEPT:
    a. Decreased levels of depression
    b. Stronger relationships
    c. Greater optimism
    d. Decreased psychotic episodes

154. When counselors are preparing their clients for termination once treatment goals have been met, what would be the most beneficial information to convey?
    a. The counselor's enjoyment when working with the client
    b. The option of coming back in the future should the need arise
    c. The importance of the client remaining independent of the therapist so as not to create an unhealthy dependency
    d. A reminder that the client should focus on other problem areas even though the treatment goals were met

155. Which type of psychological group deals with long-standing pathology?
   a. Tertiary
   b. Secondary
   c. Primary
   d. Psychoeducational

156. A counselor is working with a client who suffers from anxiety. The client is a Buddhist who is considering dating a Muslim. Which of the following would NOT be a helpful focus for this client?
   a. Having the client go through a value-sorting card set
   b. Discussing the similarities and differences between the religions
   c. Having the client consider what the familial implications could be
   d. Discouraging the client from dating the person because it might escalate their anxiety

157. The Gottman Method is a type of therapy used for what kind of benefit?
   a. To enhance self-direction
   b. To incorporate a holistic view of people's environments
   c. To gain awareness of the present moment
   d. To strengthen relationships and improve interactional patterns

158. How does negative reinforcement encourage specific behaviors?
   a. Removing unwanted stimuli
   b. Adding desired stimuli
   c. Punishing clients for unwanted behavior
   d. Extinction of stimuli

159. Which term refers to how well a person can maintain a sense of identity and acknowledge/accept their own feelings and thoughts?
   a. Ego identity
   b. Emotional capitulation
   c. Superego formation
   d. Differentiation

160. Which of the following would be an unhealthy coping mechanism for stress management?
   a. Progressive relaxation
   b. Avoidance of all stress-related thoughts and emotions
   c. Deep breathing practice
   d. Exercise

Answer Explanations #1

1. C: Avoiding the feared object or situation will only solidify the fear in the client's mind. The remaining choices are all components of helping a client overcome a phobia.

2. A: Worldview. One's worldview is typically comprised of personal beliefs, values, and attitudes about the world around them and beyond. Choice B, cultural encapsulation, refers to a viewpoint wherein the individual refuses to take into account other beliefs and cultures that differ. Choice C, ethnicity, is belonging to a certain group that has a common cultural tradition. Choice D, ethnocentrism, is a belief that one's culture is superior to another's.

3. B: The United States Department of Veterans Affairs helped expand services after World War II in order to help returning servicemen transition back into civilian life and civilian workforce.

4. C: This is an example of psychoeducation. The counselor is describing research on language differences in young children. Choice A, racism, and Choice B, gender bias, are not evident here. Choice C, shaping, is not what the counselor is attempting to accomplish since they are not slowly changing the client's behavior.

5. D: This is an example of building communication skills. Sometimes counselors educate their clients by demonstrating appropriate behaviors. The remaining choices are incorrect.

6. A: Bereavement, ageism in the workforce, and unemployment. These are some issues older adults face and report discussing in counseling as they begin to lose friends and family, or if they are forced into retirement or made redundant in their workplace.

7. C: Avoidance would not be an appropriate way to handle impending termination because it does not address the emotional and psychological issues that may arise for the client when she completes treatment. Choice A would be appropriate because it would remind the client that she has met her treatment goals. Choice B would be appropriate because it would allow the client to bring up any issues that have not been addressed in treatment yet. Choice D would be appropriate because the counselor should prepare the client for the variety of potential feelings that might arise after treatment ends.

8. C: Developmental age is a more appropriate consideration than chronological age since babies cannot control their elimination and yet are not diagnosed with either condition. Choice B is incorrect since the diagnosis can be given whether the symptoms are voluntary or involuntary. Choice D is not a relevant factor; the diagnosis can be appropriate whether the elimination occurs during the day or night.

9. D: All of the above. Harlow, a theorist in mother-offspring attachment, noticed all of these qualities in monkeys who were given a wire mother substitute and were not shown warmth and affection. He theorized that newborns of many species, including humans, had an innate need to bond in this way in order to develop healthy personalities and attachment bonds.

10. A: A reduction in the primary symptoms that initially led the client to seek counseling is a positive outcome of group therapy. Choice B is incorrect; group therapy aims to help clients advance toward their goals. Choice C is the opposite outcome; group therapy encourages independent client coping. Choice D is incorrect because termination of group therapy should be a joint decision by its members.

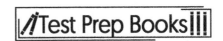

11. A: The counselor should talk with the client about his short temper. This would help the client learn how he comes across to others, and he can begin to work with the counselor on that matter. Choice *B* would not be the most beneficial option because the client may lack self-awareness in this area, or he may falsely believe that it is appropriate to talk this way. If the counselor handles the interchange appropriately, the therapeutic bond will likely not be damaged. Choice *C* would be an unhealthy way for the counselor to teach the client how to change his temper, and it may recapitulate childhood traumas. Choice *D* would be inappropriate because it could send a message of abandonment to the client.

12. D: The treatment may be working, but alterations to the treatment plan may be needed because the client's progress is insufficient. Choice *A* is not something that a counselor could conclude based on these test results. Choice *B* is incorrect because the BDI has empirically established validity. Choice *C* is incorrect because suicide risk is not indicated by the information given. Furthermore, counselors should only refer clients to other counselors under special circumstances due to the risk of emotional abandonment and feelings of rejection.

13. D: The correct sequence is tension building, explosion, and honeymoon. First, the tension escalates, leading to a violent altercation, after which the abuser showers the victim with kindness, affection, and/or gifts. Choice *A* presents the phases in the wrong order. Choice *B* is incorrect because it leaves out the explanation phase. Choice *C* is incorrect because the honeymoon phase includes reunification.

14. A: Asking the client to show the counselor her personal journal could possibly harm the client because she may not want to share this personal record with anyone. Choice *B* could show the client the progress she is making progress toward her treatment goals. Choice *C* could help the client see her physical progress. If the tests show improvement, she can see how her body is recovering from her past food deprivation. Likewise, if the tests show no improvement, the client can see that she has more work to do. Choice *D* would be beneficial when evaluating the effectiveness of treatment, especially if the eating disorder has caused tension between the client and her family members.

15. A: Signs of hopelessness, when accompanied by other warning signs, may indicate that the client is suicidal. The remaining choices are all possibilities, but the greatest concern for the counselor would be the potential for suicide.

16. B: Parentification occurs when a child fulfills a parent's role within a family system. Choice *A*, Electra Complex, is the Freudian term describing a daughter's competition with her mother for her father's affection. Choice *C*, Paradoxical Intervention, is when a counselor encourages continuation of a negative symptom, therefore showing the client their ability to control it. Choice *D*, Motivational Interviewing, is a form of therapy.

17. C: Biological, social, and psychological are known as the biopsychosocial realms of functioning, and they encompass the areas that counselors should assess to obtain a holistic view of their clients. The remaining choices do not adequately cover the entirety of the human condition.

18. B: Choice *B* correctly describes what occurs during pre-group preparation. Choices *A* and *C* are incorrect because clients are not always told what other group members' diagnoses are. Choice *D* is incorrect because clients do not sign a waiver of confidentiality; instead, they are told about the limits of confidentiality in group counseling.

19. A: Previous suicide attempts put a person at a higher risk for suicide than someone who has never attempted suicide. Choice *B* is incorrect; if a client is thinking about suicide but has no definite plan, this

alone does not put them at high risk for suicide. Choice *C* is incorrect. A client who has been diagnosed with depression is not necessarily suicidal. Choice *D* is incorrect; lack of a healthy support system does not by itself make the client a suicide risk.

20. D: Fails to reject; false. A type II error in statistical testing occurs when the researcher fails to reject a null hypothesis that is false. This type of error in a test will indicate that there is no relationship between two variables when there actually is.

21. C: In 1983, the ACA launched the National Board for Certified Counselors. The establishment of this credential was key in defining fundamental standards for the counseling profession.

22. A: Approximately 65 percent of second marriages end in divorce. The remaining choices are incorrect. Approximately 50 percent of first marriages and 75 percent of third marriages end in divorce.

23. A: Cognitive defusion is a term from Acceptance and Commitment Therapy. The remaining choices are incorrect.

24. C: Contributing to the next generation is the goal of individuals in the Generativity vs. Stagnation phase. Choice *A* is part of the Trust vs. Mistrust phase. Choice *B* is part of Identity vs. Identity Confusion. Choice *D* is part of Autonomy vs. Shame and Doubt.

25. A: Gestalt is a holistic model that helps clients focus on the present and work toward personal growth and balance. Person-centered, Choice *B*, is a group method designed to help members increase self-awareness, self-acceptance, and openness, and decrease defensiveness. These groups have less structure and focus on listening and reflecting. Rational Emotive group therapy, Choice *C*, is based on cognitive behavioral theories. The focus is on the present with the goal of improving cognitive, emotional, and behavior functioning. Group members focus on adaptive behaviors. Jungian, Choice *D*, is a form of therapy but not a specific group therapy. In Jungian therapy, the therapist is an analyst who works with the client to merge the unconscious parts of the psyche with the conscious parts of the self.

26. B: Eating non-nutritive substances for at least one month is a sign of pica. Admitting the client to a hospital is not warranted based on this information alone, nor is sending the client for a brain scan. Therefore, Choices *A* and *C* are incorrect. The client is not showing symptoms of anorexia nervosa, so Choice *D* is also incorrect.

27. A: Groups that provide guidance, problem prevention, and skills building are psychoeducational and may also be called guidance groups. Structured groups, Choice *B*, refer to how the group is set up—whether it is rigid in how it operates or more fluid. Gestalt groups, Choice *C*, are an alternative to intense psychoanalytic groups. Group members work on emotional awareness, freedom, and self-direction. Psychodynamic groups, Choice *D*, are long-term therapeutic groups made up of individuals who all have similar mental health diagnoses.

28. D: Negative transference can result in clients becoming angry and hostile toward the counselor. Although transference is an essential part of psychoanalytic counseling, negative transference can be difficult to manage and must be dealt with in order for therapy to progress. Choice *A*, when counselors project feelings onto clients, is called countertransference. Choice *B*, when clients project feelings toward another person in the past onto the counselor, is known as transference. Choice *C*, when multiple roles exist between a counselor and client, is known as a dual relationship.

29. B: Hallucinations (both auditory and visual) are symptoms of schizophrenia. Choice *A* refers to dissociative identity disorder. Choices *C* and *D* are not common diagnostic symptoms of schizophrenia.

30. A: Cyberbullying includes the use of electronic media and technology. Choice *B* would include physical assaults or property damage. Choice *C* is the intent to discredit another person's reputation. Choice *D* is not a defined form of bullying.

31. B: Choice *B* is not an appropriate course of action because the counselor cannot break confidentiality with the client's neighbor; they can only break confidentiality with the appropriate authorities (e.g., the police) in the event of possible self-harm by the client. The remaining choices are all possible steps the counselor could take, depending on the situation, such as consent having been given to contact the fiancé if a situation like this should arise.

32. B: Probability sampling uses randomization. In probability sampling, anyone who is eligible to be in the sample has an equal chance of getting randomly selected, whereas non-probability sampling may choose participants based on convenience, referral, volunteerism, etc., making Choices *A, C,* and *D* incorrect.

33. D: Issues with sexual satisfaction can occur during the desire, arousal, orgasm, and resolution phases. Choice *A* is incorrect because sexual dysfunction can happen during any phase of the sexual cycle. Choice *B* is incorrect because sexual dysfunction may be a result of psychological concerns. Choice *C* is incorrect; more than 40 percent of women and 30 percent of men experience some form of sexual dysfunction.

34. C: Cultural values and beliefs should be researched and learned when working with clients from a different culture. These values should then be used as strengths during goal development to aid the client in making the changes they desire.

35. A: Blocking refers to a group leader blocking or putting a stop to negative behavior of a group member. This can be harmful comments or anything that violates confidentiality or group norms. Members being disruptive to the process, Choice *B*, would be an example of conflict within the group. The leader locking the door to prevent exiting, Choice *C*, is not a technique used in group therapy. Existing members not welcoming new members, Choice *D*, could be an example of scapegoating a group member.

36. D: Joe's reaction is an example of transference. Joe is transferring feelings toward his father onto his therapist, which may be beneficial in resolving his childhood issues. Choice *A* is incorrect; remorse is a feeling of deep regret or of a wrong committed, and does not make sense in this context. Choice *B* is incorrect; in Freudian theory, fixation occurs when a child is unable to progress from one psychosexual stage to the next. Choice *C* is incorrect; negative reinforcement is a learned behavior meant to avoid negative stimulus.

37. A: If the client is unable to perform their daily responsibilities, this may indicate a need for intensive treatment in a residential facility. Choice *B* is incorrect because a counselor should not talk with a client's family members (unless the client has signed a HIPAA form for each member of their family). Choice *C* is incorrect because receiving a DWI does not necessitate residential treatment. Choice *D* is incorrect because there are other forms of outpatient addiction groups that the client could attend instead of going to a residential facility.

38. D: The length of time that symptoms are present is the key difference between Major Depressive Disorder (MDD) and Persistent Depressive Disorder (PDD). In PDD, the symptoms must occur on most days over at least a two-year period. For an MDD diagnosis, the symptoms must be present on most days for at least two weeks. The remaining choices could all be present in either PDD or MDD.

39. A: Maslow's hierarchy of needs is composed of five levels. The fourth level is esteem needs and was updated to include cognitive and aesthetic needs. This includes the need for self-esteem, status, prestige, knowledge, and an appreciation for beauty and balance. Level 1 is the need for food, shelter, warmth, air, sex, and sleep. Level 2 is the need for safety, personal security, stability, laws, and social order. Level 3 reflects the need for love and a sense of belonging. Level 5 of the pyramid is self-actualization.

40. B: Nihilistic delusions are beliefs that a major catastrophic event will occur. Persecutory delusions are beliefs that one is being or will be harmed by another person or agency. Grandiose delusions are beliefs that one possesses talents, beauty, or power that are not supported by objective evidence. Referential delusions are unwarranted beliefs that impersonal gestures or things occurring in the environment are directly related to oneself.

41. D: The counselor should consider using another treatment method because the Adlerian therapy method has not proven successful with this client. Choice *A* would not be appropriate because shyness is not treatable with medication. Choice *B* could possibly harm the client since she might interpret the referral as a rejection, further entrenching her fear of being with people. Choice *C* is incorrect because the empty chair technique would be an insufficient method to improve shyness after several months of treatment.

42. D: Authenticity is difficult to determine in a mental status examination because the counselor may not be able to verify the report's truthfulness. The remaining choices contribute to the overall picture of the client's functioning and are pertinent to a mental status exam.

43. B: Emotional Quotient. Also known as EQ, this index is lesser known than its IQ counterpart. People with high EQ tend to have better interpersonal and leadership achievements. Choice *A* is an index that measures someone's cognitive and critical thinking abilities, so this choice is incorrect. Choices *C* and *D* are too broad and do not refer to a measurement of emotional intelligence.

44. A: EMDR would not be helpful in teaching social skills. The remaining choices are all techniques or tools that the counselor could use.

45. A: Neural pathways in the brain are formed through repetition (this is also known as the Hebbian principle). This describes the process by which behaviors and thoughts become engrained. The remaining choices are not described by the given phrase and are incorrect.

46. A: Feeling the need to urinate is not a symptom of anxiety. The remaining choices are all symptoms of anxiety.

47. C: No, informed consent has not been satisfied. Susan did not have a document outlining what counseling would entail, including the risks and limitations. She also did not have Claudia sign such a document to become part of the chart. Documentation of informed consent protects both the client and the counselor.

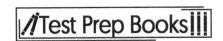

48. C: Homogenous society; heterogeneous society. A homogenous society is one where the people are very similar in background, attitudes, and beliefs; a heterogeneous society embodies a great deal of diversity within its people.

49. B: Risky shift phenomenon refers to groups becoming less risk-averse or riskier in their decisions. The act of sharing the risk among others makes individuals less conservative in their actions. Group leaders encouraging members to take more risks, Choice *C*, would fall under therapeutic techniques. Closed groups considering taking on new members, Choice *D*, would involve completely changing the type of group from closed to open.

50. C: Studies show that, due to previous abuse, a lack of security, caregiver deprivation, or early trauma, adopted children are almost twice as likely to develop behavior problems as those who are not adopted. Choice *A* is not the sole contributing factor to the client's behavior. Choice *B* is incorrect because extreme behavioral issues are not a normal trait of development. Choice *D* is not indicative of adoption issues.

51. B: Reflection is when a counselor restates the client's words so the client knows that the counselor is listening and understands. The remaining choices are incorrect.

52. C: Asking open-ended questions is important because it encourages clients to clearly describe what brought them to counseling and what their presenting symptoms are. Choice *A* may not be possible in the initial interview because more data may need to be gathered in future sessions before a diagnosis can be established. Choice *B* is important but likely would not occur in the first meeting. Choice *D* is not possible because permission to break confidentiality is not required when a client becomes suicidal.

53. D: Cognitive Information Processing (CIP) asserts that content and process are the main components of the career decision-making process. The content is what an individual must know to make a decision (such as self-assessment and knowledge of careers and options). The process is what an individual needs to do to make a decision.

54. A: Horizontal interventions in group counseling are referred to as *interpersonal* and define when the leader works with the group as a whole rather than as individuals. Intrapersonal, Choice *B*, is another term for vertical interventions, which occurs when the group leader focuses on individuals rather than the group.

55. A: The stages of positive interaction are exploration, consolidation, planning, and termination.

- Stage 1. Exploration of feelings and definition of problem: The counselor will use rapport-building skills, define the structure of the counseling process and relationship, and work with the client on goal setting.

- Stage 2. Consolidation: The client integrates the information and guidance from the counselor, allowing him or her to gain additional coping skills and identify alternate ways to solve problems.

- Stage 3. Planning: The client begins employing techniques learned in counseling and prepares to manage on his or her own.

- Stage 4. Termination: This is the ending of the therapeutic relationship, when the client feels equipped to manage problems independently and has fully integrated techniques learned in counseling.

56. A: *Tarasoff vs. Regents of University of California* is the correct answer. In this 1976 case, the therapist failed to notify the intended victim of the threat of harm. After the client had stopped seeking treatment, he then attacked and killed Tarasoff, prompting her family to sue the University and therefore establishing the duty to warn. None of the other cases directly relate to duty to warn.

57. B: This is an example of negative reinforcement. This type of behavioral technique involves changing a behavior by removing its unwanted consequence. It intends to teach that the behavior (leaving late for work) is associated with an unfavorable experience (being stuck in traffic). The negative aspect is the act of removing, as opposed to positive reinforcement that adds a consequence, such as a reward for a desired behavior, which makes Choice *C* incorrect. Choice *A*, modeling, is when a counselor models a behavior for a client so they can behave in a similar fashion. Choice *D*, classical conditioning, is when two stimuli are paired repeatedly, and the response over the first stimulus will eventually also become a response to the second stimulus by itself. This is shown in Pavlov's dog, where eventually the dog salivates to the sound of a bell, even if there is no food paired with it anymore.

58. A: Choice *A* is not a good strategy because this allows the child to see where the alliance has broken down between the parents, and the child will possibly take sides. The remaining choices are all possible solutions that the counselor could offer.

59. C: Clients are motivated and ready for change during the preparation stage, so counselors are able to effectively work with clients in this stage. Choice *A* describes clients who are still in denial and not considering change. Choice *B* is when clients are only considering making a change. Choice *D* is the end stage after changes have been implemented.

60. D: The counselor is evaluating the client's judgment. Choice *A* is not being evaluated because the question does not address memory. Choice *B* is incorrect because the question relates to a concrete, hypothetical situation. Choice *C* is incorrect because spatial orientation involves identifying objects or oneself in a point of space/environment; this is not the focus of the question.

61. C: Multigenerational Transmission Process. This concept explains how the variance in differentiation of self between parents and children over time leads to a widespread difference in beliefs between the oldest generation and the youngest generation of the family. Choice *A* is incorrect; differentiation of self refers to how much an individual's personal beliefs differ from that of his or her group's beliefs, and Jake is identifying with his peers here. Choice *B* is incorrect; family projection process refers to how parents project emotional conflict onto their children. Choice *D* is incorrect; emotional cutoff is the act of failing to resolve issues between family members by reducing or eliminating contact with one another.

62. A: Choice *A* would be inappropriate because counselors do not give advice. The remaining choices are appropriate actions that the counselor could take.

63. B: ADHD in adults can affect personal relationships and workplace success as a result of mood swings, short temper, and difficulties coping with stress; interpersonal conflict results from being off task, trouble with paying attention, or controlling other impulses. Choice *A* is a possible condition that

190

develops from having ADHD but is not a focus area when providing therapy. Choice *C* is a type of counseling intervention. Choice *D* is not characteristic of ADHD.

64. D: It would never be appropriate for a counselor to yell at a counselee. It would be appropriate (and necessary) for the counselor to address the belligerent group member, but not in a hostile, demeaning way. The remaining choices are incorrect.

65. D: Recall, Empathize, Altruistic Gift, Commit, and Hold are the five steps of the REACH forgiveness model. Choices *A, B* and *C* are not part of the model.

66. D: It is appropriate to discuss spiritual issues when the client has agreed to discuss them. The remaining choices are irrelevant when determining whether spiritual issues can be discussed in counseling.

67. A: This kind of statement would be made by a counselor to model appropriate feedback. The remaining choices are incorrect.

68. A: Competence is the reason that social workers need to be continually educated. This is important so that the counselor can provide the services in which they are trained and remain up-to-date on research and practice. While the other answers may be true, they are not the strategy specifically implicated for being an effective counselor.

69. A: The counselor should ask the client what he would like the focus to be because clients control their treatment goals. Choice *B* takes the power away from the client, which is detrimental to treatment. Choices *C* and *D* may or may not be warranted; the counselor would need more information before taking either of these actions.

70. A: Professional counselors are legally and ethically required to report matters pertaining to harm of self or others. Choice *B* is symptomatic information that can be used for assessment and diagnosis. Choice *C* violates the client's privacy unless the client has provided written consent. Choice *D* is incorrect because clients are free to terminate the relationship at any time while maintaining confidentiality of their records.

71. A: Confidence and pragmatism; seeking approval from others. Bowen discusses this idea under the concept of "Differentiation of Self." This refers to how much an individual's personal beliefs differ from that of his or her group's beliefs and plays an important role in whether someone develops a strong or weak sense of self.

72. D: A combat veteran is not likely to display psychosis as a symptom. The remaining choices are common symptoms of PTSD, which is common among combat veterans.

73. B: Denial, anger, bargaining, depression, and acceptance are the five stages of grief according to Kubler-Ross. Sadness, frustration, and resolution are not part of her stages, making Choices *A, C,* and *D* incorrect.

74. B: Unconditional positive regard is when a counselor accepts all aspects of a client, whether good or bad. The remaining choices are incorrect.

75. B: Avoidance of the object or action of fear is NOT one of the stages of desensitization. Exposure to the object, creating a fear hierarchy, and learning relaxation techniques while being exposed are stages of systematic desensitization.

76. D: Critical Incident Stress Debriefing (CISD) is best suited to secondary trauma victims. First-degree victims need more direct assistance, making Choice A incorrect. HR professionals and first responders can provide needed help, making Choices B and C incorrect.

77. D: One year of sobriety is not a protective factor against suicide; in fact, recent addiction may put the person at a greater risk for suicide. SAMHSA considers the remaining choices to be protective factors against suicide.

78. B: This would be appropriate if the counselor believes the client is not complying with the treatment directives. The client needs to understand that compliance is required for progress to be made. Choice A is incorrect because whether the psychiatrist agrees with the counselor has no bearing on the decision to speak with the client about treatment compliance. Choice C is incorrect because compliance with the counselor's directives is vital to symptom improvement just as medication compliance is essential. Choice D is incorrect because the length of treatment is irrelevant in this case.

79. C: A client's self-report of symptoms is one of the main considerations when formulating a diagnosis. Choice A (socioeconomic status) is not a diagnostic criterion. Choices B and D (cultural background and psychometric assessments) can contribute to the formulation of diagnoses, but they are not central factors.

80. D: Autocratic leaders are most likely to lead with control and power. Democratic leaders use consensus and belonging, making Choice A incorrect. Laissez-faire leaders operate with little to no structure, making Choice B incorrect. Choice C is not a group of characteristics for any main style of leadership.

81. A: Initiative vs. guilt occurs between the ages of three and five. Choice B, trust vs. mistrust, occurs in the first year of life. Choice C, autonomy vs. shame and doubt, begins around eighteen months and lasts until about two or three years of age. Choice D, identity vs. confusion, occurs between the ages of twelve and eighteen.

82. A: Choices B, C, and D are all goals of family therapy. Resolving intrapsychic conflicts is a function associated with psychoanalysis and not family therapy.

83. C: The Outcome Rating Scale (ORS) should be introduced at the beginning of the session to obtain the client's sense of well-being in regard to therapy. The scale assesses areas of life that can change as a result of therapeutic interventions. The four items assessed are interpersonal well-being, symptom distress, social roles, and overall well-being. Choice A assesses the counselor's skills development and professional competencies; clients are not involved in rating a CCS. Choice B is a feedback tool that should be given to the client at the end of the counseling session. Choice D is for clients in group therapy to report their experience in relation to overall cohesion, approach, and goals; it helps to measure group therapy alliance.

84. A: Susan has knowledge that Christine has a history of drug abuse. Christine has shown signs of possible relapse. Susan also has safety concerns for Christine's children based on what she has seen and the way Christine has behaved. Due to her concerns, Susan must refer to the NCC code of ethics

handbook that says serious harm to another individual must be revealed. Susan will be required to break confidentiality in this situation.

85. B: Choice *B* is correct because additional treatment should be initiated by the client. The remaining choices would be appropriate ways for a counselor to check in with a client and show care. Choice *D* would be especially appropriate if the client had done marriage counseling with the counselor.

86. C: Sleep diaries can pinpoint triggers that cause disturbances in sleep and assist in developing positive sleep hygiene practices. Choice *A* can give the client more anxiety if he or she is not able to meet a certain goal. Choice *B* should be a collaborative intervention with the client's medical doctor if needed. Choice *D* is incorrect; sleep-wake schedules should remain as consistent as possible to encourage healthy sleep hygiene.

87. C: Cultural encapsulation. This refers to a narrow viewpoint of global cultures or any culture differing from one's own. Choice *A*, acculturation, refers to the process of group-level change that can occur when two or more cultures meet. Choice *B*, assimilation, refers to the process of one or several people from a minority group accepting and modeling characteristics of a larger group. Choice *D*, worldview, refers to the set of basic presuppositions that someone holds about the nature of reality, the world, culture and society on a domestic and global scale.

88. C: Although challenges with clients (Choices *A*, *B*, and *D*) can contribute to counselor burnout, the main reasons for burnout are overwork and lack of appropriate supervision.

89. B: Choice *B* would be unethical because the counselor cannot break confidentiality under this circumstance. Choice *A* would be appropriate because it provides the client with support without pressure. Choice *C* is acceptable because, even though a counselor can encourage a client to break the cycle of shame by sharing with appropriate people, it is ultimately the client's decision when to share and with whom. Choice *D* is appropriate because it would allow the client to speak freely about it.

90. C: A healthy attachment will result in distress when the caregiver leaves the room; this is a normal response with a secure attachment style. Choice *A* is a type of attachment style in which children are wary of strangers and will become highly distressed when the caregiver is not in the room. Choice *B* is not a type of attachment style. Choice *D* will result in no distress; children with an anxious-avoidant attachment style do not seek closeness and will not show preference for caregivers over strangers.

91. C: Yalom's three-stage model included orientation, conflict/dominance, and development of cohesiveness. Corey's stages included initial, transition, working, and termination, making Choice *D* incorrect. Forming, norming, storming, and performing are included in Tuckman's theory, making Choice *A* incorrect. Choice *B* is a mixture of all of these stages.

92. A: Cognitive reframing is a technique that helps clients identify and change the way ideas, emotions, and experiences are viewed; clients are encouraged to look at situations from a different perspective and empathize with the decisions made by others. Choice *B* is incorrect; reminiscence therapy is used to treat severe memory loss and would not prove helpful in this situation. Choice *C* is incorrect because cognitive processing helps clients process traumatic events and is beneficial for clients with posttraumatic stress disorder. Choice *D* explores the different roles and identities that can impact behavioral patterns; the given situation does not depict this behavior.

93. A. The client is likely experiencing auditory hallucinations. The remaining choices are not evident in the given situation.

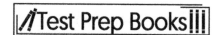

94. B: The inability to focus on video games is not part of the diagnostic criteria for ADHD. In fact, although individuals with this condition are unable to focus on many activities, they are sometimes able to focus on video games. The remaining choices are all elements of the diagnostic criteria.

95. D: Nothing. Practitioners will serve clients from all backgrounds and should not make any assumptions from intake information. Practitioners should be aware of any personal biases they may hold and make all inferences about the client's situation from information that comes directly from their sessions.

96. D: This is not part of any specific marriage therapy. There is not a specific form of marriage therapy that encourages clients to yell at each other during their sessions. The remaining choices are incorrect.

97. A: Emotional forgiveness is akin to forgiving someone from the heart and requires an emotional release of the wrongdoing. Choice *B*, decisional, is the first type of forgiveness; it is an intellectual move toward forgiveness. Choice *C*, situational, and Choice *D*, conditional, are not components of the forgiveness paradigm.

98. C: The validity of the test ensures that the tool is measuring what it is intended to measure. Choices *A*, *B*, and *D* do not play a role in the worth of the test.

99. C: Launching adult children. Empty nest syndrome is characterized by feelings of sadness and purposelessness that parents may feel when their children leave the family home and begin adult independence. Choice *A*, independence, occurs when the individual leaves the family unit into which he or she was born to establish independence. Choice *B*, parenting, is when a couple adds children to the family unit and raises them. Choice *D*, retirement, is the stage that focuses less on caretaking and professional work.

100. A: If an individual diagnosed with cyclothymia has a major depressive episode, then their diagnosis of cyclothymia is dropped. The remaining choices are incorrect because they indicate that the original diagnosis is kept while another is added.

101. A: Vertical interventions occur when the group leader focuses on individuals rather than the group (also referred to as *intrapersonal*). Choice *B* is incorrect; when the group leader focuses on the group as a whole rather than individuals, this is known as horizontal interventions, or interpersonal.

102. B: Choice *B* is correct because it is unethical to refer a client to another counselor based on religious preference. Counselors must demonstrate acceptance and respect for their clients' religious preferences. The remaining choices describe ethical practices.

103. B: EMDR would be an inappropriate treatment method because it is primarily used for trauma recovery. Choice *A* would be appropriate because CBT (cognitive behavioral therapy) entails rationally addressing and altering one's thoughts. Choice *C* would be appropriate since clinical studies have demonstrated effectiveness when using this method to treat emotional dysregulation. Choice *D* would be appropriate because social connectedness is often a good antidote for ruminations and sadness.

104. B: Ethical guidelines regarding counselor self-disclosure indicate that it should occur only when beneficial for the client. Choice *A* is too broad of a statement. Choices *C* and *D* may or may not be true, depending on the client.

105. B: Alfred Adler. Adler believed that birth position and the context of one's sibling relationships played a pivotal role in shaping one's personality. Choice *A*, Abraham Maslow, created Maslow's Hierarchy of Needs, a pyramid that depicts biological and psychological needs. Choice *C*, Albert Bandura, was a psychologist who theorized that learning takes place socially through observation and imitation of others and that not all behaviors are conditioned. Choice *D*, Anna Freud, was a psychoanalyst that focused on the ego and child development.

106. C: The distinguishing characteristic between bipolar I and II is whether the client has ever had a full manic episode. Individuals with bipolar I have experienced a full manic episode while those with bipolar II have experienced only a hypomanic episode. Choice *A* (a decreased need for sleep) can be present in both bipolar I and II. Choice *B* (excessive shopping, gambling, sexual activity during a depressive episode) would occur during a manic episode, not a depressive one. Choice *D* (a full major depressive episode) is not a distinguishing feature because it can occur in both bipolar I and II.

107. C: Carl Rogers was responsible for developing and influencing many of the theories related to understanding humans holistically. Choice *A*, Wilhelm Wundt, was a German physician who founded the Institute of Experimental Psychology. Choice *B*, Sigmund Freud, is considered the founder of psychoanalysis. Choice *D*, Raymond Cattell, is known for his exploration into empirical psychology and is known for developing theories on fluid and crystallized intelligence.

108. D: Safety plans are useful for clients who experience harmful thoughts or situations. Choice *A* does not provide enough information to determine if this client is in danger. Choice *B* is a healthy coping mechanism to alleviate the problem. Choice *C* is not displaying repetitive behavior that requires a safety plan.

109. D: Choice *D* is not a component of creating a healthy support system. The remaining choices describe potential places where clients can develop relationships that might become part of their healthy support system.

110. C: Strengths-based counseling can help the client identify positive attributes they have used in the past and apply them to present problems. Choice *A* refers to Cognitive Behavioral Therapy. Choice *B* is not implied here since the gestalt approach would focus on awareness of current situations, not methods used in the past. Choice *D* refers to looking into one's childhood issues to resolve present problems.

111. C: Contempt, criticism, stonewalling, and defensiveness are the four communication styles that can predict the end of a relationship. Choices *A, B* and *D* are not part of Gottman's formulation.

112. C: Choice *C* lists the correct stages of Motivational Interviewing. The remaining choices are incorrect.

113. D: Groups help clients practice honesty and communicate their feelings openly. Choice *A* is incorrect; the goal is for members to act on their own instincts and not be dependent on others. Choice *B* is incorrect because clients should never be forced to participate; free-form dialogue allows members to willingly express their thoughts. Choice *C* is not a guarantee after clients attend group therapy.

114. B: Americans with Disabilities Act of 1990 (ADA). This law requires that workplaces in the United States provide the necessary accommodations and structures for access, unless doing so places an unreasonable burden on the entity. In the building above, there are no accommodations for individuals with physical handicaps to enter the building or access any offices. Choice *A*, Individuals with Disabilities

Education Act, was enacted in 1975 and also provides communities with extra funding to provide resources for disabled children. Choice C, Workforce Innovation and Opportunity Act, is designed to streamline training programs in the workforce. Choice D, the Hidden Job Market, is a term used for jobs that aren't advertised.

115. B: The counselor is trying to reframe the client's perspective in less drastic terms. Choice A, confronting, is when a counselor challenges a client. Choice C, mirroring, and Choice D, underestimating, are not therapeutic techniques.

116. C: Choice C would not be a healthy way for a trainee counselor to counsel families. The remaining choices are possible ways that a trainee counselor could manage a highly conflictual family.

117. C: Transference is the process whereby someone projects onto the counselor a previous relationship. Choice A, resistance, does not apply here as it pertains to reluctance to take part in the counseling process. Choice B, countertransference, is when a counselor has emotional reactions to a client based on a previous relationship. Choice D, role reversal, does not apply. This would involve the client swapping roles with the leader or another member of the group.

118. D: School-aged children establish either industry or inferiority in this stage of development; poor relationships in school can lead to feelings of inferiority. Choice A can potentially happen during infancy when needs are not being met. Choice B happens during early childhood when asserting independence. Choice C occurs during the preschool years when a parent's reaction impacts the child's attitudes and behaviors.

119. B: Choice B would be inappropriate. Since she has suffered sexual abuse, she may feel threatened if the counselor initiates physical contact. The remaining would facilitate trust with the counselor.

120. A: Choice A is incorrect; this violates counselor/client confidentiality laws. Ensuring the client's needs are within the counselor's scope of practice, helping the client gain a better understanding of themselves, and evaluating the effectiveness of counseling interventions are all reasons a counselor would administer a test to a client.

121. B: Using nonsexist language and gender-sensitive skills while counseling is encouraged by the ACA. Choice A will not build trust and rapport with the client. Choice C displays counselor bias toward a specific belief. Choice D is incorrect because counselors should facilitate client knowledge about how gender-role stereotyping and sexism affect their physical and mental health.

122. A: When working with counseling clients online, you must encrypt all client intake information, communication, evaluations, and other related records. Encryption works by securing messages sent online so that only the sender and the target audience are able to see the information. Choices B, C, and D won't help maintain the client's privacy.

123. B: Balancing a career and family, self-esteem, and mitigating societal expectations/pressures. Men, on the other hand, are more likely to discuss work pressures, time commitment to family, work-life balance, and verbally expressing fears and concerns.

124. D: Modeling occurs in the counseling process when counselors demonstrate (or model) appropriate reactions and behaviors for clients to follow. Modeling is nonverbal and helps clients learn appropriate behavior through observation.

125. B: This is an example of the leader trying to develop empathy between group members. The remaining choices are incorrect.

126. D: Choice *D* is not a central component of Carl Roger's therapy model. The remaining choices list the three main components of his method.

127. A: Choice *A* is correct since the client has developed an addiction and needs treatment. Choice *B* is incorrect because if a person's use of marijuana interferes with their daily functioning, then it is an addiction that requires treatment regardless of whether the substance use is legal. Choice *C* is incorrect because drug use is not a reportable issue for which the counselor can break confidentiality. Choice *D* is not a good treatment decision because the client should learn to break the addiction without medication.

128. C: A regular sleep routine helps to establish a consistent cycle, making it easier to fall sleep and wake up on time. Exercising for thirty minutes before bedtime does not give the body time to relax and get ready for sleep, so Choice *A* is incorrect. Choice *B* is incorrect because staying away from screens that emit blue light for at least twenty minutes before bedtime is not long enough; it is recommended to turn off screens at least one or two hours before bedtime. Eating chocolate left on one's pillow might sound romantic, but chocolate contains caffeine and should be avoided before bed. Therefore, Choice *D* is incorrect.

129. C: Counselors should never offer medication or supplements of any kind to clients since it is out of their scope of practice. The remaining choices are all suitable options for counselors to explore.

130. A: Communicating via email is ethical so long as the email server is secure and no one in the counselor's home has access to it. Choice *B* is incorrect because a counselor may hold licenses in multiple states, allowing them to counsel clients across state lines. Choice *C* would not be an ethical safeguard against potential violations of confidentiality. Choice *D* is incorrect because email communications are allowed.

131. B: Cognitive behavioral therapy can be used with individuals who have some compromised intellectual functioning. The remaining choices are forms of therapy that would not be suitable for this individual.

132. D: Critical Incident Stress Debriefing (CISD) is most effective when offered within 24 to 72 hours of an event. It can be provided by any trained individual, including HR or mental health professionals, and is intended for groups of secondary trauma victims.

133. A: Auditory hallucinations can often direct the client to self-harm or become homicidal; counselors should assess suicidal or homicidal intent. Choices *B, C,* and *D* are all important to ask to establish common occurrences, distraction methods, and aggravating factors; however, safety should be prioritized prior to establishing patterns.

134. B: Modal behavior. Similar to the term *mode*, which indicates the number that occurs the most often in a dataset, modal behavior describes behaviors that occur most often within a group of people. Choice *A*, culture, refers to the beliefs, customs, and arts of a particular people. Choice *C*, tripartite, refers to awareness, knowledge, and skills of multicultural counseling. Choice *D*, ethnology, is a branch of anthropology that systematically studies and compares the similarities and differences between cultures.

135. A: Genograms are diagrams that display familial patterns across multiple generations. The remaining choices do not accurately represent the purpose of genograms.

136. C: Assessments, establishing rapport, and identifying cause of crisis. Briefly, Roberts's seven phases of crisis management are:

- Biopsychosocial assessments
- Making contact and quickly establishing rapport
- Identifying problems and possible cause of crisis
- Providing counseling
- Working on coping strategies
- Implementing an action plan for treatment

137. C: Choice *C* is correct because females develop language earlier than males. The remaining choices are all incorrect.

138. D: Occupations are not considered when formulating diagnoses, though some occupations may put individuals at greater risk for the development of certain diagnoses. Choice *A* (mental health history) provides clinicians with information about the type, length, and severity of symptoms; this information is necessary when formulating a diagnosis. Choice *B* (length of time that symptoms have been present) is a defining characteristic of certain conditions such as persistent depressive disorder. Choice *C* (cultural background) must be a consideration because symptoms occurring in the Western world may not be considered unhealthy in other regions of the world.

139. B: The counselor should ask additional questions about the client's alcohol consumption to determine what the client needs. The remaining choices are all potential options after the counselor has ascertained more information.

140. B: Having a structured day allows for a sense of productivity and normalcy. Choice *A* is incorrect because clients should continue to feel a sense of independence. Choice *C* is incorrect; if clients decide to continue working, they should be encouraged to work in a less stressful job. Choice *D* will lead to boredom and disillusionment.

141. C: Talking to the child's teacher would be unethical because it violates confidentiality. The counselor is only required to report abuse to the local authorities. The remaining choices are all valid options.

142. C: The client's symptoms are all common to PTSD, and EMDR is an empirically established method of treatment for that condition. Choice *A* would be inappropriate because Psychoanalysis is not an empirically established treatment method. Choice *B* is incorrect because reoccurring nightmares are not a typical symptom of major depressive disorder. Choice *D* is incorrect because there is no indication that the client is faking symptoms.

143. C: The ACA Code of Ethics addresses technology and its limitations with maintaining confidentiality; encryption methods should be used to minimize data breaches. Choice *A* should be addressed in the informed consent prior to delivering services. Choice *B* can still be established virtually through verbal and nonverbal communication. Choice *D* is not a requirement; professional or personal social media accounts are optional and must be kept separate.

144. D: Depression manifests itself differently in older adults, and symptoms such as fatigue, loss of interest in sex, and pain often go unnoticed. Choice *A* is incorrect because older adults are still capable of developing coping mechanisms to deal with depression. Choice *B* is incorrect because depression occurs in every age group. Choice *C* may require a more in-depth assessment, but older adults are capable of seeking treatment.

145. A: There is thought to be two types of grieving: instrumental grieving and intuitive grieving. Instrumental is more thinking-based and about solving problems rather than feeling, and is viewed as a more masculine approach to grief. Intuitive is more emotional and about sharing and processing feelings, and is considered a more feminine approach to grief.

146. A: Medication management is not within the counselor's scope of competence. The remaining choices are all appropriate and within the counselor's scope of practice.

147. A: The Myers-Briggs Type Indicator (MBTI) is an example of an objective personality test that evaluates multiple personality dimensions based on statistical analysis of client responses. Choices *B, C,* and *D* are all symptom checklists.

148. C: Based on the information given, referring the client to a psychiatrist for medication is not warranted. Choice *A* would be helpful because he could learn to counter his thoughts with realistic or alternative appraisals of his situation. Choice *B* is a good option because it would teach the client to notice how his thoughts are impacting his physical stress and how to calm his body and thoughts. Choice *D* could be helpful for the client to process with his former employer (in an imaginary way) how he feels about losing his job.

149. C: Substantive advice can be considered directive and may involve the counselor imposing his or her opinions onto clients. Process advice is more empowering and helps clients navigate options for solving their own issues. In some situations, it may be appropriate for the counselor to offer process advice; it is less likely that substantive advice should be given.

150. A: Safety plans are created for clients to use during crisis situations; clients should be able to initiate coping strategies, such as music, meditation, and exercise, and be able to identify family, friends, or professional organizations that can help. Choices *B* and *D* are incorrect; interventions during crisis should always be client-centered. Choice *C* is only partially correct; the plan must incorporate interventions to perform during a crisis.

151. C: It's important for a counselor to consult with other professionals if they feel they're outside the scope for their practice area. Being in the LGBT community is not necessary, although awareness and respect for the culture is.

152. B: If a client is hallucinating, then they are unable to make the rational decisions necessary to take care of basic needs; therefore, hospitalization is needed. Choices *A* and *C* are incorrect because homelessness and high levels of depression are not grounds for hospitalization. Choice *D* is incorrect; if a client has recently beaten his wife, then a report should be made with the police, but hospitalization is not necessary.

153. D: Gratitude has not been clinically demonstrated to decrease psychotic episodes. The remaining choices have all been found to be associated with gratitude.

154. B: It is important for counselors to give clients the option of coming back in the future should the need arise because clients should know that they can return to counseling without feeling any sense of failure. Choice *A* is something that the counselor could disclose, but it is not necessary. Choice *C* is incorrect because clients should know that they are welcome to return if any other issues arise. Choice *D* would be unhelpful and potentially harmful to clients. Instead, they should be congratulated on meeting their treatment goals.

155. A: Tertiary groups deal with long-standing pathology; think of it as the third and most acute level. Tertiary groups are used to facilitate long-term personality change or rehabilitation. Primary groups are educational in nature, making Choice *C* incorrect. Secondary groups are focused on counseling, making Choice *B* incorrect. Psychoeducational group structure refers to a type of group designed to teach individuals to develop or maintain specific skills, making Choice *D* incorrect.

156. D: Choice *D* would be inappropriate because counselors do not give advice. The remaining choices are appropriate measures the counselor could take with the client.

157. D: The Gottman Method is a type of therapy that identifies and addresses the natural defenses that hinder communication and bonding; the technique enhances a sense of understanding, empathy, and interpersonal growth by practicing conflict management and positive interactions between couples. Choices *A, B,* and *C* are all characteristic of Gestalt therapy, which is designed to help clients increase mindfulness, focus on the present, and understand the different aspects of an experience, mental health issue, or conflict.

158. A: Negative reinforcement encourages specific behaviors by removing unwanted stimuli. An example of this is putting on a seat belt to remove the sound of the car dinging (reminding you to fasten your seat belt). Choice *B*, adding desired stimuli, is considered positive reinforcement. Negative reinforcement does not include punishment for unwanted behavior, which makes Choice *C* incorrect. Negative reinforcement also does not include extinction of stimuli (Choice *D*), but the removal of unwanted stimuli; the "unwanted" here is important.

159. D: Differentiation is the process whereby individuals maintain a sense of who they are in relation to those with whom they are in intimate or close relationships. Instead of losing oneself and conforming to others, one maintains their personal identity, thoughts, feelings, and behaviors. The remaining choices do not describe this phenomenon.

160. B: Studies have demonstrated that avoiding painful thoughts and emotions is not an effective long-term solution and may create bigger problems; therefore, Choice *B* is correct. The remaining choices are all healthy coping mechanisms.

Practice Test #2

1. Which theorist developed ideas on fluid and crystallized intelligence?
   a. John Ertl
   b. Alfred Binet
   c. Sir Francis Galton
   d. Raymond Cattell

2. Robert Carkhuff wrote *Toward Effective Counseling and Psychotherapy*, a book wherein he discovered that therapeutic interventions did not always have a long-term positive impact on clients. Carkhuff also created a five-point empathy scale, designed to measure what?
   a. Counselor's ability to accurately reflect
   b. Effectiveness of counselor
   c. Defensiveness of counselor
   d. Adequate structuring of sessions

3. The storming phase of group development refers to which activities?
   a. Anxiety from some members of the group and difficulty opening up
   b. Group termination and moving on
   c. Use of role-playing
   d. Vying for leadership and group conflict

4. A client verbalizes shortness of breath and heart palpitations every time they meet a new group of people. The counselor recognizes that the client is displaying physical signs of anxiety. Which of the following counseling techniques can be used with the client during therapy sessions?
   a. Exposure therapy
   b. Interplay
   c. Positive psychology
   d. Reality therapy

5. Which of the following is NOT a symptom of Post-Traumatic Stress Disorder (PTSD)?
   a. Intrusive thoughts or images of the traumatic event
   b. Efforts to avoid thoughts of the traumatic event
   c. Duration of symptoms for longer than one week
   d. Reckless or self-destructive behavior

6. A counselor is working with a client who is suffering from grief after the loss of her mother. The counselor can do all of the following EXCEPT:
   a. Encourage the client to connect with her religious organization for support.
   b. Encourage the client to create a memory book of her mother.
   c. Encourage the client to join a grief support group.
   d. Agree to meet weekly for lunch with the client until her grief has passed.

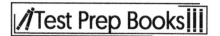

7. For many years, Abraham Maslow, who developed the hierarchy of human needs, described self-actualization as the highest level of achievement. In later years, he adjusted the model in order to add another level, which is referred to as what?
   a. Peace and serenity
   b. Spiritual attainment
   c. Self-determination
   d. Self-transcendence

8. A client confides in his counselor that he has been unfaithful to his wife for the past fifteen years. The counselor should do all of the following EXCEPT:
   a. Call the client's wife since she has been attended previous counseling sessions.
   b. Provide a non-judgmental attitude.
   c. Encourage the client to tell his wife.
   d. Ask the client to have his wife come to a future counseling session where he can confess to the affair.

9. When should the therapeutic alliance between a counselor and a client be established?
   a. During the first couple of counseling sessions
   b. When the counselor notices the client is not a good match for therapy sessions
   c. At the end of all counseling sessions
   d. The time when the alliance should be established is not important.

10. Which of the following entities publishes the International Classification of Diseases (ICD)?
    a. The World Health Organization
    b. The United Nations
    c. The International Journal of Health Sciences
    d. The United States Agency for International Development

11. A married couple has been in counseling for four months, and the counselor believes that they are not making enough progress. The couple are first generation Mexican immigrants. The couple will likely NOT respond well to which of the following treatment methods?
    a. Referral to group therapy
    b. Inclusion of their parents, who live with them, in the counseling process
    c. Encouragement of spiritual practices
    d. Education about Gottman's Four Horsemen of the Apocalypse

12. Which of the following stereotype(s) exist regarding older workers?
    a. The idea that older workers will take more absentee and sick days
    b. The idea that older workers are resistant to new technology
    c. The idea that older workers are slower to learn new information
    d. All of the above

13. What is the function of the helping relationship in the counseling process?
    a. It works by giving advice to the client.
    b. It allows the counselor to set goals for the client independently.
    c. It helps create a climate for change.
    d. It helps counselors maintain power in the counseling relationship.

14. Counselors should use all of the following methods to formulate their diagnoses EXCEPT:
    a. Psychometric tests
    b. Client's neighbor's report
    c. Mental status exam
    d. Client's self-report

15. Those who research self-image throughout the life cycle report which of the following?
    a. Most people's self-image tends to peak around the age of sixty.
    b. Adolescents have the highest likelihood of a positive self-image when compared with other age groups.
    c. There is very little change in self-image once middle school is completed.
    d. Young adults who are completing high school and entering the work force or college show an increase in self-image.

16. Which therapeutic modality uses the miracle question?
    a. Cognitive behavioral therapy
    b. Psychodynamic therapy
    c. Solution focused brief therapy
    d. Person centered therapy

17. When processing difficult emotional issues with a client, a counselor can do all of the following EXCEPT:
    a. Be aware of the time left in the session so he can wrap things up with the client by the end of the session.
    b. Allow for periods of silence during the session so the client can experience his emotions.
    c. Cancel all afternoon clients so the counselor can spend the rest of the day with the client.
    d. Offer homework so the client can continue to work through his emotions between sessions.

18. Which of the following is NOT a collateral source?
    a. Family members
    b. Police Officers
    c. Client
    d. Other medical providers

19. According to Elizabeth Kubler-Ross, there are five stages of grief. They occur in what order?
    a. Denial, anger, bargaining, acceptance, depression
    b. Anger, depression, denial, isolation, and bargaining
    c. Refusal, denial, isolation, anger, acceptance
    d. Denial, anger, bargaining, depression, acceptance

20. Dr. John Gottman's predictors of marital distress take the form of which of the following?
    a. The Wind and The Rain
    b. The Four Love Languages
    c. The Four Horsemen of the Apocalypse
    d. The Seven Stages of Marital Decline

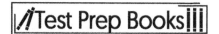

21. During couples counseling, the counselor discovers that the wife is unhappy with the mother-in-law's suggestions for disciplining the couple's children. The wife shares these thoughts with the husband and expects him to address the issue with his mother. What tactic is the wife displaying?
    a. Strategizing
    b. Pattern interruption
    c. Separation
    d. Triangulation

22. What therapy modality was developed by Steve de Shazer and Insoo Kim Berg?
    a. Psychodynamic therapy
    b. Cognitive behavior therapy
    c. Rational emotive therapy
    d. Solution focused brief therapy

23. A group of clients who are in group therapy where the group cannot be altered and the group does not allow new members is called what?
    a. Closed group
    b. Open group
    c. Stagnant group
    d. Gated group

24. A client verbalizes that she is unable to forget negative experiences in her past and they are interfering with her new relationship. What kind of theory-based therapy might benefit this client?
    a. Adlerian psychotherapy
    b. Gottman Method
    c. Humanistic psychology
    d. Gestalt therapy

25. A therapist asks a client about how he has reacted to problems in the past and what he tends to do when problems arise. What is the therapist assessing?
    a. Coping skills
    b. Communication skills
    c. Motivation
    d. Resistance

26. According to Erikson's stages of development, what is the dichotomy experienced during maturity (sixty-five years or older)?
    a. Intimacy vs. isolation
    b. Industry vs. inferiority
    c. Ego integrity vs. despair
    d. Generativity vs. stagnation

27. The following statements about standardized instruments are true EXCEPT?
    a. Examples of standardized instruments include police reports and physician's reports.
    b. Standardized instruments are crucial to providing a uniform, reliable method of providing a comprehensive screening.
    c. Standardized instruments can be used to facilitate ongoing clinical evaluation.
    d. Standardized instruments are tools to measure client behaviors, knowledge, and other affects.

28. What is the first item to focus on during the client interview?
   a. What the client wants to discuss first
   b. Historical influences that contribute to the presenting problem
   c. Family dynamics and social supports (or lack thereof)
   d. Medical diagnoses that complicate the presenting problem

29. Payment that is based on the client's income is known as which of the following?
   a. Private pay
   b. Sliding fee scale
   c. Health savings account
   d. Private insurance

30. During a discussion of substance use, a client states that he no longer drinks alcohol because he has a chronic, progressive condition called alcoholism. Which theory of addiction is the client's statement expressing?
   a. The learning model
   b. The moral model
   c. The medical model
   d. The biopsychosocial model

31. Rationalization, intellectual capacity, creativity, and drive are all examples of what?
   a. Interpersonal skills
   b. Cognitive skills
   c. Coping skills
   d. Internal supports

32. When two individuals with children from a previous marriage get married, what is the best way to begin the parenting process?
   a. Allow the biological parent to discipline his/her own children until the new family unit has bonded.
   b. Allow the father to be the main disciplinarian so the mother can be seen as the nurturer in the home.
   c. Adapt a style of permissive discipline so the children will feel accepted and loved.
   d. Adapt an authoritarian style of discipline so the children will feel secure and protected.

33. Alexa is a young woman receiving treatment from a therapist for anxiety. Alexa is hopeful that she can get better and knows that changing some of her behaviors is in her best interest. She acknowledges being nervous about change but has consistently been willing to take small steps in the right direction. She sometimes comes to her weekly sessions five minutes late due to her school schedule, but she participates fully and does not miss sessions. Based on this information, what are Alexa's levels of motivation and resistance?
   a. High motivation/high resistance
   b. Low motivation/low resistance
   c. Low motivation/high resistance
   d. High motivation/low resistance

34. _____ centered approaches usually involve behavioral modification and may be broken down into steps for the client.
   a. Goal
   b. Task
   c. Partialization
   d. Client

35. Controlled observation can be best defined as which of the following?
   a. Picking up on non-verbal cues in the surrounding environment for a holistic assessment
   b. Recalling interactions with the client to fill in gaps of information
   c. Purposely targeting a client's behaviors in a pre-determined setting
   d. Looking at facial expressions and mannerisms to gain insight on communicative deficits

36. In addition to past personal issues, the following factors are also important to review when gathering a client's history EXCEPT?
   a. Previous or current physiological health diagnoses
   b. Employment history and related financial status
   c. Review of psychological development
   d. Past experiences with substance abuse

37. Problem solving, self-confidence, the ability to empathize, and relationship sustainability are all examples of what?
   a. Internal supports
   b. Cognitive skills
   c. Coping Skills
   d. Extrinsic factors

38. A client verbalizes to the counselor that he plans to commit suicide by jumping off a building that night. What action should the counselor perform next?
   a. Perform an in-depth suicide risk assessment and contact the crisis team if the client has clear intent.
   b. Contact the client's family and let them know the client plans to end his life.
   c. Tell the client to go home and rest and return in the morning.
   d. Ignore the client's statement and change the subject to help the client forget about his plan.

39. Which of the following is NOT an indication of a client's resistance to change?
   a. Minimizing the problem
   b. High self-confidence
   c. Skipping therapy
   d. Refusal to try new behaviors

40. According to Murray Bowen's family systems theory, the concept of the Nuclear Family Emotional System refers to four different relationship dynamics. These are which of the following?
   a. Conflict, distance, child-adult interactions, and proximity
   b. Marital conflict, dysfunction in one spouse, impairment in one or more children, and emotional distance
   c. Happy, conflicting, grieving, and joyous
   d. Parent-child conflict, spousal conflict, full family conflict, and sibling conflict

41. When working with a group, confidentiality is _____ group members.
    a. guaranteed by
    b. fluid within
    c. true for
    d. dependent upon

42. A counselor is working with a client diagnosed with bipolar disorder who was recently hospitalized after having a psychotic episode. Which of the following should the counselor do first?
    a. Refer the client to a psychiatrist for medication.
    b. Have the client take several psychological assessments to ensure the correct diagnosis was given.
    c. Begin working with the client on their history of childhood trauma.
    d. Have the client sign a HIPAA form and then contact the hospital to obtain information about the psychotic episode, how it was treated, and the hospital's recommendation for future treatment.

43. The methods used to develop an intervention/treatment plan are problem definition, problem causation, _____, and obstacle/risk identification.
    a. objective development
    b. risk assessment
    c. solution identification
    d. information gathering

44. When reviewing the problem history, which of the following is not one of the three key areas?
    a. Progression
    b. Severity
    c. Performance
    d. Onset

45. Which two phases indicate client readiness for change?
    a. Pre-contemplation and contemplation
    b. Action and termination
    c. Contemplation and preparation
    d. Maintenance and recycling

46. A client tells a therapist that, growing up, his father was "like a drill sergeant." The father made the rules, and the children obeyed without question. He insisted on respect, hard work, and discipline. Punishments were frequent. Reflecting on his upbringing, the client states that it made him excel, but he never learned to be happy. What parenting style did the client experience from his father?
    a. Permissive
    b. Authoritarian
    c. Authoritative
    d. Uninvolved

47. Which of the following is NOT an example of ego strength?
    a. Divulging medications being taken
    b. Moving forward after a loss
    c. Empathizing with others without minimizing the pain
    d. Being aware of and accepting one's own limitations

48. Interventions matched to client problems are based on _____ and empirical data gathered by the social worker.
    a. biopsychosocial assessment information
    b. behavioral approach
    c. problem causation
    d. solution identification

49. All of the following items are used in the flow of an ecomap, EXCEPT?
    a. Solid lines
    b. Dotted lines
    c. Triangles
    d. Arrows

50. Which therapy modality is favored by insurers and managed care companies as more evidence based?
    a. Cognitive behavioral therapy
    b. Psychodynamic therapy
    c. Person centered therapy
    d. Narrative therapy

51. Mistrust of others, fear of going home, presence of marks, and frequent vomiting are indicators of what?
    a. Physical neglect
    b. Physical abuse
    c. Sexual abuse
    d. Psychological abuse

52. Receiving a diagnosis of a serious pulmonary illness can have many biopsychosocial impacts. Some things a therapist will want to address with a client who has just received a diagnosis of this nature may include which of the following?
    a. Asking why he or she continued to smoke, even after being told by a doctor it was affecting the respiratory system
    b. Insisting that the client discuss the diagnosis with all immediate family members within twenty-four hours
    c. Providing support and encouraging ventilation of emotions, especially grief and anger
    d. Accompanying the client to his next medical appointment to make sure the information is accurate

53. Excessive desires to be a people pleaser, low self-esteem, and fluctuation between aggression and passiveness are indicators of what?
    a. Physiological malfunction
    b. Cognitive deficits
    c. Sexual abuse
    d. Psychological abuse

54. Which of the following statements is NOT true about co-occurring disorders?
   a. Co-occurring disorders may also be known as dual diagnoses.
   b. Co-occurring disorders are less prevalent in clients with a history of substance abuse.
   c. Co-occurring disorders may be difficult to diagnose due to symptom presentation.
   d. Symptoms possibly appear related to another disorder.

55. What is the primary difference between atypical and typical antipsychotics?
   a. Atypical antipsychotics were developed decades after typical antipsychotics and generally have fewer side effects.
   b. Typical antipsychotics were developed decades after atypical antipsychotics and generally have fewer side effects.
   c. Atypical antipsychotics were developed decades after typical antipsychotics and generally have more side effects.
   d. Typical antipsychotics were developed decades after atypical antipsychotics and generally have more side effects.

56. Factors linked to the body's physiological response are known as what?
   a. Psychological factors
   b. Biological factors
   c. Social factors
   d. Environmental factors

57. Changes that occur in a normal family life cycle tend to cause a re-alignment of relationships and roles within the family unit. This is because of what?
   a. At some point, the adult child is expected to provide more care and support to the parent than the parent can provide to the adult child.
   b. Families often split apart due to disagreements over money and relationships.
   c. Most parents view their adult children as being incapable of properly raising children and feel they must intervene.
   d. Some elderly people are constantly critical when their adult children are having a more successful career than the parents had.

58. Being able to relate to the client's experiences as if one is in their shoes is called what?
   a. Sympathy
   b. Pity
   c. Empathy
   d. Relatedness

59. The intake form contains all of the following information about the client, EXCEPT which of the following?
   a. Client's household
   b. Client's age
   c. Client's food allergies
   d. Client's gender

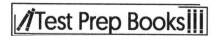

60. Observing the antecedents, behaviors, and consequences is known as what?
    a. Functional analysis
    b. Formal observation
    c. Formal analysis
    d. Controlled observation

61. When the therapist uses information and asks finding questions to better understand where the client is emotionally, while distinguishing the facts related to the situation, he or she is using what?
    a. Controlled data
    b. Objective data
    c. Subjective data
    d. Qualitative data

62. Self-regulation, the ability to multi-task, temperament, and optimism are all examples of what?
    a. Internal supports
    b. Problem-solving skills
    c. Coping skills
    d. Extrinsic supports

63. Which of the following statements about Jean Baker Miller's relational-cultural theory is NOT accurate?
    a. It explores how culture impacts relationships.
    b. It describes the characteristics of "growth-fostering relationships."
    c. It views relationships as the vehicle for change and growth.
    d. It was based on men's experiences, but can be applied to women also.

64. Which of the following is NOT a characteristic of a good treatment goal?
    a. Subjective
    b. Specific
    c. Measurable
    d. Achievable

65. What does the biopsychosocial model stand for?
    a. Biorhythm, psychotic, social welfare
    b. Biological, psychological, social
    c. Biotine, psychological, socioeconomic
    d. Biotrons, psychomatic, sociocultural

66. Which of the following tools is most useful for taking a family history?
    a. Ecogram
    b. Genogram
    c. Medical records
    d. Family tree

67. When the client provides their perspective on what happened and the correlated feelings and experiences felt, it is known as what?
    a. Measurable data
    b. Objective data
    c. Subjective data
    d. Planning data

68. You are running a therapy group for teenage girls who have been sexually abused by a family member, and one common thread you have noted is that most of the girls experience feelings of shame and unworthiness, as well as a sense that they are different from most of their peers. Which of the following is NOT a learning goal of therapy within this group?
    a. They have been deeply betrayed by someone who was supposed to love and protect them.
    b. These feelings are normal and are experienced by most people who have been sexual assault victims.
    c. Most people who engage in therapy eventually feel better about themselves and can learn to make peace with what happened.
    d. Assess why self-defense did not come into play so that next time they will be better prepared to fight back.

69. The acronym for the Health Insurance Portability and Accountability Act of 1996 is what?
    a. HIPPO
    b. HIPAA
    c. HIPPAA
    d. HI1996

70. Stress can manifest itself in the following symptoms: cognitive, emotional, _____, and behavioral.
    a. irrational
    b. vocational
    c. physical
    d. mutable

71. A therapist notices that one of her clients sometimes comes to therapy restless, talking quickly, and with dilated pupils. Other times he appears irritable and tired. He has been sniffling constantly for two months, which he attributes to a lingering cold. He has been getting into trouble for missing work. He used to be involved in several community groups but has stopped participating. His wife recently confronted him about the fact that he is often up late into the night then falls asleep randomly during the day. She checked their bank account and discovered that he has been spending large amounts of money that he refuses to explain. What is the most likely explanation for this client's behavior?
    a. Psychosocial stress
    b. Alcohol use disorder
    c. Cocaine use disorder
    d. Narcolepsy

72. Which of the following is NOT true?
    a. Social context refers to one's environment and how this influences behavior.
    b. What appears normal in one culture may appear bizarre or disgusting in another.
    c. The neighborhood where one resides has no bearing on behavior.
    d. Certain behaviors are acceptable in some social contexts, but the exact same behavior in a different social context might cause a person to be shunned or excluded from certain circles.

73. Which of the following is harmony and agreement in communication with the client?
    a. Congruence
    b. Affluence
    c. Way of being
    d. Being in tune

74. Which of the following statements describes 12-step groups for addiction?
    a. They are the most effective addiction treatment.
    b. They are free to attend and widely available.
    c. They are facilitated by a mental health professional.
    d. They require members to believe in God.

75. All of the following are the best methods to assess a client's strengths and weaknesses, EXCEPT?
    a. A verbal report with open-ended questions
    b. An intake form with specific, closed-ended questions for accuracy
    c. Parroting back responses during the interview
    d. Using finding questions during the interview

76. How many main sections make up the *DSM-5-TR*?
    a. One
    b. Two
    c. Three
    d. Four

77. Who is one of the founders of family centered therapy?
    a. Sigmund Freud
    b. Carl Jung
    c. Salvador Minuchin
    d. Albert Ellis

78. What defense mechanism occurs when a negative feeling is covered up by a false or exaggerated version of its opposite?
    a. Reaction formation
    b. Displacement
    c. Projection
    d. Denial

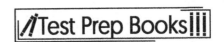

79. Janelle is a therapist at a nonprofit agency, and she is supervised by Susan, who meets with the executive director each month to alert her of any issues. Janelle has been seeing Brad for over a year for individual therapy. Brad wanted to focus on marital issues, but his wife refused to join him, telling him the issues in their marriage were because of his own personal problems. Brad told Janelle he wanted to improve himself to be a better husband. Last week, Brad's wife moved out and filed for divorce. She told him he had not improved himself during the last year of therapy. Brad believes this is Janelle's fault and has filed a malpractice lawsuit against Janelle. Legally, could Brad do anything else regarding malpractice?
    a. No. You can't sue someone because your wife left you.
    b. Yes. Brad could also file suit against Janelle's supervisor and go up the chain of command, naming even the executive director in the lawsuit.
    c. Yes. Brad can also file suit against Janelle's direct supervisor.
    d. No. Brad can only sue Janelle, because she was his therapist.

80. The phallic stage of Freud's psychosexual model of development is characterized by all of the following EXCEPT:
    a. The genitals becoming the focus of pleasure and gratification
    b. Oedipus and Electra complexes possibly emerging
    c. Potty training being a source of internal conflict
    d. Experiencing this stage between ages three and six

81. When a client is resistant to change and not thinking about change as an option, they are at what stage of change?
    a. Contemplation
    b. Action
    c. Pre-contemplation
    d. Maintenance

82. A therapist is providing counseling to a 10-year-old boy whose parents are going through a divorce. He recently had a doctor's appointment at the suggestion of the school nurse who said the boy was coming to her office several times a week complaining about a sore tummy. The doctor did a full evaluation and determined that the boy is healthy and has no signs of gastrointestinal illness. The boy continues to complain about tummy aches frequently and the therapist has observed that these episodes appear genuinely painful. The therapist does not believe that the boy is faking his symptoms. What is the most likely explanation for the tummy aches?
    a. A medical condition missed by the doctor
    b. Factitious disorder
    c. Hypochondria
    d. Somatization

83. Studies have shown that those who embrace spirituality tend to live longer and happier lives. The benefits of being a spiritual person include all of the following EXCEPT?
    a. It increases the likelihood of connection with others.
    b. It increases the likelihood of being artistic.
    c. It increases the likelihood that the client will find purpose in their lives.
    d. It increases the likelihood of self-actualization.

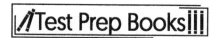

84. Jane is working with a client whose goals are based on his personal values. Jane finds her own values in direct conflict with the client's values. Jane has tried to self-reflect and work through this issue, but she finds herself having a harder time putting her own values aside each session. What should Jane's next step be?
   a. Termination
   b. Consultation
   c. Speaking to the client about the conflict she is having
   d. Personal exploration

85. In Skinner's theory of operant conditioning, the term *shaping* refers to which of the following?
   a. Placing a neutral stimulus before a reflex that occurs naturally
   b. Changing behavior through rewarding the person each time an approximation of desired behavior occurs
   c. Exploring superstitions that might impact willingness to make behavioral changes
   d. Giving a person a reward when the desired behavior is perfected

86. Hypervigilance, disturbing dreams, and eruptions of anger are symptoms of what psychiatric disorder?
   a. Claustrophobia
   b. PTSD
   c. Borderline personality disorder
   d. Severe anxiety with panic attacks

87. Which interviewing technique is used to bring together important points that have been discussed, reflect on progress made, and ensure that the therapist and client are on the same page at the end of a session?
   a. Asking open-ended questions
   b. Validating
   c. Clarifying
   d. Summarizing

88. What kind of group allows prospective members into the group most of the time, does not have specific beginning and end dates, and group members are not heavily vetted before being permitted into the group?
   a. Closed
   b. Open
   c. Archaic
   d. Affluent

89. When people experience a major life-changing crisis, such as an earthquake or a terrorist attack, which of the following is NOT true?
   a. Children are more resilient and, therefore, less likely to experience the negative impact as severely as adults.
   b. Some immediate reactions may include disorientation, disbelief, or a sense of helplessness.
   c. As the event and its aftermath are processed, more symptoms, such as insomnia or withdrawal, may begin to surface.
   d. Most events of this nature are sudden and unexpected, and there is no way to prepare for them emotionally.

214

90. Which statement is NOT true about indicators of motivation?
    a. Indicators of motivation are very basic and transparent.
    b. A client's level of engagement with the practitioner is an indicator.
    c. A client involuntarily coming for mandated treatment consistently indicates high motivation.
    d. Time progression will reflect the level of motivation.

91. Counseling interviews should always be focused and purposeful. Which of the following is NOT one of the three purposes of a counseling interview?
    a. To gather information about a client
    b. To determine a client's level of honesty
    c. To provide or update a client's diagnosis
    d. To provide therapy to a client

92. A manager tells an employee to hurry up and finish his work. The employee feels angry and disrespected, but nods and says ok. He spends the next few hours feeling angry and deliberately working less efficiently. He leaves the office at the end of the day having not completed his work. What type of communication style did the employee use?
    a. Aggressive
    b. Assertive
    c. Passive-aggressive
    d. Passive

93. During a mental status exam (MSE), assessing how well the client pays attention is an example of what main element of the MSE?
    a. Psychomotor behavior
    b. Mood and affect
    c. Cognition
    d. Thought patterns

94. If a therapist overidentifies with the client or views the client as an important figure in their life, the therapist is encountering what?
    a. Countertransference
    b. Transference
    c. Negative transference
    d. Nullification

95. A client's view of an experience and/or self is an example of which of the following?
    a. Psychological factors
    b. Physiological factors
    c. Social factors
    d. Person-in-environment

96. What progression do almost all theories of spiritual development have in common?
    a. Persecution to salvation
    b. Egocentrism to universalism
    c. Resistance to obedience
    d. Atheism to theism

97. Clients who are resistant to treatment will do all of the following, EXCEPT:
   a. Provide rationalizations for behaviors.
   b. Appear disengaged.
   c. Arrive late or cancel frequently.
   d. Request assistance outside of business hours.

98. One's cultural background is based primarily upon all of the following EXCEPT?
   a. Where one was born
   b. At what point in time one was born
   c. Sociological practices and standards in which one was raised.
   d. Genetic predispositions inherited at birth

99. Dan is seeing a therapist about his depression. They have met for a couple of sessions during which the therapist asked a lot of questions and had Dan complete the Beck Depression Inventory. Together they have come up with goals for Dan, and now they are talking about different ways they could accomplish those goals. The therapist has suggested some evidence-based interventions, and they are determining which one would work best for Dan's situation. Which phase of treatment is Dan in?
   a. Engagement
   b. Evaluation
   c. Planning
   d. Implementation

100. Excessive sleepiness, untreated medical problems, excessive hunger, and reports that no one is around to provide care are indicators of what?
   a. Physical neglect
   b. Biological assessment flaws
   c. Sexual neglect
   d. Starvation

101. What is the medical term for problems with understanding, speaking, reading, or writing due to brain injury?
   a. Aphasia
   b. Agnosia
   c. Acalculia
   d. Prosopagnosia

102. In the field of personality theories, which researcher proposed that personality develops as a result of striving to become the best one can be, combined with the importance of self-perception?
   a. Eric Ericson
   b. Sigmund Freud
   c. Carl Rogers
   d. Gordon Allport

103. Which of the following is an example of indirect discrimination?
    a. An employer who tosses a resume in the trash because the name on it is commonly held by persons of the Muslim religion
    b. A school requiring all students to come to school on Saturday for a make-up day despite having Jewish students who observe Saturday as a day of rest
    c. A restaurant owner who refuses to serve a customer because the customer is black
    d. A landlord who tells an interracial couple seeking an apartment that there are no vacancies, even though there are several empty units ready to be rented

104. During a mental status exam (MSE), assessing the client's cooperation is an example of what main element of the MSE?
    a. General appearance
    b. Mood and affect
    c. Speech
    d. Level of consciousness

105. All of the following are strategies to maintain effective professional boundaries EXCEPT:
    a. Limiting self-disclosure with clients or colleagues
    b. Setting clear expectations with clients about the role of the client and the therapist
    c. Using supervision to address boundary issues as they come up
    d. Engaging in self-care to promote work-life balance

106. All the following are reasons a social worker might request a client's educational records EXCEPT:
    a. To determine if problems at home affect school performance
    b. To assess a client's level of intelligence
    c. To diagnose developmental disabilities
    d. To determine when a client's symptoms began

107. The goal of crisis intervention is to bring the client back to what?
    a. Eloquence
    b. Equilibrium
    c. The house
    d. Justice

108. Perception of family relationships, mental functioning, occupation, and social class are elements that help guide which of the following?
    a. The assessment process
    b. Formal observation
    c. Diagnosis
    d. Life span development

109. Therapists sometimes do research involving human subjects. In order to be considered ethical, all the following conditions need to be met EXCEPT:
    a. The study participants are protected from harm.
    b. The study participants are compensated fairly for their participation.
    c. The researchers get full informed consent from all participants.
    d. The study will provide some benefit to the public and the profession.

217

110. A man asks his wife, "Does this outfit make me look fat? Be honest, don't just tell me what I want to hear." The woman feels trapped. If she says her husband looks fat, he will be unhappy. If she says he does not look fat, he will suspect she is lying, and he will be unhappy. What is the name for this type of no-win situation in communication?
    a. Passive-aggression
    b. Double bind
    c. Latent communication
    d. Cognitive dissonance

111. A therapist is creating a treatment plan for a client. The client is a member of a different cultural group than the therapist. The therapist wants to ensure that the treatment plan is culturally appropriate. The therapist should take all the following steps EXCEPT:
    a. Ask the client to talk about how their culture views health and illness. Explore how to incorporate healing practices from the client's culture in the treatment plan.
    b. Explain why it is important for the client to collaborate in treatment planning and encourage questions, suggestions, and feedback.
    c. Acknowledge the cultural differences and discuss them with curiosity, empathy, and openness.
    d. Counterbalance the power differential by asking the client to recommend a treatment modality. If the client is not familiar with any, encourage them to do their own research.

112. When a client presents with co-occurring substance use disorder and mental illness, what should be treated first?
    a. The substance use disorder should be treated first.
    b. The mental illness should be treated first.
    c. Both should be treated at the same time.
    d. It depends on the substance being abused and the mental illness.

113. What is NOT included in a treatment plan?
    a. The problems that are going to be addressed
    b. The goals that are going to reduce the impact of the problems
    c. The interventions that are going to be used
    d. Proof that the interventions are evidence-based

114. The psychodynamic approach originated with which one of the following?
    a. Skinner
    b. Jung
    c. Freud
    d. Ellis

115. Which of the following may be a dysfunctional family pattern?
    a. Scapegoating a child
    b. Affirming a child
    c. Undermining a child
    d. Disavowing a child

116. Psychoanalytic groups focus on what specific solution?
   a. Decreasing anxiety
   b. Resolution of childhood issues
   c. Resolution of current relationship issues
   d. Increasing daily functioning

117. A genogram is most useful for what?
   a. Determining the occurrence of behaviors
   b. Establishing peer support systems
   c. Pinpointing significant life events
   d. Understanding life events and familial patterns

118. The first stage of the therapeutic process is what?
   a. Change
   b. Termination
   c. Commitment
   d. Storming

119. The learning theory of addictions is based on the premise that addictions are developed due to which of the following?
   a. A need to reduce feelings of shame and poor self-esteem
   b. Operant conditioning, classical conditioning, and social learning
   c. An inability to be morally strong or to use willpower to overcome the addiction
   d. The interplay of social and cultural factors and one's genetic makeup

120. What does it mean for a therapist to be congruent in their communication with a client?
   a. The therapist maintains professional detachment and objectivity.
   b. The therapist and the client have the same understanding of the client's problems.
   c. The therapist matches the client's body language and speaking style.
   d. The therapist's verbal and nonverbal communication is real and genuine.

121. Which approach theorizes that thoughts and behaviors influence emotions?
   a. Cognitive behavioral
   b. Psychoanalytic
   c. Miracle approach
   d. Dialectical behavior therapy

122. Which of the following statements is NOT true about a client's developmental level?
   a. It describes a client's ability to function in different domains at any given time.
   b. It can change over time.
   c. It is not as important as the client's age when choosing interventions.
   d. It can be delayed or advanced in some areas of functioning but not others.

123. What is the FIRST thing a therapist should do to assist a client with sexual dysfunction?
   a. Ask whether the client has experienced sexual abuse.
   b. Refer the client for a medical evaluation.
   c. Assess the client for depression and anxiety.
   d. Ask about medications, lifestyle, and stress.

124. Which type of abuse involves the use of shame and manipulation to control a person, such as yelling, constant criticizing, or belittling, threatening, or name-calling?
    a. Physical Abuse
    b. Vocal Abuse
    c. Psychological Abuse
    d. Critical Abuse

125. A client with bipolar disorder requires regular blood tests to check his kidney and thyroid function as well as his blood levels of a medication. Which medication is this client taking?
    a. Lithium
    b. Lamictal
    c. Seroquel
    d. Wellbutrin

126. Xavi is a 28-year-old Latino man whose parents immigrated to the United States from Colombia when he was a child. He is fluent in English and speaks Spanish at home. He is seeking treatment for co-occurring benzodiazepine use disorder and major depression. What treatment would be most effective for Xavi?
    a. Treatment that involves the whole family
    b. Integrative treatment for dual diagnoses
    c. Treatment based on Catholic values
    d. Bilingual 12-step group treatment

127. All the following are guidelines therapists should follow when requesting feedback from clients, EXCEPT:
    a. Pay attention to informal feedback in the form of verbal and nonverbal cues.
    b. Use a standard feedback form for every client.
    c. Request feedback at different times throughout the treatment process.
    d. Clearly explain the purpose of the feedback and how it will be used.

128. Sarah is a fifteen-year-old high school student who says her parents are making her go to therapy even though she does not want to. What kind of client is Sarah?
    a. Voluntary
    b. Involuntary
    c. Non-voluntary
    d. Mandated

129. Which of the following is included in the biological section of a biopsychosocial assessment?
    a. Coping skills
    b. Marital problems
    c. Developmental history
    d. Educational background

130. A normally developing child will demonstrate all of the following behaviors and abilities by age one EXCEPT:
    a. Having knowledge of at least 50 words
    b. Responding to their name
    c. Smiling socially
    d. Sitting up on their own

131. What factor can cause family members or those outside the family to be judgmental toward a person suffering from mental illness?
    a. Ease
    b. Confusion
    c. Ambiguity
    d. Stigma

132. Sigmund Freud and his daughter Anna developed a lengthy list of defense mechanisms, including denial, projection, rationalization, and sublimation. They proposed that the need for people to employ defense mechanisms was for which of the following reasons?
    a. Because they were dishonest and did not want others to see the real person.
    b. Because if they admitted the truth about themselves others would no longer accept them.
    c. Because the defense mechanism allows one to avoid perceiving or accepting something very unacceptable about themselves, which they are not yet ready to address.
    d. Because using defense mechanisms gives one an emotional advantage over others and makes it easier to exploit them.

133. In an initial session with a therapist, John, who is a new father, tells a funny story about his baby. The therapist tells him that almost the exact same thing happened when his first child was a baby and quickly relays the anecdote. What is this an example of?
    a. Dual relationship
    b. Self-disclosure
    c. Boundary violation
    d. Empathic communication

134. What is the focus of problem-solving approaches, such as brief, solution-focused therapy?
    a. To understand how thoughts, feelings, and behaviors influence each other
    b. To explore unconscious and subconscious motivations and drives
    c. To find practical solutions to current problems
    d. To help clients identify their values and act in accordance with them

135. Which of the following is NOT a common characteristic of a perpetrator of abuse?
    a. Uses/abuses drugs or alcohol
    b. Has a learning disorder
    c. Tends to be controlling toward others
    d. Has a history of mental illness

136. Which of the following is sometimes but not always included in a biopsychosocial assessment?
    a. Spiritual beliefs
    b. Psychiatric diagnoses
    c. Medical history
    d. Presenting problem

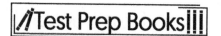

137. At the beginning of treatment, a therapist and client agreed on a rule that the client would show up for sessions on time. Recently, the client has been showing up later and later. They had a conversation about it and agreed that if the client was more than fifteen minutes late, the session would be cancelled. The client arrives twenty minutes late for the next session but is extremely apologetic, saying that they were stuck in traffic. The therapist does not want to negatively affect the therapeutic relationship. What should the therapist do?
  a. Remind the client of their agreement and cancel the session.
  b. Do not cancel the session because the traffic was out of the client's control.
  c. Warn the client that the next time this happens, the session will be canceled.
  d. Compromise by doing a half session.

138. Celia is seeing a social worker for help with anxiety that started after she was involved in a public scandal. The social worker thinks he could provide treatment more effectively if he knew more about what happened. He knows that a quick internet search would turn up all the details. Would it be ethical for him to look up Celia's name on the internet?
  a. Yes, but only to look for information that directly relates to her treatment.
  b. No, that would be a violation of her privacy.
  c. Yes, but only if he seeks supervision and he and the supervisor agree that it is necessary for treatment.
  d. Yes, but only with Celia's permission.

139. Which reinforcement schedule is most effective at producing the desired behavior and least susceptible to extinction?
  a. Continuous
  b. Variable ratio
  c. Fixed ratio
  d. Fixed interval

140. Factors that are present in one's immediate physical surroundings and social systems are known as?
  a. Physiological factors
  b. Psychological factors
  c. Biological factors
  d. Social factors

141. A therapist has a client with a history of domestic abuse and battery charges. He confides in the therapist that he believes his new girlfriend is cheating on him. He says that he plans to follow her and that if he catches her, he's going to kill her and her partner with the gun he keeps in his car. What should the therapist do first?
  a. Have the client involuntarily committed.
  b. Contact the client's girlfriend and warn her.
  c. Do not let the client leave the office until he has calmed down.
  d. Inform the client that the therapist will contact his girlfriend.

142. What is an example of a negative punishment technique?
  a. A time-out
  b. A token economy
  c. Spanking
  d. Cancelling chores

222

143. Which theorist is most known for their work on children's cognitive development?
    a. Erikson
    b. Freud
    c. Skinner
    d. Piaget

144. Encouraging a client to take a more active role in their treatment is likely to result in all the following, EXCEPT:
    a. A more equitable relationship between client and therapist
    b. More positive treatment outcomes
    c. The client feeling empowered
    d. The client feeling overwhelmed

145. Sandra tells a therapist that she feels like something is wrong with her. No matter how hard she works, she never gets promoted or feels respected at work. Her husband and children treat her like a maid. When she was younger, she had to deal with men sexually harassing her on the street. She expected that getting older and receiving less male attention would be freeing, but she just feels invisible. Her husband does not seem to be struggling with any of the same things and dismisses her concerns, telling her that she is too sensitive. The therapist reframes her issues by asking Sandra to think about where these problems come from. Are Sandra's struggles evidence that something is wrong with her, or could it be that something is wrong with the culture in which she lives? Why might it be that her husband's experience is so different? How are gender and power related? In asking these questions, what theoretical model is the therapist using?
    a. The moral model
    b. Conflict theory
    c. Feminist theory
    d. Systems theory

146. Which of the following is NOT a component of a mental status examination?
    a. Appearance
    b. Affect
    c. Speech
    d. Psychiatric history

147. A therapist has been meeting with Jerry weekly to treat his depression. He sought services voluntarily. After a month of treatment, he announces, "The treatment isn't working. I still feel terrible. This whole thing was a big waste of time and money. I just came to let you know that I'm done, and I'm not coming back." What is the best way for the therapist to respond?
    a. Empathize with Jerry's frustration and suggest creating a new treatment plan together.
    b. Explain that treatment takes longer than one month and encourage Jerry to continue.
    c. Explain the risks of terminating without completing treatment and document the encounter.
    d. Apologize and offer to reimburse Jerry for a percentage of the treatment.

148. What does *orientation* mean in the context of a mental status examination?
    a. The client's awareness of people, places, time, and events
    b. The client's sexual orientation
    c. The client's beliefs and feelings about treatment
    d. Informing the client of the purpose of the examination

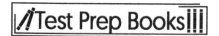

149. Carol Gilligan created an adaptation of Lawrence Kohlberg's theory of moral development based on her research of women's moral development. What was the main change she made to Kohlberg's original theory?
   a. Women view morality more in terms of relationships than men do.
   b. Women go through the same stages in a different order than men.
   c. Women achieve a higher level of moral development than men.
   d. Women go through additional stages that men do not.

150. The process of social development as defined by Lev Vygotsky suggests that one's development in life is deeply impacted by:
   a. Income Status
   b. Birth order and gender
   c. The variety of social institutions, such as family, school, or church, to which someone is exposed throughout life
   d. Physical stamina and overall health

151. According to Freud, what type of problem will be experienced in adulthood by a child whose parents are too strict about toilet training?
   a. Binge eating disorder
   b. Disorganization and messiness
   c. Excessive cigarette smoking
   d. Rigid and obsessive thinking

152. Sarah is a licensed therapist in private practice. She receives a subpoena from an attorney requesting one of her client's records. How should she respond?
   a. Claim privilege on behalf of the client.
   b. Ignore the request unless it is accompanied by a court order signed by a judge.
   c. Release the client's records but not the psychotherapy notes.
   d. Inform the client and release the records.

153. What kind of therapy involves the revelation of unconscious drives, such as sex or aggression?
   a. Psychodynamic
   b. Solution focused brief therapy
   c. Cognitive behavioral therapy
   d. Rational emotive behavior therapy

154. All the following statements about dementia are accurate EXCEPT:
   a. It is a cognitive disorder common in elderly people.
   b. It can cause mood changes including irritability and apathy.
   c. It starts suddenly and progresses quickly.
   d. It causes problems with memory.

155. A therapist has a client who is a young, black male living in a mostly white, suburban community. Growing up, the young man behaved like the white children around him. After a series of racist incidents, he has become more aware of race and more interested in exploring his black identity. Lately, he has pulled away from his white friends stating that they are "nothing but hillbillies and racists." He started wearing traditional African clothing and threw out all his books and music produced by white people, stating that black culture is superior. According to Atkinson, Morten, and Sue's theory of racial and cultural identity development, which stage is the young man currently experiencing?
    a. Dissonance
    b. Conformity
    c. Resistance and immersion
    d. Synergistic articulation and awareness

156. What should therapists be aware of when working with involuntary clients?
    a. Goals are set by the court, not the client and therapist.
    b. Motivation is likely to be high due to fear of legal consequences.
    c. Therapists should help clients see that they still have choices.
    d. There is no difference between working with voluntary and involuntary clients.

157. The ABCs of a problem can be described as what?
    a. Antithesis, Behavior, Coordinate
    b. Articulate, Behavior, Consequence
    c. Antecedent, Behavior, Consequence
    d. Antecedent, Boredom, Collaboration

158. A therapist is conducting research to determine the effectiveness of a new tool for measuring symptoms of depression. The tool asks a series of questions and assigns each participant a number from 0 to 10, with 10 indicating the highest level of depression and 0 indicating no evidence of depression. The tool is used multiple times for each participant and produces consistent results; however, the results do not accurately reflect each participant's depressive symptoms. What can be said about this tool?
    a. It lacks reliability.
    b. It lacks validity.
    c. It has internal validity but not external validity.
    d. It has external validity but not internal validity.

159. Cognitive approaches of psychotherapy address cognitive _____.
    a. distractions
    b. disenchantment
    c. distortions
    d. tracking

160. Which class of medication can cause tardive dyskinesia?
    a. Antidepressants
    b. Mood stabilizers
    c. Antipsychotics
    d. Antianxiety medications

Answer Explanations #2

1. D: Raymond Cattell proposed the concept of fluid and crystallized intelligence in the 1940s. John Ertl, Choice A, invented a neural efficiency analyzer that measured the speed and efficiency of electrical activity in the brain using an EEG. Alfred Binet, Choice B, developed the first test to determine which children would succeed in school. Sir Francis Galton, Choice C, believed that intelligence was genetically determined and could be promoted through selective parenting.

2. B: Effectiveness of counselor. Carkhuff's scale measured the degree to which a counselor was providing empathy, genuineness, concreteness, and respect. The scale measures effectiveness but refers to how defensive a counselor is toward the client. Choice A, accurate reflection, is a counseling skill, but not one measured by Carkhuff. Defensiveness of counselor is incorrect, Choice C. Choice D, structuring of sessions, is important, but it is not the correct answer.

3. D: Storming is the vying for leadership and conflict in the group. Storming involves conflict, discord, and struggles to agree upon a leader. Choice A refers to the forming phase. Forming is the stage where the group members are just beginning to get acquainted and may be anxious and less vocal. Choice B is adjourning, which is the point in which the group is terminated. Role-play is not relevant to group development but is a technique used in therapy to help clients work through how they would handle conflict with individuals.

4. A: Exposure therapy helps clients experience social situations progressively; it is done in time increments to lessen the physical effects of anxiety. Choice B is used to increase self-awareness and encourage better life choices; the client in the scenario is struggling with social anxiety. Choice C is not appropriate for the scenario because positive psychology is a theory that aims to help clients identify happiness from moment to moment. Choice D is a technique used to encourage problem solving and meet personal needs such as power, freedom, and survival.

5. C: For a diagnosis of PTSD, the symptoms must last for at least one month. The remaining choices are all criteria for PTSD.

6. D: The counselor should not agree to meet weekly with the client for lunch because the client could interpret such interactions as the development of a friendship or more intimate relationship. The counselor should keep the relationship strictly professional. The remaining choices are acceptable methods of working with a client.

7. D: Maslow devised his last level during his later years and referred to it as Self-transcendence. Achievement of this goal relies on experiencing a greater sense of spiritual growth and practicing one's beliefs on a deeper level. Previously, self-actualization was the ultimate achievement in Maslow's hierarchy of needs. In later life, as he worked on his own spiritual evolution, he believed this went beyond the process of self-actualization and deserved to be added to his original model of human needs. Self-transcendence refers to elevating one's self to a state of spiritual enlightenment in which there is greater clarity and understanding of certain spiritual truths. Choices A and B are factors that contribute to the Self-transcendence Level, but these are not listed in Maslow's hierarchy of needs theory.

8. A: Calling the client's wife would be unacceptable because it is the client's decision to reveal this information. The remaining choices are possible options for the counselor.

226

9. A: In order to predict a positive counseling relationship, the therapeutic alliance should be established as early as possible. Choices *B and* C are later than desired; the alliance needs to be established early to improve counseling outcomes. Choice *D* is incorrect; the timing of a therapeutic alliance is crucial for a good counseling outcome.

10. A: The World Health Organization publishes the International Classification of Diseases (ICD) as an international resource for medical and epidemiological data, health statuses, and other health information. The United Nations, Choice *B*, is a global union of members dedicated to confronting, managing, and solving world problems. The International Journal of Health Sciences, Choice *C*, is a peer-reviewed journal dedicated to all aspects of health. The United States Agency for International Development, Choice *D*, administers civilian foreign aid when needed.

11. A: Choice *A* is correct because the culture they come from does not generally encourage the disclosure of personal struggles to strangers. The remaining choices could be beneficial to them.

12. D: All of the above. These stereotypes are a form of ageism that exist toward older workers. These ideas include that older workers may need extra accommodations to work, may not understand new technologies, or may have health issues that lead to more absentee days or higher health insurance costs.

13. C: Creating a climate for change generates opportunities for reflection and facilitates the client's awareness of possibilities. Choice *A* is incorrect because counselors should help clients uncover solutions to their own problems. Choice *B* is incorrect because setting goals should be a collaborative effort. Choice *D* is incorrect because clients should maintain the power of the relationship while counselors use it to assist clients in developing strategies for change.

14. B: A report from the client's neighbor would not be considered when formulating a diagnosis because the counselor would not discuss the client with their neighbors. The remaining choices are useful sources when formulating a diagnosis.

15. A: Self-image does change throughout the life cycle, and while this varies from individual to individual, age sixty represents a change in roles from being an actively engaged parent and successful member of the work force to an empty nester who will soon face retirement. In our society where youth, beauty, and wealth are revered, there is often a shortage of several of these when one enters the sixties. Even those who are financially fit will begin to experience physical changes, such as less energy, more body fat, and the onset of a variety of medical conditions that prevent one from doing some of the things that were once simple, such as lifting a three-year-old grandchild. Gracefully accepting these changes is difficult and painful. Choices *B*, *C*, and *D* all represent stages that consist of great change and challenging transition and often fail to correlate with a positive self-image.

16. C: Solution focused brief therapy includes the miracle question, scaling questions, exception questions, and past success questions. Solution focused brief therapy is often used because it is time sensitive and allows clients access to self-direction.

17. C: Cancelling all afternoon clients so the counselor can spend the rest of the day with the current client is likely to foster unhealthy dependency and communicate that the client is unable to handle his emotions independently. Choice *A* is a healthy strategy aimed at helping the client re-enter the world when the session is over. Choice *B* provides opportunities for the client to learn how to manage his

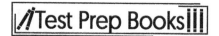

painful emotions. Choice *D* is important because much of the work of counseling is accomplished between sessions.

18. C: The question asks which of the answer choices is not a collateral source. Let's look at the answers that do qualify as collateral sources:

Collateral sources are persons outside of the client like family members, Choice *A*; police officers, Choice *B*; friends; or other medical providers, Choice *D*, who can provide information related to the client's levels of functioning, life events, and other potential areas of significance in the client's treatment. Choice *C* is the only answer choice that is not considered a collateral source.

19. D: Denial is first so that the person has a moment to process the loss, followed by anger at others or self for causing the loss to occur. The grieving person in desperation tries to bargain with their God or others in hopes of bringing back that which was lost. As reality sets in, the person grieves the loss and experiences sadness and depression. Resolution occurs when the person accepts the loss and is ready to move on, with an understanding that in spite of that which is gone, they will be fine in the long run. The other responses do not outline the order correctly.

20. C: The Four Horsemen of the Apocalypse are contempt, criticism, stonewalling, and defensiveness. When partners communicate using these four styles, they increase the likelihood of the relationship ending. The remaining choices are not part of Gottman's theory.

21. D: Involving a third person in a conflicting situation is known as triangulation; manipulating the third person to resolve the conflict is not beneficial for dealing with extended family issues. Choice *B* is a positive technique used to develop alternative solutions to stagnant routines. Choices *A* and *C* are not terms used in the management of extended family conflicts.

22. D: Solution focused brief therapy was developed by Steve de Shazer and Insoo Kim Berg. This brief therapy involves changing cognitive perceptions through Socratic style questioning techniques. Clients are allowed self-direction in the change process and reduction of symptoms may be viewed as a success instead of elimination or abstinence.

23. A: A closed group is formed when clients are specifically chosen by the agency, and new clients cannot enter the group. Open groups permit the fluctuation of new members who are welcome during each meeting.

24. D: Gestalt therapy helps clients focus on the present as opposed to the past or future. Choice *A* focuses on values clarification, self-worth, and acceptance; the client in the scenario is experiencing different issues. Choice *B* is a type of therapy that identifies and addresses the natural defenses that hinder communication and bonding; the scenario does not depict communication issues. Choice *C* focuses on the hierarchy of needs and explores morality and ethics; the scenario does not speak to such issues.

Permissive households tend to be low on expectations and high on warmth. Children brought up by permissive parents tend to experience difficulties at school, at work, and in relationships. Choice *C* is incorrect because authoritative parenting involves high expectations and high warmth. There are rules and structure, but children are given some input into the rules and decisions that affect them. There are consequences to breaking rules, but punishments are not too severe. Children raised in authoritative households tend to experience the most positive life outcomes. Choice *D* is incorrect because uninvolved parenting is often seen in dysfunctional families. It involves inconsistent rules and

228

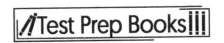

consequences without warmth or guidance for children. This parenting style tends to leave children confused about how they are supposed to behave. Children raised by uninvolved parents tend to experience problems throughout the lifespan.

25. A: Coping skills are the strategies people employ to deal with their problems. Asking about how clients handled problems in the past and identifying patterns in how they react to difficult situations can reveal how healthy their coping skills are. Choice *B* is incorrect because communication skills are assessed by paying close attention to a client's verbal and nonverbal communication in the context of their culture and history. Choices *C* and *D* are incorrect because motivation and resistance are assessed by observing a client's behavior and determining which stage of change they are in.

26. C: Erikson devised eight stages of psychosocial development. He emphasized the importance of social context, asserting that family and environment are major contributors to child development. During maturation (aged sixty-five and above), ego integrity vs. despair is the struggle. Important life tasks, such as child rearing and career, are being completed. Reviewing and evaluating how one's life was spent and success over the course of one's life provides a sense of fulfillment, while failure emerges if one is dissatisfied with accomplishments, which leads to depression or despair.

27. A: The question asks which statement concerning standardized instruments is not true. Let's look at the following statements that are true:

Standardized instruments are crucial to providing a uniform, reliable method of comprehensive screening, Choice *B*. Standardized instruments can also be used to facilitate ongoing clinical evaluation of clients in social work practice, Choice *C*. Finally, standardized instruments are defined as tools to measure client behaviors, knowledge, or other affects, Choice *D*.

Police reports and physician's reports are not examples of standardized instruments, which means Choice *A* is the answer that is not true concerning standardized instruments.

28. A: The first item to focus on during the client interview is what the client wants to discuss first. The client should be empowered to guide the focus of discussion. Choices *B*, historical influences that contribute to the presenting problem; *C*, family dynamics and social supports; and *D*, medical diagnoses that complicate the presenting problem, are all good to focus on, but should not be forced at the beginning of the interview by the social worker.

29. B: Sliding fee scale is a method of determining fees based on the client's income. Choice *A* is payment with cash or credit card. Choice *C* is a savings account that allows money to be set aside pre-tax. Choice *D* pays the counselor directly after a claim is reviewed.

30. C: There are several competing theories or explanations of what addiction is and why/how it occurs. The medical model views addiction as a chronic, progressive brain disease. This model informs 12-step groups, such as Alcoholics Anonymous. The learning model views addiction as a learned behavior that is reinforced through operant conditioning. People see others consuming substances, try them themselves, feel good, and learn to continue with the behavior. The moral model views addiction as a conscious choice to do the wrong thing. The model assumes that people make this choice because they are weak, bad, or sinful. This model is neither accurate nor helpful; however, unfortunately, moralistic attitudes toward addiction persist. Therapists must work to combat the stigma. The biopsychosocial model views addiction as arising from the interplay of genetic, social, and psychological variables. The biopsychosocial model is most suitable for counseling practice.

31. B: Cognitive skills include rationalization, intellectual capacity, creativity, and drive. Choice *A*, interpersonal skills, are skills someone would use to get along and interact with others. Choice *C*, coping skills, are skills a person uses in order to deal with stressful events or situations. Choice *D*, internal supports, are what the client uses to deal with situations, such as strengths and coping abilities.

32. A: Choice *A* allows the children to adapt to the new parent gradually. Choice *B* may cause the stepchildren to rebel against the father in the newly formed unit. Choices *C* and *D* are incorrect because permissive and authoritarian styles of discipline do not encourage stability or attachment to the new stepparent.

33. D: Alexa demonstrates high motivation and low resistance. Evidence of high motivation includes feeling hopeful about getting better, acknowledging the need for change, being willing to take small steps to change behavior, participating fully in sessions, and not missing sessions. Most clients show at least some degree of resistance. In Alexa's case, she is fearful, but she acknowledges her fear and still wants to change. Coming to sessions a little late could indicate resistance, but in this case, her tardiness is clearly explained by her school schedule, and she is diligent about attending and participating. Choices *A*, *B*, and *C* are incorrect because they do not describe Alexa. Choices *A* and *B* are unlikely to describe most clients because typically motivation and resistance have an inverse relationship.

34. B: Task centered approaches may assist the client in behavioral modification and the client may engage in partialization in order to carry out tasks in a step-by-step approach. Task centered approaches may be beneficial for more concrete thinkers.

35. C: Controlled observation can best be defined as purposely targeting a client's behaviors in a pre-determined setting. A client may be observed in a setting such as a school environment or home to allow the therapist to get a better understanding of how the client functions in their natural environment.

36. B: Employment history and related financial status are not commonly explored during the gathering of historical data. Choices *A*, previous or current physiological health diagnoses; *C*, review of psychological development; and *D*, past experiences with substance use, should all be explored when gathering a client's history.

37. A: Problem solving, self-confidence, the ability to empathize, and relationship sustainability are all examples of internal supports. Choice *B*, cognitive skills, involve a person's rationalization, intellectual capacity, creativity, and drive. Choice *C*, coping skills, are the methods one uses to deal with stressful situations. Choice *D*, extrinsic factors, refers to factors that exist external to the client and are reviewed in counseling assessment and diagnosis.

38. A: Direct suicide ideation statements should be taken seriously, and help should be obtained for the client promptly. Choice *B* may be an option after a suicide risk assessment has been performed and the client discloses his support systems. Choices *C* and *D* are dangerous interventions that may cause the client to harm themselves if not assessed properly.

39. B: High self-confidence indicates motivation rather than resistance to change. It is important for clients to believe that they can improve their lives. Therapists can help clients increase their self-confidence by focusing on their strengths, resources, and goals, and by celebrating every small step in the right direction. Choices *A*, *C*, and *D* are incorrect because they are all indications that a client is resistant to change. When clients exhibit resistance, the therapist should explore the resistance and

230

where it is coming from. Then, they should assess which stage of change the client is in and tailor their interventions accordingly with the goal of moving the client towards readiness for change.

40. B: Marital conflict, dysfunction in one spouse, impairment in one or more children, and emotional distance. These four dynamics refer to four different relationship patterns in the Nuclear Family Emotional System, and they affect how family units handle various problems.

41. D: When working with a group, confidentiality is dependent upon group members. In a group therapy situation, everyone must agree to keep confidential any information that is discussed in the group. It is impossible, however, for the therapist to guarantee that each group member will abide by that agreement and maintain confidentiality.

42. D: The counselor should have the client sign a HIPAA form so they can contact the hospital. The hospital could provide the counselor with valuable information that would aid in treatment planning. Choice *A* is incorrect because the client is likely already on medication from the hospital. Choice *B* is incorrect; while psychological assessments might be helpful later, they should not be the first step. Choice *C* is incorrect because this approach may or may not be appropriate for this particular client.

43. C: Solution identification is the third method used to develop an intervention/treatment plan. This is where the practitioner works with the client to suggest solutions towards which to work. Three goals included in this solution are Choice *A*, objectives developed for the goal Choice *B*, developed objectives that are SMART (specific, measurable, achievable, relevant, and time-specific); and Choice *C*, activities developed in an effort to assist the client in achieving goals.

44. C: Performance is not one of the three key areas when reviewing the problem history. Choice *A* (progression), Choice *B* (severity), and Choice *C* (onset), are the three key areas of the problem history. The history of the problem is important to address because it provides clarification on the factors contributing to what the client describes as the presenting problem, as well as the actual problem. Gathering background information on the problem history is also helpful for developing interventions.

45. C: Contemplation and preparation indicate that the client is ready to make changes. Pre-contemplation indicates resistance and unwillingness to change. Action phases suggest that the client is already engaged in the change process and not contemplating or preparing.

46. B: The client's upbringing is an example of authoritarian parenting. This parenting style involves the parent as dictator of the house, making all the rules and decisions. Children are meant to obey and face punishment for questioning or failing to abide by the rules. Authoritarian households tend to have high expectations and low warmth. Children brought up in this environment are often capable but unhappy. Choice *A* is incorrect because permissive parenting is basically the opposite of authoritarian parenting. Permissive parents do not set or enforce many rules—and when rules are broken, there do not tend to be serious consequences. Children in permissive households are free to behave as they wish.

47. A: Divulging medications being taken is not an example of ego strength. Ego strength is exhibited when a client demonstrates the ability to utilize a skill or set of characteristics that deal with highly demanding, stressful situations. Choice *B*, moving forward after a loss; Choice *C*, empathizing with others without minimizing the pain; and Choice *D*, being aware of and accepting one's own limitations, are examples of ego strength.

48. A: The components of the biopsychosocial assessment drive the data pertinent to designing interventions that match the client's problems, such as client strengths and risk factors. In turn, these

231

strengths and risk factors help guide the practitioner in the selection of a theoretical model to apply (in an effort to enhance client functioning and improve the client's overall well-being).

49. C: The question asks which item is not used in the flow of an ecomap. Let's look at the items that are used in the flow of an ecomap:

When the client constructs the map of social relationships, the client connection between the self and relationships is demonstrated with Choice *A*, a solid line. Choice *B*, the dotted line, would indicate a fractured relationship. Arrows may be used to add more detail to the relationship status and help the client and social worker understand the overall function of the relationships.

Triangles, Choice *C*, are not used in the flow of an ecomap.

50. A: Insurers and managed care companies sometimes consider cognitive behavioral therapy as the most evidence-based therapy for practice. Insurers are becoming more and more time focused and are favoring brief therapies and evidence-based therapies for practitioners.

51. B: Mistrust of others, fear of going home, presence of marks, and frequent vomiting are indicators of physical abuse. Indicators of Choice *A*, physical neglect, may be the appearance of being malnourished, excessive sleepiness, or untreated medical problems. Victims experiencing Choice *C*, sexual abuse, may have mistrust or fear of those who bear resemblance to the abuser or may have severe alterations in behavior such as depression, anxiety, or fearfulness. Choice *D*, psychological abuse, is indicated by extreme fluctuations between aggression and passiveness, manifestation of emotional stress, people-pleasing, or developmental delays.

52. C: Providing support and encouraging talking about the issue, but only at the chosen pace of the client, is the correct response. The person receiving a frightening diagnosis needs time to process thoughts and feelings. Choice *A* would be a form of shaming the client about the smoking addiction and does nothing to help the individual make peace with the diagnosis. Choice *B* is inappropriate because family is not always the client's first choice for support, and the client should decide when and with whom to share this news. Choice *D* puts the therapist in a sticky situation in terms of boundaries. There may be some settings in which this could be helpful, but generally this is not an expectation of either client or therapist.

53. D: These symptoms are indicators of psychological abuse. Psychological abuse may be one of the more difficult types of abuse for a social worker to detect. Choice *A*, physiological malfunction, has nothing to do with people-pleasing or low self-esteem. Cognitive deficits, Choice *B*, are also unrelated to the question and have to do with an intellectual disability beginning in childhood. Choice *C*, sexual abuse, is indicated by severe alterations in behavior such as depression, anxiety, or fearfulness, especially around the abuser or those who resemble the abuser, such as other adults.

54. B: The question asks which of the statements is not true concerning co-occurring disorders. Let's look at the statements that are true:

Co-occurring disorders may also be known as dual diagnoses, Choice *A*. It may be difficult to diagnose substance use due to symptom presentation, which may appear related to other disorders, Choices *C* and *D*.

Co-occurring disorders are more prevalent in clients with a history of substance use; Choice *B* states that co-occurring disorders are less prevalent in clients with a history of substance use, which makes Choice *B* the false statement.

55. A: Atypical antipsychotics were developed in the 1990s and have been shown to have less severe side effects. Typical antipsychotics were developed in the 1950s. They can be used if atypical antipsychotics don't work for the client, but they usually have severe side effects.

56. B: Factors linked to the body's physiological response are known as biological factors. These factors may present in the form of fluctuations in heartbeat, sweating, shortness of breath, digestive issues, and/or brain functioning. Choice *A*, psychological factors, refer to cognitive processes, such as thoughts, beliefs, one's view of an experience, and one's view of self. Choice *C*, social factors, and Choice *D*, environmental factors, are present in one's immediate physical surroundings and social systems such as work, school, home, and peer group.

57. A: At some point, the adult child is expected to provide more care and support to the parent than the parent can provide to the adult child. This is a painful process for both parent and adult child. While most adult children are willing to lend a helping hand to parents, parents sometimes feel diminished and awkward as the roles shift. When assistance is in the form of direct care, such as bathing and dressing, it can be even more difficult for the parent to accept care from their child. Choices *B*, *C*, and *D* may each be true in terms of causing realignments of roles, but the process of caring for aging parents, who sometimes become quite childlike and difficult in later years, is at the core of relationship realignment.

58. C: Empathy is being able to relate to the client as if in their shoes while also remaining objective. If a therapist cannot be empathetic toward a client, then the therapist should work through the issue or refer the client to another therapist.

59. C: The intake form does not contain information about the client's food allergies. The assessment form includes identifying information about the client's household, age, and gender, as well as a brief description of the problem in the client's own words. Clients are generally asked to complete an assessment form prior to the first session. The social work practitioner may review this form before or after meeting with the client to gain additional insight into the client's needs.

60. A: Observing the antecedents, behaviors, and consequences is known as functional analysis. Choice *B*, formal observation, is a method that includes functional analysis, but also includes other methods where specific data is collected on the client in a pre-determined setting. Choice *C* is also incorrect. Choice *D*, controlled observation, is purposely targeting a client's behavior in a pre-determined setting.

61. B: Objective data is correct. The social worker collects objective data to determine the facts in a client's situation. Subjective data, Choice *C*, is when the client provides their perspective on what happened and the experiences felt. Controlled data, Choice *A*, and qualitative data, Choice *D*, are not relevant to the context of the question.

62. C: Self-regulation, the ability to multi-task, temperament, and optimism are all examples of coping skills. Choice *A*, internal supports, are the inner resources the client uses to cope. Problem-solving skills, Choice *B*, involve working through a problem in order to achieve a solution. Extrinsic supports, Choice *D*, involve support outside of the client.

63. D: Relational-cultural theory (RCT) was developed by Jean Baker Miller in the 1970s based on her research on women. RCT is a feminist theory and has been used to describe women's experiences of

233

depression. RCT views humans as inherently social beings who seek out relationships with others. Culture shapes the relationships people develop. Baker coined the term "growth-fostering relationships" to describe healthy relationships that promote personal growth. These relationships are the vehicle through which individuals change and grow. RCT considers how societal-level relationships and power dynamics can encourage, discourage, or otherwise shape people's ability to form the kind of relationships they need for psychological health.

64. A: *Subjective* is not a characteristic of a good treatment goal. Choices *B, C,* and *D* make up the first three letters of the acronym regarding SMART goals: Specific, Measurable, Achievable, Relevant, and Time-specific. The client and practitioner must both agree on the measurability of a goal with specificity. Measurable terms used in writing the goals should focus on the type of behavior the client wants to achieve. The type of language used to plan and the objectives themselves should be relevant to the client. Objectives should be both short and long-term. Short-term objectives should only be a few weeks in length. The timeframe for completion should align with the nature of the objective.

65. B: The biopsychosocial model is a common model used in counseling today to encompass multiple areas of a client's life. Spiritual and gender aspects may also be included in this model.

66. B: A genogram is a tool that can be used to identify patterns in a family. It is a visual representation of a client and their family that tracks generational patterns of behavior, emotions, relationships, psychosocial functioning, and tendencies. Choice *A* is incorrect because an ecogram is a visual representation of a client and various aspects of their environment. Choice *C* is incorrect because medical issues are only one of many components of a family history. Choice *D* is incorrect, because it does not cover the depth and breadth of information that a genogram does.

67. C: Subjective data is when the client provides their perspective on what happened and the correlated feelings and experiences felt. The social worker may use the information to tease out facts related to the client's situation, which is known as objective data, Choice *B*. Measurable data, Choice *A*, and planning data, Choice *D*, are not relevant to the context of the question.

68. D: It is important to acknowledge the girl is not in any way at fault and that the act of sexual assault upon a minor is a felony. Choices *A, B,* and *C* plant a seed of hope that through sharing feelings in a safe setting. One can begin to move down the path to healing the emotional pain. It is helpful to normalize the experience to some extent so that the child realizes one in four girls are victims of some form of sexual abuse. The therapist should never blame the victim for abuse, regardless of the circumstances.

69. B: HIPAA is the acronym for the Health Insurance Portability and Accountability Act of 1996. All therapists need to be familiar with this Act because it affects electronic record confidentiality for the client.

70. C: Stress can manifest itself in the following symptoms: cognitive, emotional, physical, and behavioral. Stress may result from a threat to the client's functioning, both real or imagined. Some common factors contributing to biopsychosocial stress are natural disasters or disruption of relationships, such as divorce, death, break-ups, or moving.

71. C: Cocaine use disorder is most likely because of the client's combination of physical symptoms (sniffling, dilated pupils, restlessness, talking quickly, irritability, sleep disturbance, mood, and attitude changes) and increasing negative life consequences (missing work, arguing with wife, overspending, withdrawal from previous activities). Choice *A* is incorrect because his behavior is causing problems

234

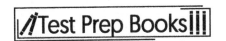

rather than the circumstances of his life causing stress. Choice B is incorrect because, although alcohol use disorder shares similar negative consequences, the physical signs are different. The sniffling, dilated pupils, and talking quickly are especially indicative of cocaine use. Choice D is incorrect because narcolepsy is a medical condition that causes daytime sleepiness, but not any of the other issues he is having.

72. C: The neighborhood in which one lives has great impact on things, such as education quality, exposure to crime, access to drugs or alcohol, and the type of role models one is exposed to. Social context shapes behavior, expectations, and morals. Choices A, B, and D are all true and reflect various aspects of social context that can significantly influence behavioral choices, such as differences from one culture to another and how these can be impacted by different social contexts.

73. A: Congruence is harmony or agreement in communication with the client. Congruence is an important part of counseling practice because it may determine treatment success with a client. If there is not congruence in communication with a client, the therapist and client must work on developing this process.

74. B: 12-step addiction groups, such as Alcoholics Anonymous (AA), are the most well-known addiction treatment currently available. Social workers should have a basic understanding of how these programs work so that they can assist clients and their families. A major benefit of 12-step programs is that they are free and available in most communities and online 24 hours a day. They are open to anyone with a desire to stop using, and they can provide a helpful social network to people in recovery. Many people assume that 12-step programs are the best or only way to treat addiction, but this is not true. Their effectiveness varies and is difficult to measure, but research suggests that treatment that combines multiple modalities is more effective than 12-step groups. One issue is that different groups can vary significantly in size, composition, and focus, as they are run by members, not mental health professionals.

12-step groups were developed based on the experiences of white men with alcohol use disorder in the 1930s. People who are not white men sometimes find that 12-step programs do not fit with their personal experience and needs. For example, there is an emphasis on taming the ego. One of the steps is admitting that you are powerless, which many women find damaging since powerlessness was one of the stressors that contributed to their addiction. 12-step groups do not require members to believe in God; however, God is referenced frequently, which can make people who are not religious uncomfortable. 12-step groups claim to be based on the medical model of addiction and yet they call addiction a spiritual malady, and require members to confess their character flaws, take a personal spiritual inventory, and submit their will to a higher power. In sum, the popularity of 12-step groups has created the impression that they are the best and only way to treat addiction. Therapists must be aware that the truth is more complicated.

75. B: The question asks which method is not the best way to assess a client's strengths and weaknesses. Let's look at the methods that are considered the best to way to assess a client's strengths and weaknesses:

The client is encouraged to provide a verbal report answering an open-ended question about what aspects he/she views as current strengths and weaknesses, Choice A. The social worker may parrot back to the client the strengths heard in the narrative and response, Choice C. Finally, practitioners are encouraged to use finding questions and phrases to guide the client to share personal reactions to the

event, discuss what favorable actions were taken, and examine what alternative actions could have been taken, Choice *D*.

Intake forms with specific, close-ended questions for accuracy are not the best method to assess client's strengths and weaknesses, Choice *B*.

76. C: The *DSM-5-TR* has three sections: one that explains an overview of the changes, one that lists the classes of and criteria for disorders, and one that covers areas for future research.

77. C: Salvador Minuchin is one of the founders of family therapy. Therapists who work with families may want to be familiar with his techniques. Minuchin's work is seminal to the field of family therapy and many family therapy models are based on Minuchin's ideas.

78. A: Reaction formation is when a person displays an exaggerated version of the opposite emotion to what he or she is really feeling. For example, a person may display strong feelings of love toward someone, though internally and unconsciously he or she detests that person. Displacement is when the feeling someone has toward one person is displaced to another object or person, such as a dog or spouse. Projection happens when one's own feelings are viewed as actually being someone else's. Denial is the refusal to admit something exists, such as painful facts or situations.

79. B: During malpractice suits, the liability goes all the way up the chain of command. This means that not only the social worker at the heart of the lawsuit, but also any supervisors or persons above them, can be held liable and named in the lawsuit.

80. C: According to Freud's theory of human psychosexual development, children go through five stages, each of which is defined by a focus on a different part of the body as a source of pleasure. The third stage is the phallic stage, which takes place between ages three and six, Choice *D*. During this period of development, children explore their bodies and become interested in their genitals as a source of pleasure, Choice *A*. Children develop what Freud called a pseudosexual interest in the parent of the opposite gender. The child sees the same gender parent as a competitor or rival for the opposite gender parent's love and sexual attention. This leads to one of Freud's major concepts: the Oedipus and Electra complexes, Choice *B*. In Greek mythology, Oedipus killed his father and married his mother.

The Electra complex refers to a girl wanting to kill her mother and marry her father. These desires are symbolic; Freud was describing an internal tension in children this age where sexual desire for one parent creates tension and conflict with the other. Freud's theory has largely fallen out of favor among professionals. For one, there is very little evidence to support it. Also, his theories are centered on the male, heterosexual experience in atomic family units, which is not necessarily representative of how most people grow up today. It is easy to see these limitations when one considers how his theory would apply to a single-parent family or a family with homosexual parents, a homosexual child, or a transgender child. Choice *C* is the correct answer because potty training is not part of the phallic stage; it occurs during the second stage, the anal stage, which takes place from ages 18 months to three years.

81. C: The client is in the pre-contemplation stage of change and is resistant to the idea of change and doesn't want to change during this time. The contemplation phase is when the client is actively thinking about changing, and the action phase is when the client is taking action to change. The maintenance phase occurs when the client has completed the change and is reiterating the change in their life.

82. D: Somatization is when a person's psychological distress manifests as physical symptoms. People experiencing somatization are not aware that their symptoms have a psychological origin and often seek

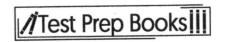

medical treatment, only to be told that there is nothing wrong with them. The stomach aches are most likely a manifestation of the boy's distress about his parents' divorce. Choice A is unlikely because the doctor did a full workup to rule out gastrointestinal issues, and because the symptoms occurred in conjunction with the divorce. Choice B is unlikely because factitious disorder involves faking symptoms or intentionally making oneself sick out of a desire for attention. The therapist believes that the boy is genuinely experiencing stomach pain and there is no evidence that he is causing or faking his symptoms. Choice C is unlikely because there is no indication that the boy is experiencing health anxiety or excessive worry about his symptoms.

83. B: Spirituality tends to increase the likelihood of someone being connected to other people, the likelihood that the client might have a greater sense of purpose, and the likelihood of self-actualization. It also can provide hope to the hopeless, help reduce anxiety, aid in healing from emotional pain, and contribute toward a greater optimism. Being more artistic is not a factor connected to levels of spirituality.

84. B: If Jane has been unable to rectify the situation through self-assessment, she should then turn to consultation with colleagues regarding her values conflict. If the consultation proves ineffective, she may ultimately need to consider termination and referring the client to another social worker. Social work as a profession prides itself on practitioners putting personal values aside, even when those values conflict with client values. Social workers must not engage in discriminatory practices or condone the discriminatory practices of others.

85. B: Changing behavior through rewards for approximation of desired behavior is the correct answer. Skinner demonstrated that behavior could be learned by rewarding actions that are similar to the desired behavior. If one wants to teach a dog to chase and catch a Frisbee thrown to the end of a field, the dog must first be rewarded for sniffing the Frisbee, then grasping the Frisbee, and then catching it when thrown four feet, then six, then ten. This process is called successive approximation. Choice A refers to a classical conditioning. Choice C refers to superstitions, meaning that one can sometimes be confused as to which behavior is soliciting the reward. Some athletes wear the same pair of "lucky" socks each game, thinking this behavior leads to the reward of winning. In reality, the behavior that leads to the win can be anything from practicing harder to playing a team that is not highly skilled; therefore, the behavior is superstitious. Choice D is a poor form of teaching a person to learn a new behavior because it may take much trial and error before perfection is achieved.

86. B: The three symptoms noted are common experiences for persons diagnosed with Post Traumatic Stress Disorder (PTSD). Along with these, PTSD survivors can be triggered into a state of anxiety or panic when exposed to stimuli associated with the trauma such as smells, sensations, or sights. Those diagnosed with PTSD may be easily startled, and they can even have periods in which they feel they are re-experiencing the traumatic event. Choice A, claustrophobia, is a fear of small spaces. Choice C is incorrect; although persons with borderline personality disorder (BPD) may have a history of PTSD, the common symptoms of BPD don't align with the ones provided. Choice D can be a symptom of PTSD, but it is generally seen as a completely different diagnosis with a different set of criteria.

87. D: Summarizing is an interview technique in which the therapist restates the important points of a discussion. Summarizing can be done at any time, but it is especially effective at the end of a session to make sure that the therapist and client are on the same page about how the session went and what the next steps are. Summarizing also helps focus the discussion on important issues to address while highlighting the progress that has been made. Choice A is incorrect because asking open-ended questions is a technique used to elicit additional information from a client. Choice B is incorrect because

validating is a technique used to affirm a client's feelings and statements about their experiences. Choice *C* is incorrect because clarifying is an interview technique that involves paraphrasing what a client has said and asking questions to make sure the therapist understands.

88. B: An open group allows membership to ebb and flow and usually does not have a distinct starting point or closing point. Members are permitted to enter as they wish and there is not as homogenous a criterion to enter the group as in closed groups.

89. A: Children have fewer resources for processing events of this nature because they have limited life experience and, therefore, fewer tools to help them adapt. Children are also less equipped to identify and share the emotions, memories, or thoughts they are experiencing than adults. The other responses are correct in that disorientation and disbelief are common in the beginning, and in the aftermath of disaster, other symptoms begin to emerge. Such events are indeed difficult to predict; therefore, one cannot easily prepare for trauma of this nature.

90. C: The question asks which statement is not true about indicators of motivation. Let's look at the choices that are true concerning indicators of motivation:

Indicators of motivation are very basic and transparent, Choice *A*. As time progresses, the client's level of engagement with the practitioner is an indicator of motivation as well, Choices *B* and *D*.

A client involuntarily coming for mandated treatment does not consistently indicate high motivation, Choice *C*.

91. B: Interviewing is a critical social work skill with three main purposes: information gathering, Choice *A*, diagnosis, Choice *C*, and therapy, Choice *D*. The same interview can serve more than one function. For example, during a therapeutic conversation, a client might reveal information that leads to a change in diagnosis. Interviews should be planned but also flexible to respond to the client's needs as they arise. Choice *B* is correct because determining if a client is being honest is not one of the purposes of social work interviewing. Sometimes social workers are concerned that their clients are lying to them or otherwise withholding information. In this situation, a social worker must reflect on why the client might be reluctant to open up and how the social worker's behavior could be contributing to the problem. Supervision can be helpful in these cases. It is not helpful or appropriate to use an interview to try to "catch" a client in a lie or omission.

92. C: The employee's behavior is an example of passive-aggressive communication. Passive-aggressive communicators outwardly display passive behavior (the employee nodded and agreed to work faster) while inwardly experiencing anger and aggression (the employee felt angry and disrespected). The employee was unable or unwilling to address his negative feelings directly with the manager. Instead, he expressed his feelings indirectly by sabotaging his work. Aggressive communicators express their feelings directly without necessarily considering the harm they could cause by doing so. Aggressive communicators make good leaders, but poor listeners. Passive communication is the opposite of aggressive communication. Passive communicators do not directly express their feelings and tend to be quiet or anxious. Passive communicators make good listeners but have difficulty getting their own needs met. Assertive communication strikes a balance between passivity and aggression. Assertive communicators express their feelings directly without harming others or infringing on others' ability to express themselves. Moving towards a more assertive communication style is a common goal for therapy clients.

238

93. C: During a mental status exam (MSE), assessing how well the client pays attention is an example of cognition. Attention, level of concentration, memory, orientation, and judgment are examples of cognition during an MSE. Choice *A*, psychomotor behavior, involves eye contact, a handshake, posture, movement, and coordination. Mood and affect, Choice *B*, involve cooperation, appropriateness, stability, and demeanor, while thought patterns, Choice *D*, include flow of thought and the ability to be present and engage in relevant conversation.

94. A: The social worker is encountering countertransference when they overidentify with a client. This needs to be worked through by the social worker or addressed in supervision. Countertransference can be destructive if left unaddressed or it can become a beneficial experience if the social worker recognizes it and can come to terms with their role in the social worker/client relationship.

95. A: A client's view of an experience and/or self is an example of psychological factors. Psychological factors refer to cognitive processes, such as thoughts, beliefs, one's view of an experience, and one's view of self. Choice *B*, physiological factors, present in the form of fluctuations of heartbeat, sweating, shortness of breath, digestive issues, and brain functioning. Choice *C*, social factors, are present in one's immediate physical surroundings and social systems, like work, school, home, and peer group. Choice *D*, person-in-environment, means learning about an individual based on the context of environmental situations in which the individual lives and acts.

96. C: Atkinson, Morten, and Sue theorized that minority youths go through five stages of racial and cultural identity development. Their theory formed the basis of many later theories of racial, ethnic, and cultural identity development. The first stage in their theory is *conformity*, Choice *B*, where the minority individual identifies with the majority (white) culture and values it above their own. This was the stage the young man was in while growing up in the white community. The second stage is *dissonance*, Choice *A*, where something happens that causes the person to question their allegiance to the majority culture.

The young man was in this stage when the racist incidents occurred and prompted him to think more about his identity as a black man. The third stage, which the young man is currently in, is *resistance and immersion*. In this stage, the person becomes heavily aligned with their minority identity and devalues the majority culture. The fourth stage is *introspection*, where the person begins questioning their total rejection of the majority culture. The final stage is *synergistic articulation and awareness*, Choice *D*, when the person can see and appreciate strengths in themselves, their minority culture, and also the majority culture.

97. D: The question asks when clients are resistant to treatment, what will they not do? First, let's look at the things they will do:

Clients who are resistant may provide rationalizations for behaviors, rather than trying to address them, Choice *A*. Additionally, a resistant client may appear disengaged during sessions or explicitly state that he or she will not take the recommended actions for an intervention, Choice *B*. Finally, resistant clients may frequently arrive late, cancel, or be a no-show for sessions, Choice *C*.

Clients who are resistant to treatment will not likely request assistance outside of business hours, Choice *D*.

98. D: Culture is a complex and multi-faceted concept and is related to when, where, and with whom one was raised. Those in the mental health field should be constantly vigilant about a client's cultural practices because these strongly impact beliefs, ethics, and behavior. Choice *D* is the best answer

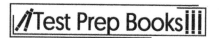

because it does not constitute an aspect of cultural identity as easily as when, where, and how one was raised.

99. C: Dan is in the planning phase of treatment. Different sources provide different labels for the phases of treatment in social work (for example, planning is also referred to as goal identification and intervention planning), but there is general agreement on how the treatment process progresses. It starts with engagement, Choice A, which involves rapport-building, then moves to assessment, where strengths, needs, barriers, and problems are identified. Based on information gathered during engagement and assessment, a treatment plan with goals and an intervention is created. Next is implementation, also called intervention, Choice D, in which the intervention is used to achieve the client's goals. In the final phases, the client's progress is evaluated, Choice B, and the process of termination and preparing the client for life post-treatment is completed.

100. A: These symptoms are indicators of physical neglect. Physical neglect can be the appearance of always being hungry, excessive sleepiness, or untreated medical problems. Other indicators of physical neglect are parents or caregivers demonstrating lack of interest or suffering from chronic illness. Usually, the home is an unsafe environment for victims who experience physical neglect.

101. A: Aphasia is a communication disorder caused by brain injury that causes problems with understanding and producing language. Someone with aphasia may have difficulties with speaking, understanding, writing, reading, or any combination of these. It is often associated with damage from a stroke. Choice B is incorrect because agnosia is difficulty recognizing familiar objects. Choice C is incorrect because acalculia is difficulty with simple math. Choice D is incorrect because prosopagnosia is difficulty recognizing familiar faces. All four of these disorders are medical issues diagnosed by a physician, not a therapist. However, therapists often provide support to clients dealing with these issues.

102. C: Carl Rogers placed much emphasis on reaching one's greatest potential and the interplay between this potential and one's perception of self. Erikson and Freud theorized that one must achieve certain developmental challenges before moving to the next level of human growth. Allport, on the other hand, believed one's destiny depended on the possession of certain clusters of personality traits. Therefore, A, B, and D are wrong. Rogers focused on the concept that humans are driven by their own need to develop into the best person they are capable of becoming.

103. B: Indirect discrimination relates to laws and policies that are applied equally but have negative consequences for certain groups. The other three answers are examples of direct discrimination since the actions are based on individual biases rather than organizational decisions. In those three scenarios, people are purposefully discriminating against others. In Choice B, the school administrators may not have even considered the negative consequence for Jewish students.

104. B: During a mental status exam (MSE), assessing the client's cooperation is an example of mood and affect. Cooperation, appropriateness, stability, and demeanor (e.g., flat, bubbly, warm, or restricted) are examples of mood and affect examined during an MSE. Choice A, general appearance, is determined by race, age, sex, body build, personal hygiene, and grooming. Choice C is incorrect because its attributes include syntax, rhythm, voice quality, and phrases used. Choice D, level of consciousness, includes alertness and presence of fatigue or lethargy.

105. A: Limiting self-disclosure is a strategy for maintaining good professional boundaries when interacting with clients; however, the same does not apply to colleagues. Developing mutually trusting

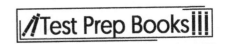

relationships with colleagues and social work peers helps social workers refine and maintain their boundaries. Strong peer relationships can help a social worker respond to challenges, improve self-care, think through ethical dilemmas, and advocate for organizational improvements.

106. B: Educational records are a type of collateral data that can provide helpful information about a client's current and historical functioning. Educational records are not an appropriate way to assess a client's level of intelligence. Although academic performance can be correlated with intelligence, there are many other factors that can affect a client's behavior at school. To assess intelligence, social workers should use an evidence-based assessment tool, such as the Stanford-Binet Intelligence Scale. Choices *A*, *C*, and *D* are incorrect because they are examples of how educational records can be used appropriately. Educational records can reveal if and how events in other areas of a client's life affect their school performance, Choice *A*. They can assist in the diagnosis of developmental disorders in children and adults, Choice *C*. They can also help pinpoint when a client's symptoms began, Choice *D*.

107. B: The goal of crisis intervention is to bring the client back to pre-crisis equilibrium and physical and emotional stability. The first treatment goals of crisis intervention are to assure the physical and emotional safety of the client.

108. C: Perception of family relationships, mental functioning, occupation, and social class are elements that help guide diagnosis. Finding questions about what is going on in the client's life and desired outcomes from therapy may help guide the diagnostic process. Choice *A*, the assessment process, focuses on the person-in-environment (PIE) and is an ongoing part of client treatment that involves review of the client's situation. Choice *B*, formal observation, is where specific data is collected on the client in a pre-determined setting. Choice *D*, life span development, refers to physical and cognitive alterations throughout a client's lifespan.

109. B: Ethical research does not require compensation or incentives to participate. There is some disagreement over whether incentives are appropriate. For example, if the potential study subjects are very poor, an incentive might be seen as coercive. On the other hand, it can be argued that an incentive would simply make participation a more viable option by offsetting the earnings lost by participating in the study.

110. B: A double bind is a type of communication between two or more people where the receiver of the message is "damned if they do, damned if they don't." The communication includes contradictory messages, and there is no way for the receiver to resolve the conflict. Double binds can be distressing, especially when they are communicated to children by parents. Choice *A* is incorrect because passive-aggression is communication that is outwardly passive but internally aggressive. Choice *C* is incorrect because latent communication involves underlying meaning and other messages that are not communicated directly through words. Choice *D* is incorrect because cognitive dissonance is when a person holds two or more conflicting beliefs at the same time.

111. D: It is extremely important to take cultural considerations into account during treatment planning. This requires the full participation and collaboration of the client. However, asking the client to recommend a treatment modality is not a good way to accomplish this. The therapist has extensive training in selecting treatment modalities that consider the client's culture, preferences, goals, lifestyle, strengths, challenges, diagnosis, and other factors. The client's role in this process is to provide as much information as possible to inform the therapist's recommendations, ask questions, suggest changes, and provide feedback until agreement is reached on an appropriate course of treatment. Choice *A* is incorrect because asking the client about cultural beliefs and practices and integrating this information

into the treatment plan ensures the plan will be appropriate. Choice B is incorrect because clarifying the client's role and the importance of collaboration is a critical step at every stage in the helping process. Choice C is incorrect because openly discussing cultural differences and how they impact the client and therapist strengthens the helping relationship by fostering mutual understanding.

112. C: Co-occurring substance use and mental disorders are common, and best practice is to treat them at the same time. This is called integrated treatment. Choices A and B are incorrect because it is best to treat both issues at the same time. Choice D is incorrect because integrated treatment produces the best outcomes regardless of which substance or mental illness a person is experiencing.

113. D: Social workers must use evidence-based interventions, but it is not necessary to prove this on a treatment plan. Instead, a treatment plan is a contract between a social worker and a client that includes the problem or problems that are going to be addressed, Choice A; the goal or goals that are going to reduce the impact of the problem, Choice B; the roles of the client and social worker in the treatment process; the interventions that are going to be used, Choice C; how progress will be monitored; situations where the contract would need to be renegotiated; and information about when, where, and how often the client and social worker will meet.

114. C: Sigmund Freud is the father of psychoanalysis or the "talking cure," from which psychodynamic theories originated. Freud's follower and disciple, Jung, took a different approach to psychoanalysis and had a major falling out with Freud. Skinner and Ellis are better known for cognitive behavioral techniques of psychotherapy.

115. A: Scapegoating a child occurs when a child is blamed for family problems and for things that are not their fault. This pattern of family dysfunction may happen in families where the problems are not being properly recognized or addressed, and members of the family seek to shift the blame. Affirming, undermining, or disavowing the child are not concepts connected to family dysfunction.

116. B: Resolving childhood issues is the crux of psychoanalytic therapy, in individuals or in groups. Decreasing anxiety, Choice A, can be a goal of individual therapy as well as Rational Emotive or psychodynamic groups. Resolution of current relationship issues, Choice C, is the goal of family therapy. Increasing daily functioning, Choice D, would be a goal of Rational Emotive as well as psychodynamic groups.

117. D: A genogram is most useful for understanding life events and familial patterns. A genogram is not useful for Choice A, determining the occurrence of behaviors. While the genogram can provide insight into the perceived relationship between the client and family and existing support systems, it does not establish peer support systems, as in Choice B, nor does it pinpoint significant life events, as in Choice C—it is only useful for understanding them.

118. C: The first stage of the therapeutic process is commitment, and the client needs to be committed to change and taking action within the therapeutic framework. The client's commitment to therapy and change are probably the most important elements of the therapeutic alliance. This phase also involves ensuring that the therapist and client are a good fit based on the client's needs and the therapist's skills and expertise.

119. B: This theory of addiction is based on the interplay of classical conditioning, operant conditioning, and social learning (observation). Choice A is not specifically a model of addiction, but rather a supposition as to why people abuse substances. C refers to the Moral Model of addictions in which the

person addicted to drugs or alcohol is viewed as weak-willed. Choice *D* refers to a hybrid of the biopsychosocial model of addiction, which focuses on the role of the environment (such as cultural and social factors), and genetic theory.

120. D: Congruence in counseling means that the therapist's verbal and nonverbal communication is both real and genuine. Incongruence means there is a disconnect between what the therapist is feeling, thinking, and showing. For example, relaxed body language and smiling while saying that one is happy is congruent, while furrowing one's brow and crossing one's arms while saying one is happy is incongruent. Congruence is a critical skill for therapists to develop because it forms the basis of an authentic and trusting relationship. It is also important to be able to recognize congruence and incongruence in a client's communication because that can reveal discrepancies between what a client says and what they actually feel.

121. A: The cognitive behavioral approach most commonly suggests that thoughts and behaviors influence emotions. The psychoanalytic approach focuses on drives and past events. The miracle approach does not exist, and dialectical behavior therapy uses some cognitive behavioral approaches, but also focuses on mindfulness and emotional self-regulation.

122. B: The question asks which statement is not true concerning the assessment process. Let's look at the statements that are true:

The assessment process focuses on the person-in-environment (PIE) and is an ongoing part of client treatment that involves review of the client's situation, Choice *A*. The assessment process should also highlight resources available to the client, in order to address presenting problems, Choice *C*. Finally, it is suggested that obtaining an accurate definition or view of the problem is essential to guiding the appropriate treatment plan and diagnosis, Choice *D*.

The practitioner's beliefs are influential in the assessment process; however, Choice *B* states that they are not, which makes Choice *B* the answer.

123. B: Sexual dysfunction describes problems with sexual desire, performance, or both. It can be caused by medical, psychological, and lifestyle factors. The first thing a social worker should do to assist a client with sexual dysfunction is refer them to a physician for a medical evaluation. It is important to determine if there is a medical problem first, before exploring other potential causes. If problems persist after medical explanations are ruled out, then it would be appropriate to explore psychological factors, Choices *A* and *C*, or lifestyle factors, Choice *D*, that may be contributing to the problem.

124. C: Psychological or emotional abuse is when the abuser uses strategies of manipulation through shame, fear, and guilt to control the other's behaviors. It also involves verbal abuse, which takes the form of yelling, constant criticisms, or belittling, threats, or name-calling. Physical abuse involves some type of physical harm. Vocal abuse is physiological disorder that occurs when a person damages their vocal cords. Critical abuse does not exist.

125. A: Lithium is a mood stabilizer often prescribed to treat bipolar disorder. Lithium has a narrow therapeutic index, which means that the difference between therapeutic and toxic levels of the drug is small. People taking lithium must get regular blood tests to make sure their lithium levels stay in the therapeutic range. Lithium can sometimes cause problems with the kidneys and thyroid, so it is also recommended to monitor the function of these organs during lithium treatment. Choices *B*, *C*, and *D* are

incorrect because none of these drugs have a narrow therapeutic index or a risk of kidney and thyroid damage, so none of them require regular blood tests and monitoring.

126. B: Xavi would benefit most from integrative treatment for dual diagnoses because this is the most effective treatment for co-occurring substance use and mental health disorders. Choice *A* is incorrect because there is no indication in the example that involving Xavi's family would be particularly beneficial. In general, Latino culture puts a great deal of importance on the family, but just because a client is Latino does not mean that they will want to involve family in their treatment.

127. B: Regular feedback from clients is essential to improving therapy practice and growing as a professional. When soliciting formal feedback, tailor the communication method to individual clients' preferences and abilities. For example, a client with limited literacy should not be given a form to fill out. For this reason, using the same standard feedback form for every client is not recommended. In addition to formal feedback, it is important to pay attention to clients' informal feedback. For example, failure to progress as expected can be considered informal feedback that something is not working as well as it could. Negative feedback is just as important as positive feedback because it provides an opportunity to learn and improve. Because of this, therapists should seek feedback at various times during treatment, not just when things are going well. Additionally, feedback should always be documented, and the client's confidentiality should be respected.

128. C: Sarah is a non-voluntary client because she was pressured into treatment by something other than the legal system. Choices *B* and *D* are incorrect because involuntary or mandated clients are required by the legal system to attend treatment. Choice *A* is incorrect because voluntary clients come to treatment on their own without outside pressure. When working with non-voluntary or involuntary/mandated clients, motivation, lack of trust, and anger can be issues. In these cases, it is particularly important that the social worker is patient, empathetic, and focused on the client's own needs and goals in addition to those imposed by outside forces.

129. C: Developmental history is part of the biological section of the biopsychosocial assessment. Choice *A*, coping skills, is part of the psychological section. Choices *B* and *D*, marital problems and educational background, are part of the social section.

130. A: Normally developing children are not expected to know at least 50 words by age one. Most children begin saying things like "mama" and "dada" around nine months. This is also when the child recognizes and responds to their own name, Choice *B*. The child gradually learns words for familiar objects over time, reaching a vocabulary of at least 50 words by age two. Not speaking at all by age two is a red flag that may indicate a developmental delay. Choice *C* is incorrect because babies begin smiling socially around two months of age. Choice *D* is incorrect because sitting up unassisted is a skill babies develop between six and nine months of age. It is important to remember that every child is unique, and although human development occurs on a predictable schedule, individual children may reach milestones at slightly different times and speeds. That said, social workers must be familiar with normal human development in order to recognize signs of potential delay and disability. Social workers should also be able to provide psychoeducation to parents about their child's development.

131. D: The stigma of mental illness can cause family members to become judgmental toward the individual who has been diagnosed, or he or she may have to deal with the misunderstandings of people outside the family. This is one of the reasons that dealing with a diagnosis of mental illness can be more complicated for a family than dealing with a diagnosis of physical illness. There is no ease associated

244

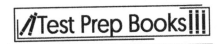

with mental illness. Even though mental illness may involve some level of confusion or ambiguity, those are not terms that best answer the question.

132. C: Defense mechanisms protect the ego from absorbing information it does not want to see, feel, or experience. This protective shield—which comes in many forms, such as rationalization, sublimation, or projection—helps reduce anxiety and guards against unwanted emotions like shame or guilt. Defense mechanisms can be helpful in reducing anxiety or can sometimes help one become immune to reality. Choices A and B imply that defense mechanisms are used to protect others from the truth about themselves, when this is not entirely accurate. Choice D suggests that defense mechanisms better allow one to exploit others. In some instances, this could apply, but for the most part, these mechanisms are acts of self-defense that keep the ego from accepting an unwanted truth.

133. B: Telling the story is an example of self-disclosure. Though inappropriate self-disclosure can be harmful to clients and lead to boundary violations, self-disclosure can be helpful when used correctly. This scenario describes an initial session, and the anecdote probably helped the therapist build rapport with John. Generally, self-disclosure is rarely required to achieve a treatment goal, and it should be used judiciously, if at all.

134. C: Problem-solving approaches focus on helping a client identify problems in their life and develop practical solutions for managing them. These approaches are generally brief and present-focused; they do not delve into the past and the origins of a problem, but instead focus on concrete solutions that can be implemented immediately. Brief, solution-focused approaches have become increasingly popular due to funding constraints, pressure from insurance companies, and client preferences. Choice A is incorrect because it describes cognitive behavioral approaches. Choice B is incorrect because is describes psychodynamic approaches. Choice D is incorrect because it describes acceptance and commitment therapy.

135. B: While the use/abuse of alcohol, a history of mental illness, and a tendency to control others are all risk factors for abuse, the presence of a learning disorder is not associated with this. There are many factors that may indicate a potential abuser, but there are no foolproof ways to identify one apart from the evidence of abuse.

136. A: The purpose of a biopsychosocial assessment is to get a holistic understanding of a client. Traditionally, this meant asking about current and past biological, psychological, and social function. It is becoming more popular to ask clients about other domains of function as well, especially spiritual and cultural, to make the assessment even more holistic. Social workers sometimes but not always include questions about spiritual beliefs, religion, and cultural traditions. On the other hand, psychiatric diagnoses, medical history, and presenting problem, Choices B, C, and D, are incorrect because they are always included in a biopsychosocial assessment.

137. A: Therapists are often reluctant to set and enforce rules, boundaries, and limits with their clients because they do not want to punish them or negatively affect the relationship. This is misguided because rules, limits, and boundaries create a predictable environment where clients feel safe and can learn to self-manage. In order to be trustworthy, therapists must do what they say they will do, and this includes enforcing agreed-upon rules. In this example, the therapist should remind the client of their agreement about lateness and cancel the session. The therapist should be empathetic and clear that this is a consequence of an action, not a punishment or an indication that the therapist does not like the client. Setting limits might be difficult in the moment, but over time, this will strengthen the therapeutic relationship and allow the client to learn and grow.

138. D: The *NASW Code of Ethics* is clear that it is unethical for therapists to do online searches for information about their clients unless they have the client's consent. This protects clients' right to privacy. The only exception would be if there is an emergency and doing a search is required to prevent harm to the client or others. In Celia's example, there is no emergency, so the therapist must get her permission to do the search.

139. B: Reinforcement schedules refer to how frequently a desired behavior is rewarded. A variable ratio reinforcement schedule means that the reward is sometimes given in response to the behavior but not every time, so it is unpredictable. Variable ratio produces the strongest behavioral response, and the learned behavior is less susceptible to extinction than it would be using a different reinforcement schedule. This is why casinos operate using variable ratio reinforcement. The gambler continues to put money in the slot machine hoping for a reward, knowing that the reward could come at any time. Variable ratio produces the most enduring behavior change. Choice *A* is incorrect because continuous reinforcement involves rewarding the behavior every time it occurs. An example would be giving a dog a treat every time it obeys a command. Continuous reinforcement is effective for teaching a new behavior, but it is less effective than variable ratio. Once the reward is no longer given, the behavior is susceptible to extinction.

Choice *C* is incorrect because fixed ratio means rewarding the behavior after a certain number of attempts. An example would be paying a farm worker $100 for every three bushels of fruit picked. Fixed ratio is less effective than variable ratio because it produces a less steady behavioral response. There is a slowdown after each reward; for example, the worker is likely to take a quick break after completing three bushels. Choice *D* is incorrect because fixed interval means that the reward is given after a certain amount of time has passed, regardless of the number of attempts at the behavior. Fixed interval produces less behavioral response and more of a pause after the reward is given. An example would be giving a lab animal a treat every five minutes in response to the animal pushing a button. The animal will push the button a lot around the five-minute mark, but much less the rest of the time.

140. D: Factors that are present in one's immediate physical surroundings and social systems are known as social factors. Social or environmental factors are present in one's social systems, such as work, school, home, and peer group. Physiological factors, Choice *A*, present in the form of sweating, shortness of breath, or digestive issues. Psychological factors, Choice *B*, refer to cognitive processes like thoughts or beliefs. Biological factors, Choice *C*, are known as the factors connected to the body's physiological response and are linked to genetics.

141. B: The Tarasoff case established that therapists have a duty to warn and to protect third parties from harm. If a therapist believes that a client poses a threat to another person, the therapist must warn and protect the person. In this example, the therapist should contact the client's girlfriend directly if possible. If the therapist cannot locate the girlfriend, they must find another way to warn her, such as contacting other people who know her or notifying the police. Choice *A* is incorrect because although it might be helpful in the long run, it does not solve the immediate problem of the threat to his girlfriend. Choice *C* is incorrect because the therapist can't prevent the client from leaving the office, and even if they could, doing so would not fulfill the duty to warn and protect his girlfriend. Choice *D* is incorrect because it could anger the client and increase the threat to his girlfriend. In general, it is best practice to inform clients when confidentiality must be broken unless doing so could result in harm, which is the case here.

142. A: A time-out is an example of a negative punishment technique. Negative punishment involves taking away something desired in response to undesired behavior; a time out takes away play and

246

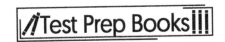

interaction as punishment for an undesired behavior. Choice *B* is incorrect because a token economy is an example of positive reinforcement. A reward (a token) is given in response to a desired behavior. Choice *C* is incorrect because spanking is an example of positive punishment. A punishment (spanking) is given in response to an undesired behavior. Choice *D* is incorrect because cancelling chores is an example of negative reinforcement. Something undesirable (chores) is taken away in response to a desired behavior. It is important to note that the use of the terms *positive* and *negative* in this context does not mean "good" and "bad." It refers to whether something is given or taken away in response to a behavior.

143. D: Piaget is most known for his work on children's cognitive development. He introduced the idea that children are not merely miniature adults; they go through a process of maturation during which different cognitive skills and abilities develop. He identified four stages of cognitive development through which children move from concrete, egocentric thinking to abstract, logical, and hypothetical thinking. This has implications for what adults can reasonably expect from children. For example, children do not learn cause and effect until the concrete operations stage between the ages of seven and eleven; a five-year-old who does not fully grasp the consequences of his actions is not being willful, he has just not learned that skill yet. Choice *A* is incorrect because Erikson is most known for his theory of social development. Choice *B* is incorrect because Freud is most known for his work on personality and psychosexual development. Choice *C* is incorrect because Skinner is most known for his work on learning through operant conditioning.

144. D: Encouraging clients to take an active role in their treatment benefits the client, the treatment plan, and the therapeutic relationship. Therapists may worry that asking a client to participate in problem formulation, goal setting, and treatment planning could make the client feel overwhelmed, but it is likely to make them feel empowered. One of the main goals of treatment is to improve a client's ability to identify and manage challenges on their own. Treatment is an opportunity for the client to practice this skill with the guidance of the therapist. Some clients will need more assistance than others in this process, and therapists must be patient and attuned to the needs of each individual.

145. C: Feminist theory looks at how gender, culture, and power relations interact. It challenges patriarchal views of men and women and seeks gender equality. Feminists believe that "the personal is political," meaning that the struggles of individual women are caused not by personal failings but rather by a society that confers privilege to men and oppresses women. Sandra is expressing a common experience shared by many American women. Feminist theory encourages women to change society rather than blaming themselves for conditions imposed on them by inequality. Feminist theory also considers how patriarchy is damaging to men and advocates for men's equality too. Choice *A* is incorrect because the moral model is a theory that addiction is caused by character defects. Choice *B* is incorrect because conflict theory holds that conflicts over power and resources drive societal change. Choice *D* is incorrect because systems theory describes how change in one part of a system affects the system as a whole.

146. D: A mental status examination provides information about a client's current mental state and function. Psychiatric history is part of the psychological section of the biopsychosocial assessment, not part of the mental status examination. Appearance, affect, and speech, Choices *A*, *B*, and *C,* are incorrect because they are all components of the mental status examination.

147. C: When clients decide to terminate before completing their treatment plan, the therapist must explain the risks of terminating and document the interaction. Documentation is important to show that

the client initiated the termination and to protect the therapist against claims of abandonment, which is malpractice. The therapist should remain objective and avoid taking the termination personally.

148. A: In the context of a mental status examination, *orientation* refers to a client's orientation to reality. This means the client's understanding of who they are, where they are, when they are (time and date), and what has happened recently. A client who can answer all these questions correctly is considered "oriented x4." Inability to answer these questions correctly indicates that the client's mental status is not optimal; the client is disoriented. The client's sexual orientation, the client's beliefs and feelings about treatment, and informing the client of the purpose of the examination, Choices *B, C,* and *D,* are incorrect because they are not related to a client's orientation to reality.

149. A: Carol Gilligan was Lawrence Kohlberg's research assistant and later become a preeminent scholar in her own right. She criticized Kohlberg's theory, which was based on men, as being sexist. Women did not often reach the postconventional stage, according to Kohlberg's theory, and Gilligan refused to believe that this was due to women being morally inferior. Her research on women's morality led her to adapt the theory to explain women's moral development. Kohlberg's theory emphasizes individual rights and justice as the highest possible moral values.

Carol discovered that women conceive of morality in terms of their connections with others and consider caring the highest moral value. While men's morality is more individualistic, women's is more relational. Gilligan did not believe that women or men were more or less likely to achieve a higher level of moral development, Choice *C.* Her theory used the same stages Kohlberg did, Choice *D,* in the same order, Choice *B.* During the preconventional stage, women are concerned with self-interest and survival. In the conventional stage, they emphasize being selfless and taking care of others. In the postconventional stage, women take control of their own lives while still placing a strong emphasis on caring and relationships.

150. C: Vygotsky believed individuals are significantly shaped by the formal and informal social groups in which they interact. These institutions teach values, how to behave in relationships, how closely one must follow rules and laws, and, in general, what is important in life. A child growing up hungry and neglected will have a very different view of life than one who is cherished and provided with love, support, and material needs. Choices *A, B,* and *D* all impact the quality of one's life, but Vygotsky leaned toward a more global explanation of social development that encompasses multiple social factors.

151. D: Freud theorized that children develop into sexually mature adults by progressing through five stages, each defined by which body part is the main source of pleasure. He believed that if the child's gratification was overly restricted or indulged during any of the stages, they would develop a fixation leading to certain predictable problems in adulthood. Toilet training occurs during the anal stage. Freud believed that a child whose parents are overly strict about toilet training will develop a fixation leading to an anal-retentive personality. Freud describes this personality type as overly controlled with rigid and obsessive thinking. On the other hand, if parents are too hands-off with toilet training, the fixation will manifest in an anal-expulsive personality marked by disorganization and messiness, Choice *B.* According to Freud, binge eating disorder, Choice *A,* and excessive cigarette smoking, Choice *D,* are oral fixations that develop as a result of parents being too strict or indulgent during the weaning process in the oral stage.

152. A: When a therapist receives a subpoena, they should try to protect the client's confidentiality by claiming privilege on behalf of the client. The therapist should refuse to release the records unless the

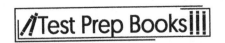

client provides written permission to do so. The therapist may eventually be legally required to release the records if they receive a second request accompanied by a court order.

153. A: Psychodynamic therapy involves the recognition of sexual and/or aggression drives. Psychodynamic therapy originated with psychoanalysis and the "talking cure" with Sigmund Freud. Modern psychoanalysis is often referred to as psychodynamic therapy.

154. C: Dementia is a cognitive disorder common in elderly people, Choice *A*, which causes changes in mood, Choice *B*; memory, Choice *D*; and thinking. Dementia is a chronic condition that starts gradually and progresses slowly over time. When these symptoms appear suddenly and progress quickly, they are more likely to be caused by delirium rather than dementia.

155. C: Atkinson, Morten, and Sue theorized that minority youths go through five stages of racial and cultural identity development. Their theory formed the basis of many later theories of racial, ethnic, and cultural identity development. The first stage in their theory is *conformity*, Choice *B*, where the minority individual identifies with the majority (white) culture and values it above their own. This was the stage the young man was in while growing up in the white community. The second stage is *dissonance*, Choice *A*, where something happens that causes the person to question their allegiance to the majority culture.

The young man was in this stage when the racist incidents occurred and prompted him to think more about his identity as a black man. The third stage, which the young man is currently in, is *resistance and immersion*. In this stage, the person becomes heavily aligned with their minority identity and devalues the majority culture. The fourth stage is *introspection*, where the person begins questioning their total rejection of the majority culture. The final stage is *synergistic articulation and awareness*, Choice *D*, when the person can see and appreciate strengths in themselves, their minority culture, and also the majority culture.

156. C: Unlike voluntary clients, involuntary/mandated clients are attending treatment due to external pressure. Working with these clients presents unique challenges, making Choice *D* incorrect. Because these clients did not choose to pursue treatment, their motivation is likely to be low. Fear of legal consequences may motivate a client to do the bare minimum to avoid punishment, but this is different than the intrinsic motivation for change typical of voluntary clients. Therefore, Choice *B* is incorrect. It is important for therapists to emphasize that involuntary/mandated clients still have choices. They can choose to participate or not and accept the consequences, and they can choose to pursue their own goals in addition to those imposed by the courts; therefore, Choice *A* is incorrect. Therapists must work harder to engage and motivate involuntary clients, as their resistance is likely to be high and their trust low. Being empathetic, acknowledging the client's situation, clearly explaining what will happen during treatment, and encouraging the client to make choices where possible are the best ways to form a positive relationship with these clients.

157. C: The ABCs of a problem refer to the Antecedent, Behavior, and Consequences linked to a client's perceived problem. The discovery of these items allows the client to specifically define the problem and examine factors affecting emotional well-being. Antecedents to a problem may be prefaced by the involvement of certain individuals in the client's life. The client may disclose interactions that led to their problematic behaviors, based on the aforementioned information in the evaluation of the antecedent. The consequences to a presenting problem are comprised of both internal (cognitive or personal) and external (environmental) interactions or reactions to the behavior.

Answer Explanations #2

158. B: The tool lacks *validity*, meaning that it is not measuring what it intends to measure. The fact that the tool produces consistent results means that it is measuring something, just not depressive symptoms. Choice *A* is incorrect because *reliability* means producing consistent results. The tool has reliability, but not validity. Choices *C* and *D* are incorrect because *external validity* means that the results from the study participants can be applied to the general population. *Internal validity* means that participant results are caused by the intervention and not by some other factor.

159. C: Cognitive distortions are cognitive aberrations that the client uses to hinder progress and change. Clients are often involved in fallacious thinking patterns and need assistance in changing these distortions into more constructive thought patterns.

160. C: Antipsychotics can cause tardive dyskinesia, especially when they are taken at high doses for a long time. Tardive dyskinesia causes involuntary movements of the face, mouth, tongue, and sometimes other body parts. Sometimes these symptoms go away when the drug is discontinued, but sometimes they persist indefinitely. It is very important for people taking antipsychotics to be monitored for tardive dyskinesia so that the medication can be changed before the symptoms become irreversible. Choices *A*, *B*, and *D* are incorrect because none of these classes of drugs cause tardive dyskinesia.

This material is provided for exam preparation purposes only and does not indicate an endorsement of any specific scientific, political, or religious point of view. © TPB Publishing. You have been licensed one copy of this document for personal use only. Any other reproduction or redistribution is strictly prohibited. All rights reserved.

Dear ASWB Bachelors Test Taker,

Thank you again for purchasing this study guide for your ASWB Bachelors exam. We hope that we exceeded your expectations.

Our goal in creating this study guide was to cover all of the topics that you will see on the test. We also strove to make our practice questions as similar as possible to what you will encounter on test day. With that being said, if you found something that you feel was not up to your standards, please send us an email and let us know.

We would also like to let you know about other books in our catalog that may interest you.

NCE

This can be found on Amazon: amazon.com/dp/1637758499

NCMHCE

This can be found on Amazon: amazon.com/dp/163775020X

We have study guides in a wide variety of fields. If the one you are looking for isn't listed above, then try searching for it on Amazon or send us an email.

Thanks Again and Happy Testing!
Product Development Team
info@studyguideteam.com

FREE Test Taking Tips Video/DVD Offer

To better serve you, we created videos covering test taking tips that we want to give you for FREE. **These videos cover world-class tips that will help you succeed on your test.**

We just ask that you send us feedback about this product. Please let us know what you thought about it—whether good, bad, or indifferent.

To get your **FREE videos**, you can use the QR code below or email freevideos@studyguideteam.com with "Free Videos" in the subject line and the following information in the body of the email:

    a. The title of your product

    b. Your product rating on a scale of 1-5, with 5 being the highest

    c. Your feedback about the product

If you have any questions or concerns, please don't hesitate to contact us at info@studyguideteam.com.

Thank you!

Made in the USA
Monee, IL
02 August 2023

40343113R00144